*A Winterthur Series Book*

CHINESE EXPORT PORCELAIN
FOR THE AMERICAN TRADE

*Tureen and platter decorated with Fitzhugh border and with a trumpeting Fame holding the badge of the Society of the Cincinnati. From dinner service purchased by George Washington. About 1786.*
Courtesy of *Winterthur Museum.*

# CHINESE

*Export*

# PORCELAIN

*for the American Trade*

*1785-1835*

*Jean McClure Mudge*

★

UNIVERSITY OF DELAWARE PRESS

1962

# INTRODUCTION

PORCELAIN MADE IN CHINA for Americans during the half century after the American Revolution is tangible evidence of a great period of trade for this country. In addition, it illustrates the meeting of two countries of almost polar contrast: America, the infant, expanding, and enterprising nation; and China, one of the most ancient, isolated, and conservative countries in the world. No other articles of trade embody the attitudes of East and West toward each other so clearly as does the export chinaware.

By its physical qualities alone, export porcelain tells its own story, but the account is quite limited without the record of its production in China and its purchase by this country. If both artistic elements and historic facts are combined, however, the chinaware may be appreciated more comprehensively than if either source is used alone.

This study tries to combine both the historic and the aesthetic approaches. It traces the historic struggle of the West to establish commercial connections in the Far East. It outlines the pattern of exchange at Canton, the only port open to foreign traders. Then it considers the porcelain itself, its special conception, its execution, and its shipment to the major East Coast ports of America. Finally, it discusses the form, decoration, and chronology of porcelain that came from China to America. Throughout this study, and especially in Chapter IV, the particular features of the export ware which make it a symbol of America's cultural relationship with China are emphasized.

# Introduction

Students of the China trade may wonder why another effort has been made to present the story of export porcelain. Homer Eaton Keyes, when editor of *Antiques*, published many vivid articles about porcelain objects; and J. A. Lloyd Hyde's *Oriental Lowestoft*, published in 1936 (second edition, 1954), was the first major book to deal with wares made for the American market. More recently, John Goldsmith Phillips' *China Trade Porcelain*, published in 1956, has contributed enlightening material on the production of porcelain, important European ceramic design sources, and many excellent illustrations of objects in the Helena Woolworth McCann Collection. Keyes' writings, however, are in the form of scattered articles about noteworthy porcelain pieces; and the books by Hyde and Phillips, distinguished by the breadth of their coverage, tell the history of the China trade from the late sixteenth century through the eighteenth century and then present the many types of porcelain objects made for the European market from the beginning of the eighteenth century and those made specifically for the American or the European market in the late eighteenth century and the early years of the nineteenth century.

The scope of this study is more limited than that of either Hyde or Phillips. It concentrates on the American adventure in the porcelain trade with the Chinese. This country's activity has been touched upon by the above-mentioned authors, but it has not been discussed in detail. Such detail has been found in contemporary manuscripts: ledgers, manifests, bills of lading, business correspondence, personal letters, and diaries. This information is important not only to describe the export chinaware made for the United States, but also to understand the significant story of the porcelain as a symbol of the feelings, thoughts, and reactions produced by the meeting of two different peoples. This aspect of the porcelain has not been treated by other writers, perhaps because of the difficulties of "getting at" the original materials. Nonetheless, a knowledge of the interrelationships between the Americans and the Chinese gives another, perhaps deeper, basis for interest in and appreciation of the whole subject of export porcelain.

Since primary research material relating to export porcelain is difficult to find, special thanks are due to those who generously and patiently aided this research. Institutions in several states provided helpful materials: In Vermont, The Bennington Museum; in Massachusetts, Essex

# Introduction

Institute, Marblehead Historical Society (Jeremiah Lee Mansion), Massachusetts Historical Society, Museum of Fine Arts (Boston), Peabody Museum of Salem, Ropes Memorial, and The Society for the Preservation of New England Antiquities; in Rhode Island, The John Carter Brown Library (Brown University), Newport Historical Society, Rhode Island Historical Society, and Rhode Island School of Design; in Connecticut, The Connecticut Historical Society and Mystic Seaport; in New York, The Grolier Club, The Metropolitan Museum of Art, The New-York Historical Society, The New York Public Library (Manuscript Division), and The New York State Library; in New Jersey, Washington Association of New Jersey and Morristown National Historical Park; in Pennsylvania, Girard College Library, Haverford College Library, The Historical Society of Pennsylvania, and The Library Company of Philadelphia; in Delaware, Historical Society of Delaware, University of Delaware Library, and The Wilmington Society of Fine Arts; in Maryland, Maryland Hall of Records and Maryland Historical Society; in the District of Columbia, The Library of Congress (Manuscript Division); in Virginia, The Mariners Museum and The Thomas Jefferson Memorial Foundation. Special thanks, too, go to the Department of Ceramics of the Victoria and Albert Museum for repeated help in research on and illustrations of European objects which served as design sources for Chinese porcelain made especially for the American market.

Many collectors of Chinese export porcelain have kindly allowed the author to discuss their objects and to use illustrations of them: Mr. and Mrs. Alfred E. Bissell, Mr. and Mrs. George P. Bissell, Jr., Dr. and Mrs. John B. Carson, Mrs. Joseph Carson, the late Mrs. Francis B. Crowninshield, Mr. and Mrs. Charles K. Davis, Mr. John Evans and Miss Margaret Evans, Ginsberg and Levy, Inc., Mr. and Mrs. Horace W. Gordon, Mr. and Mrs. Barry H. Hepburn, Mrs. Dunham Higgins, Mr. and Mrs. Rafi Mottahedeh, Mrs. Alfred Coxe Prime, Miss Elizabeth I. Richardson, Mrs. Benjamin Rush, Mr. and Mrs. Samuel Schwartz, Mr. and Mrs. David Stockwell, and the late Mr. Arthur J. Sussel.

Of special importance to this work was a manuscript, the manifest of the *Empress of China*. Permission to use this document was granted by its owner, Mr. Carrow Thibault, of Ardmore, Pennsylvania, a descendant of Captain John Green, of the *Empress*.

# Introduction

I am highly indebted to Mr. Henry F. du Pont for his interest and experience in collecting Chinese export ware brought to America. The collection he has made at Winterthur gave an exciting variety of objects and decorations to study. The staff of the Winterthur Museum has been highly cooperative; especially so was Mrs. Charles F. Montgomery, who served as adviser for the initial study. Others whose work on details was an indispensable aid include Miss Helen R. Belknap, Mr. and Mrs. Dean A. Fales, Jr., Dr. E. McClung Fleming, Miss Dorothy W. Greer, Mr. Charles F. Hummel, Mrs. Louis Moeller, Mr. Charles F. Montgomery, and Mr. Gordon Saltar. Thanks are also due to Miss Doris J. Creer, who called to my attention the Providence trader's notebook which has been used as Appendix II. I greatly appreciate the patience and understanding shown by many others, and especially by Mr. and Mrs. Bruce A. Ludgate and Miss Anne K. Bullard.

I wish especially to thank five people without whose interest, co-operation, and thoroughness this study would never have been ready for publication. I am greatly indebted to Dr. Schuyler Van Renssalear Cammann, of the Department of Oriental Studies of the University of Pennsylvania, for his careful reading of the manuscript and his scholarly guidance and many important suggestions, especially in Chapter I; to Dr. Ernest J. Moyne, Coordinator of the Winterthur Program at the University of Delaware, for his very patient and meticulous attention to the endless details of form and style and the problems of publication; to Mr. Milo M. Naeve for handling innumerable details in the process of getting this book ready for publication; and to Mr. John A. H. Sweeney for his availability for consultation on numerous problems and for his reading and criticism of the manuscript. Most especially, however, I am very happy to acknowledge the superior editorial assistance and devoted interest of Miss M. Elinor Betts, of The Henry Francis du Pont Winterthur Museum. Only her painstaking attention to verifying endless details made the publication of this book possible.

Finally, I should like to thank the University of Delaware and the Winterthur Corporation for making possible the publication of this study as the second in the Winterthur Series.

*Jean McClure Mudge*

# CONTENTS

# ILLUSTRATIONS

# Illustrations

# Illustrations

# Illustrations

# Illustrations

# Illustrations

[ *xx* ]

# Illustrations

Credit for the photographs provided for this book by museums, historical societies, historic houses, and individual owners should go to many sources, among them: *Antiques* Magazine (Fig. 133); Gilbert Ask (objects in the Winterthur Museum); Samuel Chamberlain (Fig. 80); William H. Chisholm (objects in the Peabody Museum of Salem); Lea S. Luquer (Fig. 37); Louis S. Martel (Figs. 43, 44); The Metropolitan Museum of Art (Fig. 32); Paris-Morris (Figs. 82, 89); and Photo-Illustrators (Figs. 48–50, 52, 53, 55–57, 130).

# Part One

## THE ENCOUNTER
## OF EAST AND WEST

# I

## Europe and the Far East

WHEN THE *Empress of China*, America's first ship in the China trade, returned from Canton to New York in May, 1785, completing what her log recorded as a round trip of 32,458 miles, newspapers enthusiastically reported her homecoming. In Philadelphia the *Pennsylvania Packet* of May 16 noted:

> We have the satisfaction of announcing the arrival of the ship Empress of China, captain [John] Greene, from the EAST-INDIES, at this port, yesterday, after a voyage of 14 months and 24 days. . . . As the ship has returned with a full cargo, and of such articles as we generally import from Europe, a correspondent observes, that it presages a future happy period of our being able to despense with that burdensome and unnecessary traffick, which heretofore we have carried on with Europe—to the great prejudice of our rising empire, and future happy prospects of solid greatness.[1]

As predicted, this initial joy over the successful and independent circuit to China foreshadowed a great period of trading in the next five decades. The merchandise brought back by the *Empress* was typical of the goods soon imported from China into every major city on the Atlantic Coast, and perhaps even to western ports as well. Her cargo included

[ *3* ]

black and green teas, silks, nankeens, cassia, and, in addition, 962 piculs of chinaware.[2] The porcelain pieces, on special order for citizens in Boston, New York, and Philadelphia, were the first Chinese export objects made especially for the American market.

Americans in the China trade had to follow a pattern of exchange that generations of Europeans had accepted from the Chinese. By tracing this pattern and the history of its development, we may better understand this country's interest in one of China's most famous articles of export—porcelain.

As early as the days of the Roman Empire, Europe was fascinated by the unmatched silks from China and by tales of that distant land. By the time of Augustus, the overland silk trade between China and Rome was well developed by such middlemen as the Parthians of Persia and the merchants of Alexandria. By sea, however, Roman ships went all the way to India for Chinese silks and Eastern spices. On one occasion a group of Roman merchants, perhaps from Roman Syria, even reached the Chinese Court at Loyang, claiming to have been sent by the Emperor Marcus Aurelius.[3]

Even before Rome fell to the barbarians, China also suffered invasions and underwent a period of dark ages.[4] Thus commerce between the Orient and the West died out until the seventh century A.D., when trade was resumed by land and sea. Then the Arabs and Persians went to India and even to China in trading ships. Persian merchants also helped to convey the products of China overland to the Near East, until their land was overwhelmed by the armies of Islam.[5]

By the ninth century, the exports from T'ang dynasty China included fine porcelains, which the Chinese had only recently learned to make. Fragments of them have been found by archaeologists in the old cities of India, Persia, Palestine, Asia Minor, and Egypt.[6] When the T'ang dynasty (618–906) fell, to be replaced by the Sung dynasty (960–1279), the overland routes across Central Asia were blocked by hostile powers. Thus the trade by sea became even more highly developed, and Chinese porcelains were exported from the great port of Ch'üan Chou (known to the foreigners as Zayton) in increasing quantities.[7]

When the Mongols under Kublai Khan completed their conquest of China in 1280, their short-lived empire extended across Asia into Western Europe, with the result that overland trade and commerce were once more developed to a high degree. The Venetian merchant-brothers, Nicolo and Maffeo Polo, took advantage of the new opportunity of comparatively safe East-West travel and visited Kublai Khan's court twice, taking with them on their second trip, in 1275, Nicolo's son Marco.[8] The Khan became very much interested in Marco Polo and recognized his abilities by giving him numerous commissions and even a high position in his government.[9] During a period of seventeen years Marco Polo traveled for the emperor throughout China and the adjoining regions of the Mongol Empire, taking careful note of what he saw. Later, after his return to Europe, he was taken as a captive of war to Genoa, where he dictated to a fellow prisoner his account of what he had seen and learned, mentioning, among other things, the great quantities of porcelain that were exported from the vicinity of Zayton.[10]

Marco Polo's tales were received with deep scepticism and even with scorn by fourteenth-century Europeans; but, then and later, his famous account served to arouse the curiosity and imagination of thoughtful Westerners regarding far-off China. Although other Europeans had preceded the Polos to China and had reported their experiences there, the Polos long remained almost legendary symbols of the adventure and wealth to be found in distant Cathay.[11]

With the breakup of the Mongol Empire and with Mohammedan intervention in central Asia, East-West communications by the old land route were once again interrupted in the fourteenth century, although tribute missions from Western Asia still continued to visit China by land as well as by sea, returning with silks and porcelains, during the succeeding dynasty of the Ming (1368–1644).[12] For a brief period in the early fifteenth century, the Ming Court sent out a series of maritime expeditions for exploration and trade, which carried Chinese junks as far as the Red Sea and Africa.[13] This was followed by a policy of isolation, broken only by the intermittent exchange of Chinese products for the exotic gifts brought by the tribute missions from other lands of Asia.[14]

Eventually, however, nationalistic interests in Europe led to renewed trade with China. First the enterprising Venetians maneuvered the Turks into granting trading privileges in the Black Sea and thereby generally monopolized the commerce of China and the West by land; but, after the Turks seized Constantinople in 1453, the East-West trade

routes were severed completely. It was then that other Europeans began
to look for new ways to resume the old contacts. Thus, Columbus
sailed west in 1492, hoping to reach Cathay or the Indies on behalf of
Spain. A few years later, Vasco da Gama, of Portugal, discovered a sea
route around the Cape of Good Hope to India and the Far East.[15]

The Portuguese thus pioneered in the attempt to compete with the
Venetians and by 1514 had reached the China coast. Three years later,
a Portuguese ship entered the port of Canton. A trading settlement was
established near Ningpo and another on the Fukien coast, but both were
wiped out by massacres because the Portuguese in general treated the
Chinese contemptuously and behaved little better than pirates.[16] Their
actions confirmed the impression of the cultivated Chinese that the foreign peoples of the West were merely another kind of barbarian, and
this undoubtedly led to the hostile way in which the Europeans of later
years were received by the Chinese officials.

By 1557, however, the Portuguese had gained a permanent settlement on the peninsula of Macao at the mouth of the Pearl River, which
led to Canton; they had accomplished this through annual rents paid to
the Chinese and through official subservience to them. On land leased to
them by the Chinese Government, they built a European city, but an
officer from Peking governed it as the emperor's deputy. Even though
Portuguese trade eventually declined, Macao's importance did not. By
the late eighteenth and early nineteenth century, it had become the base
of operations for all nations trading at Canton.[17]

The Spanish had less interest than had the Portuguese in the direct
trade with China, as Chinese junks came to the Spanish outpost, Manila,
to trade after the founding of that city in 1571. In the annual voyages
of the Acapulco galleon, Chinese products were carried from Manila
across the Pacific to Acapulco, Mexico, from which port they were
transshipped across Mexico and on to Spain. So many Chinese migrated
to Manila and set themselves up as small merchants there that much of
the business of Manila passed into their hands. Several times the Spaniards met this problem simply by massacring the Chinese wholesale.
These massacres and the restrictions placed by the Spanish on the
Chinese in the Philippines created extremely poor Spanish-Chinese relations and increased Oriental hostility toward Westerners in general.[18]

Another reason for the Chinese contempt toward Europeans was the disagreeable way in which the people of the various European nations acted toward each other, first observed in the attitude of the Portuguese toward the Spanish and the Dutch. In fact, it had been national competition and friction in Europe which brought the Dutch to the Far East. When Spain closed the port of Lisbon to Dutch ships in 1594, cutting off their access to Eastern products, the Hollanders had to go to the Orient themselves to obtain what they desired. They established an East India Company in 1602 and devoted most of their attention for a long time to the spice trade of the East Indies and to the trade with Japan, for which they obtained the sole monopoly after 1640. Several times during this period Dutch ships approached the coast of China to secure permission for trade with Canton, but in each instance the jealous intervention of the Portuguese blocked their attempts to accomplish this aim. The Dutch did, however, establish a settlement on Formosa (from 1624 to 1661) and conducted their trade in teas, porcelains, and other Chinese products from there.[19] Chinese porcelains were so popular in Holland that the Dutch developed their own blue-and-white Delft pottery in an attempt to imitate it. Not until 1762 did the Dutch establish a factory or trading station at Canton, a century and a half after their first efforts to make contact with China.[20]

The English were not far behind the Dutch, their chief rivals in commerce during the seventeenth century. Incorporated by royal charter in 1600, the British East India Company began activity that had a marked effect on life in England only after 1662, when Charles II married Catherine of Braganza, in whose dowry was Bombay. When the advantages of access to the harbor of Bombay were realized, trade with India increased, as did the interest of the British in products of the East and their desire for them.[21] After an earlier attempt to set up a trading station in Japan (1613–1623), the Company had gradually turned its attention to the China coast, and to trade at Amoy and Chusan because an unpleasant incident provoked by them in Canton in 1637 had made them unwelcome in that city. It was not until 1699, when a successful attempt to trade with Canton brought back a particularly rich shipment of teas and some porcelains, that the Company's interest in the Canton trade became very strong. By 1715 the British East India Company had a highly organized trading station at Canton, with a regular schedule for shipping; throughout the rest of the eighteenth century, the Company dominated the China trade.[22]

France was the last large European power to ask for trading concessions from the Chinese. She sent ships to Canton at long intervals from the late seventeenth century through the eighteenth. Most of her activities were carried on through the *Compagnie des Indes*, founded in 1719 to replace an older company that had been designed primarily for trade with India. A trading station was established in Canton in 1728, but the Company's monopoly of French trade was terminated by the French Government in 1769. France's trade passed into the hands of independent merchants, who continued to visit Canton except when the French Revolution and the ensuing wars (1789–1815) made overseas trade impossible. The French trade with China, however, was never extensive.[23]

Other nations entered the trade with minor success, if not with lasting importance. They included the Swedes, Danes, Prussians, Austrians, Hungarians, Italians, and the Parsees from Bombay, as well as the Peruvians, Mexicans, and Chileans.[24] Many European merchants, wishing to avoid direct conflict with national monopolies, sailed under the Austrian Imperial flag. This was the only way, for example, that private British merchants could trade at Canton without coming into open competition with the British East India Company's strict monopoly.[25] Ships from Indian ports, known to the British as "country ships," were also permitted to trade in certain restricted commodities.[26] (The Russians also engaged in the China trade at this time, but they used overland caravans, coming to the trade station of Kiakhta, in the Far North, where there was no competition with other Europeans.)[27]

The initial experiences of the Chinese with lawless Portuguese, arrogant Spaniards, and too-forceful British sea captains not only increased their disgust with the "barbarians," but also impressed on them the necessity of dealing firmly with the foreign traders. When the Manchus had taken over China in 1644 after the fall of the Ming dynasty, they found it convenient to maintain the old tribute system, and the foreign traders had to conform to this, although they were not always aware of the reasons for all the restrictions that so often irked them.[28] In 1757 the Chinese Court decided to limit all foreign seaborne trade to

Canton, placing it in the hands of local officials and supervisors, and instructing them to act in accordance with the old tribute regulations by which all foreign traders were to be treated as tribute-bearing representatives of vassal nations.[29]

In the light of China's paramount position in East Asia, which she had long enjoyed, and her tradition of high cultural and technological achievements, it is easier to understand the Chinese attitude of lofty superiority.[30] However, the first Americans who came to Canton, in 1784, had no knowledge of China's long cultural heritage, and they were puzzled by the haughtiness and aloofness of the Chinese officials and by the vast amounts of red tape with which they surrounded the trading activities (to be described more fully in Chapter III). Luckily, the newcomers found friends among the French and British merchants who were able to instruct them in the required procedures, helping to smooth their way. In contrast to the Chinese officials, they found many of the individual Canton merchants to be cordial, cooperative, and honest; and in time warm friendships, based on mutual integrity in business affairs, developed among them as well as among the other foreign traders.[31]

A comparatively fortunate situation thus faced the Americans in Canton in 1784. The very discovery of America had been the result of the desire of European nations to get to the Far East. Then for more than two hundred years before Americans came to China, Europe's series of national ventures cleared the way for their arrival. By the last quarter of the eighteenth century these countries were reducing their activity in China. The Portuguese were limited to Macao and were subject to Chinese credit. The Spanish kept larger operations in Manila than in Canton and were more interested in New World silver than in the products of ancient China. The French had no official company or influential consul. Swedish and Danish private traders were very few. The Germans had a company, but it was on the brink of closing. The Dutch confined their activities principally to the East Indies. Only the English, with their virtual monopoly, remained powerful in the China trade.[32]

The initial good feeling between the American traders and the British soon broke down, as an intense rivalry developed between the British East India Company and the independent Yankee shippers. In a short time, the Americans became second only to the English in the Canton trade. This position was not attained merely because all other countries were relaxing their interests. The American shipowners, their representatives (called supercargoes), and the captains who managed their ships were men of tremendous enterprise and initiative, willing to take huge risks for possible profits. Unlike the men of the British East India Company, they owned their own ships, for the most part, free from monopolistic restrictions. A little later, when the rest of the Western World was deeply involved in the Napoleonic Wars, the Americans, as neutrals, benefited by carrying Oriental cargoes for the belligerents. With their strong commercial ambitions, they competed so successfully with the British East India Company in the 1820's and early 1830's that the British crown withdrew the Company's monopoly in 1834; but even with new competition from independent British traders, the Americans still maintained control of a high percentage of the Canton trade.[33]

The very qualities of independence and reckless personal initiative which made the Americans such successful traders did not always insure their popularity at Canton. The Chinese called them "flowery-flagged devils," perhaps not solely because of the stars on the American flag, but also because the "New People" were not immune to a certain sense of self-importance.[34] Also, the unruliness of the American sailors often caused friction with the Chinese authorities.[35]

On the whole, however, the Americans accommodated themselves to the Chinese system of dealing with foreign traders to a far greater extent than did the British.[36] It was the British who finally broke the old imperial tribute system by defeating China in the First Opium War, of 1839–1842, which marked the first step toward obtaining from China the recognition of the equality of other nations.[37] After this violent act of aggression, the whole situation rapidly changed; the Chinese officials lost their power to dominate the foreign traders, while the Europeans and the Americans lost their respect for the Chinese Court and began to think of the Chinese themselves as an inferior people. Eventually, because of this war and the second one which soon followed, further Chinese ports were opened, and Canton's importance declined for foreign traders.[38]

As far as the Americans were concerned, the First Opium War marked the period of their diminishing interest in the China trade and their activity at Canton. Nonetheless, the half century of independent exchange with China which they had enjoyed since their arrival in 1784 had made a great difference to the new nation, and this story will now be considered in more detail.

# II

## *America and the Far East*

FOR AMERICA the nature and extent of exchange between America and the Orient underwent many alterations in the fifty-five years from 1784 to 1839. These developments indicate the country's domestic growth and rising international prestige. For our purposes, however, these changes are important as they reflect the pattern of the trade in chinaware. The half century may be divided into (1) a beginning period, 1784–1790, (2) a period of growth and foreign conflict, 1791–1814, and (3) a period of further expansion, 1815–1839, from the end of the War of 1812 to the beginning of the British-Chinese First Opium War.[1]

Why did the Americans enter the China trade in the first place? The answer to this question involves many aspects of the home scene and relationships with Europe, as well as the essential spirit of a people recently united in political independence from England.

Edmund Burke, speaking to the House of Commons in 1775 on conciliation with the colonies, well described the activity of New England seamen:

No sea but what is vexed by their fisheries. No climate that is not witness to their toils. Neither the perseverance of Holland, nor the

activity of France, nor the dexterous and firm sagacity of English enterprise, ever carried this most perilous mode of hardy industry to the extent
to which it has been pushed by this recent people—a people who are still,
as it were, but in the gristle, and not yet hardened into the bone of man-
hood.[2]

Despite her maritime history, however, New England did not monopolize America's shipping after the Revolution. Ports in New York,
Pennsylvania, Maryland, Virginia, and the South all depended heavily
on the exchange of goods by sea. Perhaps New England directed the
largest foreign shipping, but all sections of the eastern seaboard were
just as eager as she to resume peacetime commerce in 1783.

Colonial shipping had suffered greatly during the Revolutionary
War (1775–1783). In the first two years nine hundred vessels were lost,
and by the end of the war one hundred more were gone. In addition,
immediately following the peace (1783), British navigation laws prevented American trade in the West Indies and with England, both of
which areas had been of fundamental importance to colonial commerce.
Even more discouraging, the Articles of Confederation provided only
weak aid to the shipping industry at home.[3] Under these circumstances
it seems almost incredible that the new United States would attempt
such a far-flung adventure as trade with China so soon after the Treaty
of Paris was signed in 1783.

Yet there were many compelling motives behind America's interest
in the Far East. Blocked temporarily from her prime sources of commerce and not yet being a manufacturing country, the United States was
in need of trade. In the Orient she had nothing to fear by way of English domination, for the British East India Company's monopoly no
longer applied to Americans.[4] Moreover, a market for China's products
had already been developed in teas and other supplies during the colonial
period; and ginseng, known in North America since 1718, had great
selling power in the early years at Canton.[5]

Though the war had decimated the number of American vessels,
new shipbuilding gradually supplemented the remaining craft.[6] Of these,
many privateers existed whose owners had accumulated enough capital
and knowledge of foreign seas to look with enthusiasm toward un-
charted adventures. These men and other sailors led the ships that went

to Canton, backed by the increasing wealth of a new group of merchants at home. British trade regulations thus ultimately channeled the country's shipping and desire for gain. As Phineas Bond, the British consul at Philadelphia, wrote in 1787:

> In the restricted state of American trade it is natural for men of enterprise to engage in such speculations as are open to them, and which afford a prospect of profit.[7]

Americans were certainly aware of the possibilities in the China trade even before the voyage of the *Empress of China*. In fact, other vessels might have won first place at Canton if the schemes of certain Salem and Boston promoters had developed during 1783, or if Connecticut planners had received sufficient state funds.[8] It remained for Robert Morris, of Philadelphia, and Daniel Parker and Company, of New York, to be the first successful entrepreneurs in the trade. They outfitted the *Empress* at a cost of $120,000, employed John Green as captain, and engaged a distinguished junior officer in Washington's army, Major Samuel Shaw, as supercargo.[9] Sailing on February 22, 1784, the vessel arrived at Macao on August 23, six months and a day later. A cargo consisting mainly of ginseng was exchanged for tea and other goods; and the *Empress* returned to New York, saluting the city with thirteen guns on May 11, 1785.[10] When Shaw returned to the United States, Thomas Randall, his close friend who had served as his assistant on the first voyage of the *Empress*, remained in China to charter another vessel to bring home extra cargo, especially teas. With John O'Donnell as master, the *Pallas*, built in the East Indies, brought Randall and a cargo including teas and other merchandise to America, entering the Port of Baltimore on August 15, 1785. The arrival of the *Pallas* and the nature of her cargo were promptly announced in the *Baltimore Advertiser*.[11]

The voyage of the *Empress* was widely publicized in the country's leading newspapers. Many shippers became interested in the Canton exchange, despite the fact that the profits from this first China venture were not extraordinary.[12] When the *Empress* returned to China for the 1786–1787 trading season, four other ships joined her, all leaving their home ports in December, 1785, or early in 1786. From New York, the *Hope*, with James Magee as captain, took Samuel Shaw on his second voyage, this time as the first United States consul at Canton. Congress had recently elected him to this post "without being entitled to receive any salary, fees, or emoluments whatsoever." [13] Even though his position was merely honorary, Shaw, as the representative of the United States, was pleased with the state of the trade he found at Canton:

> On the whole, it must be a most satisfactory consideration to every American, that his country can carry on its commerce with China under advantages, if not in many respects superior, yet in all cases equal, to those possessed by any other people.[14]

A third vessel, also from New York, was the sloop *Experiment*, captained by a former privateer, Stewart Dean. The tiny craft was one of only 84 tons and, on reaching China, was mistaken for the tender of a bigger ship. That interest in the China trade had developed quickly in ports other than New York is indicated by the fact that the other ships in the 1786–1787 group were from Philadelphia (the *Canton*, Thomas Truxtun, captain) and from Salem (the *Grand Turk*, Ebenezer West, captain).[15] Growing interest was further apparent in the next few seasons. Providence sent the ship *General Washington* in 1787 to begin her activity at Canton. Boston joined her the same year with the *Columbia*, whose voyage around Cape Horn to the Northwest Coast and then to China inaugurated America's west-coast fur trade. When it was known that the *Alliance*, of Philadelphia, had brought home a cargo reputedly worth half a million dollars, merchants from her home port and from many other cities were undoubtedly stimulated to make further investments. Samuel Shaw reported seeing the ships *Asia* and *Canton*, from Philadelphia, in the trading months of 1788–1789, as well as several vessels from New York, including the ship *Jay*, whose captain was Thomas Randall, Shaw's partner on the first voyage of the *Empress*.[16]

With equal trading privileges and handsome fortunes possible, the China commerce held high attractions for Americans. A slight decline in activity did occur in this period when a market glut in China goods, foreshadowing many such miscalculations of domestic demand, discouraged shippers in 1789–1790.[17] By the end of six years of trade, nevertheless, America had sent twenty-eight ships to Canton.[18] With this number she was buying from China one-seventh of her total imports, making great gains for her seacoast merchants, and employing her best men and ships in the trade.[19]

In 1791 Americans entered a second period of expansion in the Far East with a great deal of government support, at least indirectly. In contrast to the Articles of Confederation, the Constitution provided a firm basis for aid to commerce. In addition, the Navigation Act of 1789 charged a graduated tonnage tax in favor of domestic shippers.[20] In the same year the Tariff Act placed a 12½ per cent protective fee on all East India goods imported by foreigners. Tea was excluded from the Act, but was already limited to importation only in American ships. Payments on tea duties, moreover, were allowed a two-year delay, a great asset when such fees either equaled or exceeded the prime cost of tea at Canton. The government extended liberal credits to American shippers in India or China; and in New York and Pennsylvania several protective measures were passed by the state legislatures to benefit merchants involved in the China trade.[21]

At the same time that merchants enjoyed official aid at home, they found conditions abroad quite variable and even dangerous. Though the French Revolution and Napoleonic Wars placed Europe in commercial as well as political difficulties, America did not always benefit by French and British tactics of mutual blockading, and by her status as a neutral shipper.[22] British impressment took uncomfortable tolls from the crews of American merchantmen; and Jefferson's Embargo Act of 1807, although designed to stop European attacks on American shipping, certainly did not accomplish its object without considerably reducing the country's foreign commerce.[23] Two years later the Nonintercourse Act also curtailed overseas shipping to Europe. Even earlier, the Jay Treaty with England in 1794 had restricted American activity in the West Indies and injured her commercial equality with the rest of the world.[24] The Treaty also helped aggravate friction between the Americans and the French. An undeclared naval war broke out between the two countries by 1797–1798, causing American merchants to be especially wary when sending vessels to Canton.[25] Robert Waln, of Philadelphia, wrote in 1799 of the interruption of his business by French privateering:

We have been informed via Lisbon of the capture of the Ship Pigou owned by Mordecai Lewis & ourselves, which Vessel was bound for

Canton & taken by two French Frigates when our advices came away the Frigates had arrived one at Brest, the other at L'Orient with the Cap. & part of the Crew & all the Money ship'd on board the Pigou which they took out immediately on the capture.[26]

Nearer China, American vessels also suffered under the attacks of native pirates who operated along the coast and up the Pearl River. In 1804 Ephraim Bumstead, in Canton, wrote to James and Thomas Handasyd Perkins, in Boston, "Their principles are the indiscriminate plunder of their Countrymen & massacre of foreigners." He recommended that ships be well on guard as they approached the China coast and be ready for surprise attacks.[27] The Chinese pirates continued to be troublesome. Benjamin Chew Wilcocks, American consul at Canton, 1815–1822, issued an address in 1817 to the "Commander of any American Vessel arriving in Macao Roads":

> I think it necessary to inform you that the ship Wabash of Baltimore while at anchor in Macao Roads on the night of the 26th of May last, was boarded by a Chinese Boat, man'd with fifteen men, who under pretence of furnishing a Pilot & delivering a letter, attacked, murdered, & wounded a number of the American Crew, & plundered the Ship of Specie & property to a considerable Amount.[28]

In spite of these obstacles, American commerce in the Orient prospered with government encouragement, the continuing interest of American entrepreneurs, and a few gains due to the wars in Europe. There were fourteen American ships anchored at Whampoa in 1790–1791. Beginning with the season 1795–1796, the annual number of American ships at Canton never fell below ten, with an average of between fifteen and twenty a year until 1808–1809, when only eight ships were reported. A peak year for the prewar period was 1805–1806, when approximately forty-two vessels from America arrived. Undoubtedly Jefferson's Embargo Act of 1807 and the upset of America's overseas shipping led to the sharp decline in numbers previously noted. Before the War of 1812, however, the yearly average had again risen and a total of more than four hundred voyages had been made to Canton since 1790.[29]

The second war with England meant almost a complete break in the China trade for three years. Ships were needed near home, and lone merchant vessels were vulnerable to British men-of-war. In 1814 the Chinese, bothered by encounters between belligerents at Whampoa, warned that, if the two nations were to engage in "petty quarrels," they should leave China to settle them.[30] With peace in 1815, the danger of losing a position in the trade at Canton was averted, and Americans resumed operations at a great pace. Thirty American ships arrived at Canton in 1815–1816. Only three seasons later an all-time high in the American totals at Canton was reached, with forty-seven vessels registered in 1818–1819.[31]

Yearly arrivals at Canton in the period from 1815 to 1839 numbered in the thirties and forties. Forty-three vessels were recorded in both the season immediately preceding and the season immediately following 1835, the final year of this study. Beginning in the late 1830's, before the great era of the China clippers, voyages dwindled slightly, with only twenty-eight ships noted in 1840–1841.[32] In the period of a little more than fifty years under consideration, a great deal of trading occurred between America's East Coast and Canton. During that time approximately 1,260 ships unloaded at Whampoa. By 1830 these vessels were responsible for $3.5 million of the total $43 million involved in the entire China trade, and America was still second only to England in numbers of ships and in tonnage.[33]

It should be remembered that for America the China trade often involved much more than a direct voyage to Canton and back. Post-Revolutionary trade in the East Indies meant stops at Île de France, Bombay, Calcutta, Batavia, and innumerable other places in Southeast Asia. Moreover, all these trips were related to America's total foreign trade with Europe, Africa, and South America.[34] The determining factor in the multiplication of routes was, of course, the search for goods that would be salable at Canton.

The Chinese were fairly self-sufficient, with little interest in the wares that Americans first offered them. Cargoes like that of the *Grand Turk*, including pitch, tar, flour, rice, tobacco, butter, wine, bar iron, sugar, oil, chocolate, spirits, hams, candles, soap, cheese, fish, and other goods, had little appeal for Asians, either for their diet or for other immediate use.[35] Americans therefore either resorted to circuitous trading in order to find products of greater demand, or changed their home cargoes. Gradually their outward loadings became simpler, with larger amounts of fewer products, mainly ginseng, furs, and specie.[36]

Specie was the American export in greatest demand at Canton. A great deal of this supply came from the Spanish West Indies, Gibraltar, Portugal, and South America, or by way of Europe; but to many in America, still influenced by a mercantilist philosophy, the outpouring of silver from the country was a dangerous financial policy. After the War of 1812 a certain group was particularly disturbed by currency valuations resulting, so they believed, from this exportation. In a committee report to the House of Representatives in 1819, it was noted:

> The whole amount of our current coin is probably not more than double that which has been exported in a single year to India, including China in the general term.[37]

In 1854 it was estimated that since 1784 the United States had shipped to China silver amounting to $180 million.[38] With the specie earned en route to Canton, this figure was probably even higher.

To supplement and eventually to replace specie exportations, Americans developed new enterprises, either by intent or by accident. These ventures included fur trading on the Northwest Coast of North America, fur searching in the waters off South America and islands in the South Pacific, and the gathering of miscellaneous products in the South Seas. In the process of exploration in the Pacific, entirely new opportunities for trade were opened to the Americans. Significantly, Spanish California entered the China shippers' routes a full thirty years before the gold rush of 1849.[39]

Of the two established routes to Canton—eastward by way of the Cape of Good Hope and westward by way of Cape Horn—the former became the more popular for large Indiamen from Boston, Providence, New York, and Philadelphia. They followed the *Empress'* trail rather closely, developing trading privileges along the way from St. Helena and Île de France to Batavia and Manila. Americans found that such tramp shipping was quite necessary for the final trading at Canton.[40]

The way westward, however, was soon opened by the two Boston ships, the *Columbia* and the *Lady Washington*, which established fur-trading connections with the Northwest Coast Indians in 1788. By the time of the *Columbia*'s second voyage, in 1792, the commerce in sea-otter skins, mainly conducted by Bostonians, was well under way. Chinese courtiers, nobles, and officials lined and trimmed their winter robes with the furs.[41] Profits from the pelts, which sometimes brought as much as $60 or more at Canton, sent increasing numbers of "Nor'west-men" by way of the Pacific route. The high point of exchange there was reached by 1800, when sixteen United States vessels were engaged in the trade. Certainly the period of greatest adventure in the Northwest pre-ceded the Embargo Act, with sixty-eight being the total number of ships noted from 1795 to 1804.[42] This figure, well above the British number, indicates the advantages of independent shipping in contrast to the prob-lems resulting from the restrictions of a trading monopoly such as the British East India Company.

By 1825 sea-otter skins became increasingly difficult to obtain be-cause of Russian competition, poor relations with the Indians, and the near extinction of the sea otter.[43] Even ten years earlier, there had been some danger that the trade would fall off. Benjamin Shreve, at Canton, in 1815 wrote to merchants in New York:

> This market will disappoint many shippers of skins this season. They had reason to suppose after a three years war that the market would be bare of skins; but too many calculated so, for almost every vessel has brought out more or less Fox & Otter Skins, and they are in so many hands, the price is not likely to rise much, but no one can make any calcu-lations with regard to this market, it is one of the most uncertain in the world.[44]

In search of additional skins, ships looked north and south along the coast, stopping at several places in California in the first few years of the nineteenth century, despite the illegality of trading there.[45] Ships estab-lished connections at Monterey, Santa Barbara, and San Diego; and in later years western hides and tallow were used in the trade between New England and California and in the Hawaiian trade as well.[46]

The route westward gained in value and extent with the beginning of the search for sealskins off the coast of South America and in the South Pacific. The first sealing voyage from America actually predated the initial sailing of the *Empress*. In 1783 an Englishwoman living in Boston, Lady Haley, sister of John Wilkes, planned and financed a sealing trip of the ship *States* to the Falkland Islands.[47] The ship returned to New York with about 13,000 skins, eventually sold in Calcutta. Later adventurers soon expanded the sealing enterprise. They came mainly from Connecticut ports such as New Haven, New London, and Stonington. The process of capturing, clubbing, and skinning the seals took place near South America—the Falklands, Tierra del Fuego, Más-a-Fuera, the South Georgia and the South Shetland Islands. From these islands the search spread to almost the entire Pacific area from Santa Catalina on the California coast to islands south of New Zealand and in the Fiji archipelago.[48]

By 1812, however, seal fishing had almost ceased. The danger of encounters with the Spanish or British and the hazards of severe weather and rough seas, especially in doubling Cape Horn, discouraged a few shippers. More shippers, on the other hand, predestined their own unemployment by indiscriminate killing of both young and old animals. Thomas Pitkin, in his statistical report for the United States in 1817, noted that, though the sealing voyages had attracted many by their great profits, "the business . . . was overdone—the seal, in a few years, became so scarce, as not to be worth the pursuit." [49]

Another source of furs was the interior of North America. From the regions of the Great Lakes and the Mississippi Valley, pelts of the red and gray fox, the beaver, and the land otter were sent to various ports.[50] Exact statistics to indicate the number of furs contributed to the China trade from these areas are not available, but estimates indicate that these furs were used less in the China trade than were either sea-otter skins or sealskins. The entire fur trade was undoubtedly of great value to the young nation, which could not easily obtain Spanish dollars. From its beginning to the early 1830's, the venture in furs amounted to between $15 million and $20 million.[51]

When once the South Pacific area had been opened to seal hunters, its other natural resources were tapped. Sandalwood, gathered mainly in the Hawaiian and Fiji Islands, was a big item until about 1820. The Chinese used it to make incense and domestic furniture. Other articles included edible birds' nests for soup, *bêche-de-mer* or sea slugs, tortoise shell, coral moss, sharks' fins, and mother-of-pearl.[52]

Opium was another import of great profit to Americans, who joined the English and other Europeans in smuggling it into Canton. Ships stopped in Turkey and India, en route, to load the illegal cargo destined for all classes of the Chinese people. One observer in 1818 noted:

> Opium is a prohibited Article in consequence of improper & excessive use of it in smoking and chewing, a custom which had extended itself to the highest ranks of people. The English Ships from Bombay bring the best Opium. The Turkey Opium imported in the American Ships is much inferior to it. Both are smuggled from the Ships at Whampoa.[53]

By the 1833–1834 season the extent and variety of exports to China were quite evident in the "Statement of the American Trade with Canton . . ." for that year. Articles listed, in order of bulk importance, were textiles from India, American metals, Turkish opium, quicksilver, furs, sandalwood, and other goods. Ginseng apparently was still important, with 3,580 piculs of crude root and 415 piculs of clarified root bought by the Chinese. The total value of all goods imported amounted to $9,887,502.86.[54]

Homeward-bound ships also followed varying routes to dispose of their cargoes most advantageously. Benjamin Shreve, in Canton, was told by his Salem employers in 1816:

> The object of this voyage is, to procure a Cargo in Canton suitable for the market in Europe, such as Sugar, few Chests Tea, Cassia and Nankeens, a more particular memorandum of which will be hereto annexed.[55]

Further instructions to Shreve suggested that he touch at Gibraltar to inquire as to the most likely ports in Europe, probably Marseilles and Leghorn. For a return cargo, he was to pick up as many Spanish dollars as possible, but also to include a few items to meet the home market, "probably some bulky articles might pay a good profit."

Return cargoes carried to the East Indies, Europe, Hawaii, California, South America, or brought home, matched imports in variety; and for many decades they exceeded in expense the supplies sold at Canton.[56] Tea stood out as the most important and most valuable export from Canton. Manufactured silk, nankeens, and chinaware followed in order of importance. These were the four articles from China in greatest demand in America.[57] When, by the end of the third decade of the nineteenth century, the country's interest in China goods greatly lessened (see Chap. VIII), teas increased, rather than decreased, in demand as return cargo.[58]

Although tea, textiles, and chinaware led the list of exports from China to America, China was not of interest to the United States for these products alone. In 1818 a Philadelphia agent in Canton noted numerous other items available, including cassia, ivory, and tortoise-shell objects, lacquered ware, vermilion, white lead, and camphor.[59] In later years cargoes were equally or even more varied, with trifles appearing in increasing number. In the 1833–1834 season major items like tea and textiles were joined by such miscellaneous goods as firecrackers, fans, fire screens, sweetmeats, sugar, spice oil, and grass cloth.[60]

# III

## *The Trade at Canton*

THE FIRST AMERICANS in the China trade found a well-developed procedure of exchange for the "foreign devils" (*fan kwae*), carefully devised by the Chinese to ensure against foreign penetration. From Macao up the Pearl River past the Bocca Tigris to Whampoa and Canton, foreign ships underwent constant chaperonage. This surveillance was tolerable to both Europeans and Americans for many decades because the profits gained at Canton often meant lifetime fortunes for many merchants. On both sides, however, discontent was present from the beginning and finally erupted into the British-Chinese war over opium, 1839–1842. China was gradually forced to yield her isolation to the pressures of foreign commerce. Under concessions granted by the Treaty of Wanghia in 1844, Americans extended their trade to several other ports on the China coast.[1]

From the beginning of the America-China trade with the arrival of the *Empress of China* in 1784 to the signing of the Treaty of Wanghia, all trading activities were limited to Canton, and there only on the basis of strict supervision by the Chinese. At Macao an incoming ship first obtained a pilot for direction up the river (see map, Fig. 1). This outpost, under joint direction of Portugal and China, was almost two hundred years old when the Americans arrived. Foreigners might feel almost at home on Macao, with a bay similar to the Bay of Naples, and with extensive houses, forts, churches, a convent, and a senate house surprisingly Western in architecture and layout. A low parapet and broad esplanade, the Praya Grande, protected these buildings from the sea

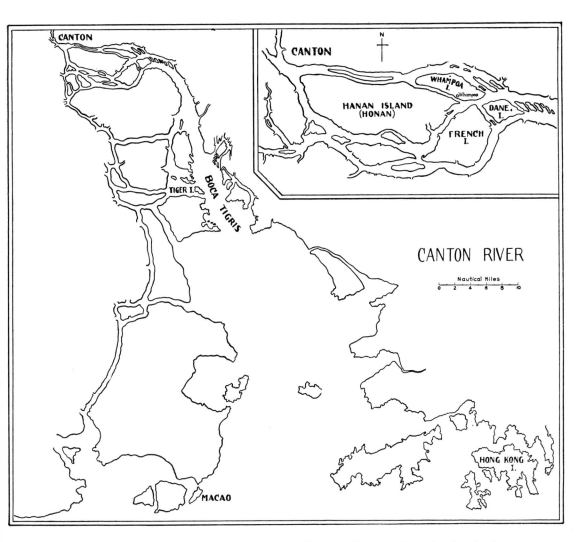

FIGURE 1. *Map of the Canton (Pearl) River, with detail of the Whampoa-Canton area, 1845. Drawing based on map facing page 145 in James Orange,* The Chater Collection; Pictures Relating to China, Hongkong, Macao, 1655–1860 *(London, 1924). Drawing by Gordon Saltar.*

(Fig. 2).[2] When spring brought the off season between trading periods, alien shippers, forced out of Canton by demand of the Chinese officials, often stayed at Macao until the next trading season. The peninsula also marked the limit of travel into China for all Western women; thus foreigners in Canton could have their company only by making the journey back to Macao.[3]

About 40 miles up the river was the Bogue, or Bocca Tigris (Fig. 3). It was the first narrow passage in the river approaching Canton; it received its name from the Portuguese word *bocca*, or mouth, suggested by the red sandstone cliffs to the left of the passage, which resembled a tiger's gaping jaw. The Chinese similarly called it the "Lion's Gate" and in later years made the name doubly relevant with the construction of forts for defense against foreigners.[4]

North of the Bogue and 12 miles below Canton was Whampoa anchorage (Fig. 4). Shallow water beyond this point prevented ocean-going vessels from further entry. As a result, foreign vessels lay at anchor there for about three months while their cargoes were being sold and new loads bought. At this bend in the river a mass of ships of all sizes filled the water, their masts making the entire area seem a floating forest.

FIGURE 2.  *View of the Praya Grande, Macao, from the south. Early-nineteenth-century water color.* Courtesy of *Mr. and Mrs. David Stockwell, Wilmington, Delaware.*

FIGURE 3. *View of Bocca Tigris, showing the forts on either side of the passage. Early-nineteenth-century water color.* Courtesy of *Mr. and Mrs. David Stockwell, Wilmington, Delaware.*

FIGURE 4. *View of Whampoa anchorage, about 12 miles below Canton. Early-nineteenth-century water color.* Courtesy of *Mr. and Mrs. David Stockwell, Wilmington, Delaware.*

Junks from the South East Indies, Philippine cargo boats, passenger and upcountry vessels, government cruisers, ferries, and barbers' boats were joined by the usual sampans, fortunetellers' vessels from Honam (Hanan) Island, and boats loaded with theatrical performers. Whampoa of the 1830's was thus described:

> . . . imagine a city afloat, and it conveys a very correct idea of the incessant movement, the subdued noises, the life and gaiety of the river.[5]

At the anchorage the traders encountered more Chinese officials, chief of whom was the "hoppo," or administrator of customs, for Canton. As district representative of the Emperor at Peking, he was outside the local Canton authority, administered by a viceroy and governor. The hoppo's job involved exacting as much as possible from the foreigners through tonnage and customs fees, not only for himself, but for many officials at the Imperial Palace to whom he owed his job.[6] The hoppo usually received a gift, or "cumshaw," in appreciation for the privilege of trading. Cumshaws were a general item for services performed, given by foreigners to many Chinese, comprador to mandarin. When the *Empress* first arrived at Whampoa, Samuel Shaw was greatly embarrassed not to have the expected "sing-songs," that is, clockwork or mechanical gadgets, that fascinated the Chinese; he recorded in the ship's logbook that the hoppo, satisfied when he knew they were from a new country, directed them to bring some when they came again.[7]

The "comprador" often deserved his cumshaw for the many duties required of him. Each vessel actually had two such agents, one engaged at Whampoa for supplying the ship, and another at Canton, who kept the factory in stock, supervised its staff, and dealt with outside tradespeople.[8] For American traders one of the most popular compradors at Whampoa was "Boston Jack," regarded by his countrymen as a very "great gun." [9] Another ship's comprador was mentioned by Thomas W. Ward, master of the *Minerva*, from Salem, in 1809:

> Tom Bull . . . is like all other Chinese you deal with, except in one particular: he is an honorable scoundrel, and will tell you how much, & why, & wherefore he cheats you. He is as good as any of them. I dealt with him considerably in selling my outward cargo, & had some trouble, but he was pretty punctual for a Comprador.[10]

Through a "fiador," or surety man, the ship's goods were contracted for a hong merchant at Canton; then the process of unloading began.[11] From this point, the entire activity of transshipment of cargoes to and from Whampoa and Canton and of the payment of customs fees was usually taken care of by the Chinese. The Americans were simply charged a lump sum, undoubtedly often unjustly high.

In this enterprise the "linguists" were also employed. They were primarily interpreters, essential to mutual exchange of orders through their "pidgin," or business English, but they also handled official business with the mandarins and obtained sampans to load and unload the ships. In the 1787–1788 season John Barry, of Philadelphia, noted that "the Linguist most uniformly preferred is named Chicqua."[12] Forty years later the principal linguists included Old Tom, Young Tom, and Alantse.[13] They were indispensable not only in commercial transactions, but also for the pleasure of the foreigners, often serving as official guides on river excursions as well as on visits to the flower gardens, and to the Buddhist temple on Honam Island.[14]

The return cargoes, also brought by sampans from Canton, were marked with the seller's seal, or "chop," which indicated to the linguist exactly who was responsible for the duty; otherwise, the purchaser had to pay for it.[15] Final approval for the whole transaction rested with the hoppo. Not until the hoppo's grand chop had been obtained certifying that all formalities, taxes, and other charges had been taken care of could the loaded vessel proceed down the river with a pilot for Macao.[16] Although actually the Emperor kept hands off the foreign trade, the grand chop, an impressive, broad-bordered clearance document, seemed to suggest imperial authority by including the dragon in the elaborate decoration in its margins.

Life in Canton itself meant additional regulations for all foreigners. They were crowded into an area less than a quarter of a mile long, about 700 feet wide, and within 300 feet of the river.[17] Along the water front was a railed-in quay or promenade called the Respondentia Walk, where the traders might exercise. From the beach, stairs and gateways led across the walk to the "factories." These were sections of the Chinese merchants' "hongs," or business houses, and were rented by the foreign factors, or chief traders, in whole or in part, during the trading season.[18]

The factories, crowded one behind another, were longitudinal buildings separated by narrow spaces; they were numbered, beginning in the front with No. 1 and continuing toward the back to Nos. 2, 3, 4, etc. Facing south toward the river, they presented a uniform line, but each was distinguished by its own flag flying from a staff in front (Fig. 5). There were thirteen factories, coincidentally corresponding to the number of hong merchants; but their several names, at least in the later periods, were merely tokens of former activity, for, by the 1780's and 1790's, only the English, Dutch, and American factories really housed their own nationals.[19]

The interiors of the factories were usually divided into three stories, with the lower floors consisting of counting rooms, storerooms, rooms for the comprador and his staff of servants, and usually a treasury. All business affairs were conducted on this ground level (Fig. 6). The second story was used for dining and living rooms; and the third, for bedrooms. Generally the factories were well built for efficiency and a certain amount of comfort, but they had little ornament, especially on the exterior.[20]

In 1787 John Barry wrote concerning renting a factory:

> On arriving at Canton one of the first things to be attended to is procuring a factory . . . the front range of factories rent from 700 to 1200 Dos the Season each—they are dominated N°. 1 & differ greatly in point of elegance—the range N° 2 immediately behind the former rent usually

FIGURE 5. *View of the factories at Canton, about 1800. Flags (left to right) are the Danish, Spanish, American, Swedish, British, and Dutch. Early-nineteenth-century oil painting.* Courtesy of *Winterthur Museum.*

FIGURE 6. *View of the first-floor interior of a factory, perhaps the American, with different stages of a tea transaction taking place. About 1830. Courtesy of* Peabody Museum of Salem.

about 200 or 300 drs less. The prospect before them is Shut up & this is the principal reason that makes them less eligible than the front ones— Ships which arrive late Sometimes meet difficulty in procuring a factory without going far back to N$^{os}$ 4, 5, or 6. A Circumstance of Greater co[n]venience than almost any other point of difference between the factories is that in Some of them their [*sic*] is a Treasury or Strongly built Appartment to keep the Silver in.[21]

As a neat border behind the trading area ran Thirteen Factory Street, which divided the factories from the city of Canton proper. On the north side, facing Old China Street, was the Council Hall of the Hong, known to the foreigners as the Consoo. It was an extensive and handsomely built series of buildings containing many suites of rooms, several with open courtyards, for receptions and business meetings. Here the hong merchants, or Co-hong, as the guild was called, conferred among themselves or with foreigners about the trade.[22]

As security agents for the government, the hong merchants were liable to fines if Europeans or Americans infringed on the regulations imposed on them. These restrictions added both physical and psychological boundaries to the foreigners' activities. The Co-hong saw that no ships of war entered the river; that no women, guns, spears, or other arms were brought by the traders; that Chinese merchants did not incur debts to the foreigners; and that the traders did not engage Chinese servants or use sedan chairs. Foreigners were not permitted to row on the river without supervision. They were to deal only with the hong merchants and to be completely under their direction as tenants in their factories. As already noted, they were forbidden to stay at Canton during the off season, though for a fee two or three could be permitted to stay behind. All others had to sail for home or stay at Macao, even paying for their departure. These rules were sometimes relaxed by the Chinese; but occasionally they were reinforced to the embarrassment of the foreigners.[23]

In 1818 Alexander McNeilledge pictured the procedure of business transactions with the hong merchants, which remained very much the same throughout the trading period. Since the Americans and other foreigners quite often had to trust their judgment in the choice of goods, knowing the reliability of each merchant was of prime importance:

> The Government enter into no immediate transactions with Foreigners, all duties etc. are paid by the Chinese when therefore you fix a price for your goods the Chinese Purchaser has the duty to pay in addition to this price and when you purchase the Price named is understood to include the Exp.ᵗ duty for which the Chinese is liable. No Goods should be delivered to a Chinese till he has deposited the Money; Nor should any money be paid him until he has delivered the Goods purchased. Trade is in this way rendered very easy; for the Stranger has no cause to enquire the Character or Credit of a Purchaser, and he can do business without paying a commission to any other person. It is however of great consequence to him to know the characters of those from whom he buys, as he is seldom or ever a competent judge of the qualities of Teas which form a portion of every Cargo.[24]

Many Americans kept track of the qualifications of all the Chinese in pocket-size trading notebooks. One can imagine that these character sketches were carefully guarded by the supercargoes, who carried heavy responsibilities in ordering return shiploads. In listings of different periods the names of several merchants reappear, often with amusing spellings. Others are new, indicating the changes due to bankruptcies or deaths. In 1816 Benjamin Shreve, of Salem, briefly described the hong merchants: [25]

| [Merchant's name (as known to the foreigners)] | [Name of his firm or hong] | [Personal comment] |
| --- | --- | --- |
| No. 1. Houqua | Ewo Hong | — very rich does most all Am business |
| 2. Mowqua | Kwonglee | — Rich |
| 3. Paunkeequa | Tongfoo | — very rich secure 1 Am Ship in 1815 |
| 4. Chunqua | Tunsing | — so so rich a great scoundrel |
| 5. Consequa | Lyachinene | — poor has failed |
| 6. Pacqua | Lyeshing | |
| 7. Manhope | Fooklyn | — cannot be depended upon at all |
| 8. Ponqua | Tongtya | |
| 9. Beaqua | Tongewe | |
| 10. Kingqua | Tingpo | — Secures several American Ships every year   Principally Opium & Skin Ships |

The name of Houqua reappears constantly in similar lists as the merchant with whom Americans were most frequently secured.[26] Actually there were four Houquas, as this name was applied by the foreign traders to four separate merchants of the Wu Family. The second Houqua, apparently the one mentioned here, maintained this favored position through most of the period under consideration. Thomas W. Ward wrote of him in 1809:

Houqua is at the head of the Hong—is very rich, sends good cargoes & just in all his dealings, in short is a man of honour and veracity—has more business than any other man in the Hong and secures 12 or 14 American ships this year. Houqua is rather dear loves flattery & can be coaxed.[27]

Eleven years later Robert Waln made a small chart in his notebook listing each merchant's standing, articles of trade, and residence. He also
found Houqua the leader of the hong, and most of the other hong merchants, located on Bridge or Thirteen Factory Street, of "No. 1" standing.[28]

In addition, Waln carefully listed the leading "outside merchants."
Distinct from the Co-hong, these men were originally meant to supply
foreigners with goods only for personal use. This privilege had long
been considerably stretched, however, to include many other items.[29]
For example, Waln recorded several such merchants as dealers in tea,
nankeens, silks, paintings, and chinaware. Included in this last group
were Fouchong and Synchong (Sinchong), both "No. 1," and Cumshong, "No. 2," all of whom lived on New China Street.[30]

Two years earlier Alexander McNeilledge had clearly stated the
relationship of outside men to the hong merchants, and the wide range
of goods in which they dealt:

> Soon after the establishment of the Hong, its Merchants found that they
> could not attend to every part of the immense business monopolized & in
> consequence the trade in *China Ware, Shoes, Clothes, Ivory & Tortoise
> Shell Works* & a few other things was thrown open. The Hong still re-
> tained the Tea and Silk trade. It was soon made the interest of some of
> the poorer Security Merchants to lend their names to less privileged
> dealers and by degrees a very large portion of the Trade fell into the
> hands of Men who not being licensed to carry on such business are called
> *Outside Men* or *Shop-Men*. Among these Outside Men are many whose
> names are a better recommendation of Teas & Silks than those of several
> Hong Merchants. They of course pay more duty than the others, but the
> large Fee paid by a Hong Merchant upon his introduction brings them
> nearly to a level.[31]

Many names are listed among the chinaware merchants in the notebooks of several supercargoes. It would be difficult, however, to approximate their total number, undoubtedly varying from year to year. In 1786
the *Grand Turk* brought home ware bought from "Echong," "Hop-
yuk," and "Souchinchiouqua." [32] These names rarely appear again and
probably indicate the turnover among smaller brokers of this sort. But
there were others who were more permanently connected with china-

ware trading. Among them was Synchong, the "Houqua" of the outside porcelain merchants. His reputation for fine quality ware and honest transactions made him very popular with the Americans despite his high prices.

Hezekiah B. Pierrepont, of New York, mentioned Synchong in 1796:

> Singshong—the most respectable China Ware or Porcelain Trader—he is very correct in Business—his worth is better than that of any other Dealer in Canton and his prices are in proportion, for Common & Cheap Goods he is not so suitable as some Other.[33]

A picture of the aged Synchong and others by Thomas W. Ward in 1809 again indicates how these outside men rated not only as chinaware dealers, but also as special and often highly humorous personalities:

> Old Synchong is head China Ware Merchant, is sometimes dearer, often a little cheaper generally better China & always best packed of any man in Canton, is a close fisted old miser, gets drunk every day, but performs his contracts & whatever you can bind him to, he will fulfill. I prefer dealing with Synchong to any other.
>
> Exching is next . . . has much business—Some manners about him—does not pack so well, and China ware not generally so good, great breakage—has considerable business.
>
> Sonyeck . . . you can make good bargains with, but he is rather slippery . . . rising in the World, active & industrious get no cyphered China of him.
>
> Fouchong . . . is a pretty good man, & well spoken of by the Philadelphians, 2% is deducted from all Bills for China Ware and payment made @ 75 Candareens pr Dollar.[34]

Another porcelain merchant engaged by the Americans was Yam Shinqua. Like other dealers, he advertised in this country, hoping to encourage specific orders for his wares. One of his advertisements appeared in the *Providence Gazette*, May 12, 1804:

> Yam Shinqua, China-Ware Merchant, at Canton, Begs Leave respectfully to inform the American Merchants, Supercargoes, and Captains, that he

procures to be Manufactured, in the Best Manner, all sorts of China-Ware with Arms, Cyphers, and other Decorations (if required) painted in a very superior Style, and on the most reasonable Terms. All orders carefully and promptly attended to.

Canton. January 8, 1804.[35]

The chinaware merchants, of course, did not make the ware themselves. They merely contracted with the purchaser to obtain pieces from the manufacturer and to have them painted according to order. Yam Shinqua, for example, made arrangements to "procure" wares, as he advertised. A tea service for which he was responsible is represented in Figure 7 both by his bill bearing another advertisement and by the saucer with the cipher of John A. Colby, of New Concord.

A detailed account of the process of purchasing chinaware, from the initial order to a final transaction with a chinaware merchant, is related in a letter to Mrs. Isaac Hazlehurst, of Philadelphia, in January, 1789, from Captain John Barry, of the *Asia*, in Canton. Since he was unable to fulfill her request, Barry apologetically explained his failure, indicating how much effort a simple order for porcelains might require of a supercargo:

On my arrival at Canton in China almost the first thing I did was to enquire for China, the same as the Pattern you sent by me, but to my great disappointment Could not find Such in Town, I then made Application to the first China Merchant there to see if he could get enough from Nankeen to Compleat your order, he told me he could very easy, I then gave him a copy of Your Memorandum, with the plate, but he had two or three dozen Plates of the same Kind, and he told me he would send one of them and Search the different China Shops, to see if he Could not Match it, I told him that I had tryed myself but I thought perhaps he might find some that I Know nothing of. I was in hopes till the very last day he would have got them, especially as we lay so long there, and I Knew the Chinese would not let any Opportunity Slip to make Money, however I was at last Grievously disappointed and obliged to lay out Your Money on the Purchase of Silks, you have herewith. I hope Madam you will not Conceive an Idea, that I did not do every thing in my Power to Serve you, for believe me, it has given me a great deal of uneasiness ever since the disappointment.[36]

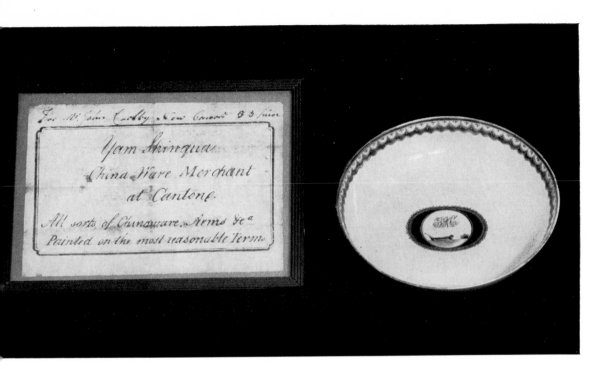

FIGURE 7. *Advertisement of Yam Shinqua, chinaware merchant at Canton, marked "For Mr. John Colby   New Concord   53 piece," referring to a tea service represented by the saucer bearing Colby's cipher JAC. About 1800–1810. From the collection of the late Mrs. Francis B. Crowninshield.*

In doing business with all the merchants, shrewd Americans followed the advice of Alexander McNeilledge. He recommended that, to ensure the most favorable purchases, a list of prices for each article be submitted by the merchants and the lowest bidder chosen.[37] Shippers also could learn from Thomas W. Ward, who was well aware of often being overcharged:

> The only way of trading with Safety is perhaps by dealing with those whose character & standing are such as to secure their honesty by ties of Interest.[38]

Americans thus defended themselves from the restrictions and possible dishonesty of the Chinese by a canny sense for commerce. Samuel Shaw established an excellent precedent for others in the first few years of the trade. In an initial encounter with a small Chinese dealer, he was firm, but polite, in obtaining the price he wished to pay for a certain article. Shaw recorded the following conversation that took place after the bargain was settled:

> "You are not Englishman?" said he. "No." "But you speak English word, and when you first come, I no can tell difference; but now I understand very well. When I speak Englishman his price, he say, 'So much,—take it,—let alone.' I tell him, 'No, my friend, I give you so much.' He look at me,—'Go to hell, you damned rascal; what! you come here,—set a price my goods?' Truly, Massa Typan [supercargo], I see very well you no hap Englishman. All China-man very much love your country." [39]

*Part Two*

# CHINESE EXPORT PORCELAIN MADE FOR THE AMERICAN MARKET

# IV

## Export Porcelain: Its Name and Special Nature

THE TERM "Chinese export porcelain" has here been chosen to identify wares produced in China especially for markets abroad and specifically for the United States. The familiar misnomer for this product, "Lowestoft" (or Sino-Lowestoft), is habitually used as a convenient name, but it is confusing and inaccurate. It derives from the work of William Chaffers, whose book on ceramics, published in 1863, tried to establish a connection between Chinese export porcelain and the ware produced in the pottery factory at Lowestoft, England.[1] This establishment was in operation for about forty-five years, from 1757 to 1802. When manufacture ceased, a former employee, Robert Allen, turned to china merchandising and also decorated blank ware, some of which may have been imported from China.[2] There was thus some reason for Chaffers to equate the two products. But no proof exists that export porcelain was decorated at Lowestoft while the factory was in operation. Moreover, according to the best evidence, the porcelain made at Lowestoft was soft-paste rather than hard-paste ware, the distinguishing feature of the Chinese porcelain.[3] Thus, to call Chinese export porcelain "Lowestoft" is not only vague, but also incorrect.

Another name for the ware, "China-trade porcelain," was used as the title of a recently published book by John Goldsmith Phillips.[4] This term improves considerably upon Chaffers' "Lowestoft," pointing as it does to the country of origin; but it does not seem to be as precise as might be wished. However cumbersome the lengthy title "Chinese export porcelain" may be, its nature and destination are made more explicit because of the word "export." It seems less ambiguous for immediate understanding than "China-trade porcelain."

Of course, names for the porcelains varied considerably from one period of trade to another. In the sixteenth century the Portuguese knew them familiarly as "Gombruns," since the ware was bought at the intermediate port of Gombrun (Bandar Abbas) on the Persian Gulf.[5] Later the British East India Company imported porcelains as "India-China" from Calcutta and Bombay to Continental Europe, England, and America. In 1813 this term was still standard for the English and for the Americans as well.[6] Some time after the American trade had begun, the term "Canton-China" became familiar and correctly stated the porcelain's first place of export. This expression referred mainly to the various sorts of blue-and-white ware so popular in this country: Canton, Nanking, Fitzhugh, and Amoy porcelain. Mandarin or medallion china, developed after the War of 1812, might also be included, but its all-over polychrome design distinguished it from the blue-and-white patterns.[7]

In the late eighteenth and early nineteenth centuries Americans commonly called every variety of porcelain object "China Ware." This term appears endlessly in letters of order, bills of lading, and invoices. Since this study is primarily concerned with the American trade, this brief and contemporary term will frequently be used as a valuable substitute for the longer, more formal, but precise title, Chinese export porcelain.

The porcelain destined especially for America keeps its significance today partly because it was one of the four major imports from China for many years; but its importance is both broader and deeper than a single statistic. It involves the special nature of porcelain in contrast to those of the tea, spices, and fabrics that accompanied it here.

In the first place, porcelain was a personal product. Whether made for the public in gross amounts or on private order, the chinaware eventually belonged to someone. This was, of course, true also of tea and textiles; but they lacked the individuality of a porcelain piece with its special form or decoration, perhaps a monogram, which announced its uniqueness and at the same time enhanced the position of its owner.

This private ownership was partial reason for a second feature of export ware—its comparative permanency. Because of their personal value, chinaware pieces were often preserved as family heirlooms. In addition, sets of porcelain were designed by their very composition to withstand a considerable amount of use. This was not true of other China goods. Tea was quickly consumed; spices were expendable; and many fragile textiles could not stand more than several seasons of hard wear.

Further, the porcelain was useful. Despite the fact that it was a romantic product of the exotic East, especially when decorated with Chinese motifs, many Americans seemed most interested in the chinaware because of its functional nature. This aspect again distinguished the porcelain from some of the other China imports, such as japanned ware and rich silks, which were luxury items designed for well-to-do consumers. While chinaware might often be made on special order for the American upper class, it was also sent to this country in bulk for middle- and lower-income groups as well.[8] By far the largest number of imported pieces consisted of dinner, breakfast, tea, or coffee services. Very few objects were purely decorative, though many, of course, were brightly painted. Chinaware satisfied, first, America's desire for the practical and, second, her enjoyment of the luxurious.

The demand for useful porcelains well indicates an apparent difference between Eastern and Western peoples. The Chinese appreciation of a vase, a bowl, or a figurine first, and sometimes solely, for its aesthetic qualities was at least partly misunderstood by porcelain buyers in this country. This did not mean that the Chinese were not practical people; they often judged a work of art on how well it fulfilled its function, rather than solely on its design. However, it was not necessary to demand a purpose for a thing of beauty. In contrast, America's primary concern in the China trade was commercial profit from useful items, and not artistic connoisseurship. This was undoubtedly a reflection of the country's age and contemporary needs, particularly in the early, precarious years of the new nation. In addition, it also indicated a certain lack of sensitivity to the delicate expression of beauty in one of the Orient's most venerated arts.

The porcelain further distinguishes itself as a special symbol of the mutual influence of China and the United States. Pieces combined Oriental forms, craftsmanship, and painting with the boldness of Western shapes and decorations and with American emblems. Eastern or Western features predominated according to the period, reflecting the changing position of the one country with regard to the other.[9]

In addition, the chinaware often reflected the attitude that each country had toward the other. Both nations met mainly for trade, with the aggressiveness of the Americans only increasing the restraint of the Chinese. Commerce was carried on in an atmosphere of suspicion and contempt. Understandably, then, the supercargoes ordered chinaware chiefly with Western forms and decorations, following the instructions of their patrons. Such preferences indicated not only a desire for useful objects and a certain artistic blindness due to European conditioning, but also an oblique, but definite, cultural imperialism. In return, the Chinese, regarding their nation as the unequaled Celestial Kingdom, never exported any of the best-quality porcelain. All the finest pieces were reserved for imperial use, and even the second-quality porcelains were often kept at home, although a few of these entered the foreign trade.[10] The Chinese stood aloof, looking at the Americans as they had looked at generations of foreigners—with an urbane and condescending attitude. Despite such signs of mutual disrespect, however, there were other indications of understanding and cooperation that constant business dealings helped to develop.

The porcelain also reflected the changing tastes of Americans in the fifty years after the Revolution. English shapes and decorative motifs for export ware had always been highly popular in this country and continued to be after 1783; but French fashions increasingly replaced them, especially in the first two or three decades of the nineteenth century. Such a change points to the fact that the ties formed with France during the Revolution were encouraged by the War of 1812 and other estrangements from the British.[11]

All these aspects of the porcelain—its individuality, permanence, usefulness, and reflection of attitudes and tastes—make it an unusually exciting and special product of the first trade relations between the United States and China.

# V

## The Porcelain at Ching-tê Chên and Canton

THE CHIEF PRODUCTION CENTER for China's distinctive ceramic art and the major source of export porcelain was the ancient establishment of Ching-tê Chên in the province of Kiangsi. One could reach Ching-tê Chên entirely by water by following the Yangtze River from the coast to the mouth of P'oyang Lake, near the city of Kiukiang, crossing the lake to Jaochow on the Ch'ang River, and traveling 30 miles up the Ch'ang to Ching-tê Chên.[1]

The town's complete concentration on the production of porcelain dated back to well over sixteen hundred years before the Americans became interested in its wares. Since the Han dynasty (202 B.C. to A.D. 220), and probably even earlier, unknown quantities of pottery had been made there; but not until the Sung dynasty (960–1279) did an imperial factory begin operations to produce special wares for the palace at Peking. By the time of the Ming dynasty (1368–1644), the high standards set by this factory meant a greater degree of artistic achievement not only in pieces destined for the emperor, but also in objects made by many private concerns.[2]

Ching-tê Chên produced many fine porcelains during the Ming dynasty, with especially outstanding wares being made at different times, as during the reign of Hsüan-te (1426–1435). With the death of Emperor Wan Li, in 1620, there began a period of conflict between the Ming and Ch'ing dynasties, with three rulers in the few years between 1620 and 1644. This time of uncertainty and transition in the government was reflected in the porcelain industry at Ching-tê Chên by a marked slowing down in production for the palace and by few, if any, improvements in the processes used by the factories. Not until the Ch'ing dynasty was well established under the emperor K'ang-hsi (1662–1722) was there any noticeable change in the situation. It was under the leadership of K'ang-hsi that Ching-tê Chên was rebuilt after a fire in 1675 had almost completely destroyed the town. The Emperor re-established the imperial factory and, in 1683, appointed Ts'ang Ying-hsüan as its director.[3] From this time, the patronage of the emperors K'ang-hsi and his son Yung-Chêng (1723–1735) combined with the talents of master potters to produce porcelain in a wide variety of rich and brilliant colors and to develop special processes such as the cloisonné enamel style which distinguished the late-seventeenth- and early-eighteenth-century works of Ching-tê Chên.[4] By the reign of Ch'ien-lung (1736–1795), under whom the great bulk of the trade in export porcelain was carried on, the town had reached its peak performance. By the closing years of the eighteenth century and especially under Chia-ch'ing (1796–1821), it had begun to decline.[5]

A description of the area was recorded in a letter written by the Jesuit missionary Père François Xavier d'Entrecolles in September, 1712, giving a picture of Ching-tê Chên which probably was still accurate seventy-five years later, when Americans were interested in its products. The settlement was located near the junction of two rivers, the Ch'ang and a small tributary, falling from mountain gorges to the north and west. To the east, a semicircle of hills enclosed the town.[6] Here were gathered almost a million people crowded into a packed, but neat, arrangement of houses. All were involved in the porcelain industry. Without the nucleus of educated and scholarly men of which many Chinese towns boasted, the population of Ching-tê Chên was singularly limited to the laborer and the businessman, except for a few officials from Peking or Jaochow.[7] The workers included great numbers of the blind and maimed, employed in specific jobs such as grinding colors.[8]

D'Entrecolles estimated that "at least three thousand" furnaces were kept active in the town, but this seems too generous a number.[9]

Probably there were about five hundred furnaces or kilns serving the three to four thousand factories that were producing wares.[10] When the kilns were in use, the whole area must have looked like a giant campsite with thousands of fires going at once. D'Entrecolles remarked:

> The sight with which one is greeted on entering through one of the gorges consists of volumes of smoke and flame rising in different places so as to define all the outlines of the town; approaching at nightfall, the scene reminds one of a burning city in flames, or of a huge furnace with many vent-holes.[11]

Even with its large population and constant activity, Ching-tè Chên could not officially be called a city because it lacked a wall. It was, however, ideally located for the special function of making porcelain; and perhaps the absence of a wall was beneficial in that it allowed for the necessary expansion of the industry. The two primary ingredients of porcelain—kaolin and petuntse, both derived from decomposed granite —were readily available in the area nearby. Petuntse was found in the mountains along the Ch'ang River, and kaolin in the district of Kaoling to the east of Ching-tè Chên.[12]

The chief differences between petuntse and kaolin lay in their molecular composition and in method of preparation. Containing quartz, petuntse came from the earth in the form of stone that had to be washed to remove loose dirt and then was broken by hand or mallet into small lumps or ground by water-driven mills into pulverized stone. Placed in tubs or bins of water, it was stirred with a wooden rake until the dregs and sediment sank to the bottom. The pure part, known as "cream," was then skimmed off and run through a fine hair sieve and allowed to congeal in bags of a double thickness of fine cloth. Pressed or pounded until the water was removed from the mass, the contents of the bags formed soft blocks, or "white bricks," ready for use in combination with kaolin. Kaolin, in contrast, came from the earth as a natural clay of remarkably fine consistency and white color; it required no breaking or grinding and less washing and purifying before it was ready for use. In combination, the two strengthened each other, the petuntse making the mixture more fusible and the kaolin providing greater ease in modeling. The two, combined in right proportion with the right amount of water added, were worked together by repeated treading, beating, or pounding until the clay became a firm mass of a consistency suitable for modeling.[13]

The fusion of the two was aided and the color improved by the addition of stone oil, made from petuntse, and by oil derived from lime and fern ashes. The whitish stone oil, when combined with the green oil, made the clay even whiter.[14] In addition, the clear water of the Ch'ang River undoubtedly added to the purity of the porcelain. Petuntse furnished the principal material for the glaze, because its quartz content contributed to the impermeable and vitreous surface peculiar to porcelain.[15]

The Chinese paintings shown in Figures 9 through 31 depict many of the steps in the porcelain industry. Seen in them are the digging of kaolin and petuntse and the processes already described for purifying the two and combining them into the raw clay used in making porcelain (Figs. 9–15); the forming of objects of various shapes and sizes by use of potters' wheels or molds, the smoothing of rough places from objects, and then the drying of long rows of raw-clay vessels (Figs. 16–19); the decorating, glazing, and drying of raw-clay objects (Fig. 20); the loading, sealing, and firing of the kilns, and then the removing of the finished porcelain from the kilns (Figs. 21–24); the grinding and mixing of colors, the applying of overglaze decoration, with a second, but shorter, firing (in an open stove for small objects and a closed stove for large) to set the paints of the overglaze decoration (Figs. 25–27); the packing of finished porcelains, the labeling of the packed tubs, and the distributing of them to Chinese merchants (Figs. 28–30).[16] Besides portraying the major processes, the pictures suggest other aspects of the industry, such as the locale of the clay fields and the factories, the number of workers and the variety of activities involved in a single step of the porcelain-making procedure, the great range in age of workers, the types of buildings and tools used. That provision was made for things other than actual work is indicated in Figure 31, which pictures workers enjoying one form of recreation, a play given at the manufactory. In this connection it is interesting to note that, according to a description published in China in 1815, the royal factory at Ching-tê Chên had in it two recreation rooms for the kiln staff and also three temples.[17]

Porcelain making involved specialized skills in the performance of particular processes with any success or speed. The factories were therefore established on a system comparable to a modern assembly line, with a division of the total labor among trained workers, each limited to his single occupation.[18] In his letter of 1712, Père d'Entrecolles noted the mass-production methods of the workers:

> I am told that a piece of porcelain has passed through the hands of seventy workmen. I can easily believe this by what I have myself seen.[19]

He found, for instance, a definite apportioning of the work merely in the shaping of the clay into round forms, either by the wheel or by single or several piece molds. The wheel and a simple mold were sufficient for circular pieces, the mold being necessary to make pieces uniform. The production of oblong objects, such as tureens and platters, required special molds because the objects could not take their basic shape from the wheel.[20] Even the making of molds was a specialized skill, for the mold had to be accurate in size and shape to allow for shrinkage in the baking of the object formed in it, the amount of shrinkage depending on variations in factors such as the type of clay used for the molded object and the type of fire used in the kiln.[21]

Specialization was further apparent in the decoration of the porcelain by different groups of painters. Again, d'Entrecolles commented:

> The painting is distributed in the same workshop among a great number of workmen. One workman does nothing but draw the first colour line beneath the rims of the pieces; another traces flowers, which a third one paints; this man is painting water or mountains and that one either birds or other animals. Human figures are generally treated the worst.[22]

The procedures described were followed for most types of porcelain, including those made for the foreign trade; but the latter pieces were frequently made of inferior materials, according to the classification of the Chinese themselves.[23] Pieces for foreigners were of two types —*hua*, or "slippery," and *ni*, or "mud." Porcelain classified as *hua* was made of slippery stone and was of good quality as far as substance was concerned; but, when glazed, it failed to show off color as brilliantly and lustrously as did the best type of porcelain, carefully reserved by the Chinese for themselves. Pieces in the *ni* group were completely lacking in quality of basic material; they were made from the earth dregs, or "brick mud," which sank to the bottom of the washing bins or gathered in the sieves in the process already described of purifying petuntse, skimming off the cream, and running it through hair sieves. Many establishments saved and accumulated this residue, known as "sweepings," which workmen sorted and sifted, taking any usable parts to make a paste, which in turn was used in making the roughest sort of pieces, especially those for the foreign trade.[24]

In baking, porcelains received treatment in proportion to their value. Only rough pieces were placed in the first two rows opposite the entrance of the kiln; they served as a screen against the most intense heat of the flames. Not until the third row from the fire was it safe to put the finer wares. In the three or four back rows coarse ware was again used to block the blaze.[25] Thus, perhaps a large portion of the export ware not only was made of the least-refined clay, but also was open to the first accidents of flame or temperature in the kiln.

The completed porcelain, some of it decorated before glazing and baking and some left plain for later decoration by special order, was packed in reeds or straw and sent north or south, depending on its destination, either to the Imperial Palace or to the factories at Canton. The dispersal pattern from Ching-tê Chên can be seen from the map in Figure 8. When chinaware was ordered for the emperor, it was shipped by way of the Yangtze to Chinkiang, then up the Grand Canal to Tientsin, and finally to Peking. Optional routes to Canton lay inland and by sea. The latter route, taken by ocean-going junks that followed the Yangtze to its mouth and down along the coast south, was a perilous voyage because pirates were a constant danger. The inland route, though perhaps safer, was more involved. Junks first brought the porcelain to Nanchang, the capital of Kiangsi province, on the Kan River southwest of P'oyang Lake. Père d'Entrecolles reported that Nanchang was filled with shops for chinaware, "its principal staple," which was distributed to all parts of China south of it.[26] Smaller boats took the porcelain up the Kan River to Nananfu, a town in the south of the province. From there it was carried on the backs of men or animals over the steep and precarious Meiling Pass to the town of Namyung, on a tributary of the North River, whence the trip to Canton could be completed by boat. It would be difficult to say which of the two very different routes was more com-

Miles

FIGURE 8. *Map showing two major routes from Ching-tê Chên to Canton.* Drawing by *Gordon Saltar.*

monly used to travel the 600 miles from Ching-tê Chên to Canton.[27]

Once in Canton, some of the pieces left blank or only partially painted received their final decoration and a final firing to set the colors. Chinese painters were located both in Canton and on the island of Honam, indicating the extent of foreign demand for their work.[28] In 1769 the American traveler William Hickey and his friends observed that the artists in Canton worked, as did the potters, in an assembly line:

> We were then shown the different processes used in finishing the China ware. In one long gallery we found upwards of a hundred persons at work in sketching or finishing the various ornaments upon each particular piece of ware, some parts being executed by men of a very advanced age, and others by children even so young as six or seven years.[29]

In 1815 John R. Latimer's description of the final decorating process at Canton indicated it to be much the same as decades before:

> The second apartment [of the pack house and paint shop of Fouchong] was the penciling room where there were a great number of men & boys employed, stowed as close & not dissimilar to a school. It is surprising with what diligence & patience a man would with a small pencil [actually a hair brush] lay on the gilding & colours of each piece. . . . In this establishment there are from 80 to 100 hands employed; the best workmen get from 8 to 10 Dolls. pr. month and their rice.[30]

In the same letter, Latimer also explained the firing process after the porcelain was painted:

> After the colours have had time to dry they are carried to the furnace for glazing, which is performed in a furnace not unlike an oven in which the ware is gradually heated untill it becomes almost red hot, & is cooled by being removed from one furnace to another of less & less heat untill it can bear the air.[31]

There were reasons enough for the porcelain to be finished at Canton. The supercargoes were, of course, concentrated at the port by force of imperial limitation; and it was much easier to have a complicated design executed by having the painter, the orderer, and the purchaser in the same place. Moreover, many Chinese artists depended solely on the foreign market for their livelihood and thus probably encouraged every aspect of it in which they might participate.

The ability of the artists in Canton was frequently commented on by American supercargoes responsible for arranging for specific work to be done. When Samuel Shaw, in Canton in 1784 as supercargo for the *Empress of China*, wished to have "something emblematic of the institution of the order of the Cincinnati executed upon a set of porcelain" by having the artist use figures taken from three engravings and from the emblems of the Cincinnati (all of which Shaw supplied the artist), he found that the best artist in Canton could copy each figure exactly, but that he was unable to combine the figures convincingly. Shaw commented in his journal concerning this experience:

> There are many painters in Canton, but I was informed that not one of them possesses a genius for design. . . . It is a general remark, that the Chinese, though they can imitate most of the fine arts, do not possess any large portion of original genius.[32]

In 1820 Robert Waln, of Philadelphia, observed the Canton painters and their style. He said of them:

> The Chinese are excellent copyists, but possess little or no inventive faculties. In the suburbs of Canton there are many Painters chiefly depending on foreigners, by whom they are almost exclusively employed. The Chinese themselves afford little encouragement to this beautiful art.
>
> But those artists who reside in, and are employed by the aliens at, Canton, possess a very respectable knowledge of their profession. Among the first of these are Hatqua, and Toonqua Sen[r] and Jun[r]: the latter devotes his talents entirely to Miniature Painting and is the only person properly qualified for the undertaking: the former copy indiscriminately any originals furnished, which they often excell.[33]

Waln may have referred to painters in general, ones who did portraits, landscapes, mythological figures, and other subjects, and not specifically to porcelain painters. However, the style of the export-ware decorators is almost identical with that of the other artists, judging from remaining works of both groups. Also, it is not altogether unlikely that an artist could do paintings on paper, canvas, and glass as well as on porcelain.

Ching-tê Chên probably did not monopolize the production of export porcelain for America. Evidence indicates that pieces designed for the European market and presumably for the American market as well were also made in several other areas. China's extensive ceramic industry, though spread throughout many provinces, seems to have had centers of concentration in the provinces of Honan, Kiangsi, Chekiang, Fukien, and Kwangtung.[34] In Fukien, and especially at Têhua, about 75 miles north of Amoy, factories had been operating since the Sung and Yüan dynasties, as cited by Marco Polo.[35] Works from Têhua (especially figurines) were exported to Europe during the seventeenth and eighteenth centuries, notably the pure white and highly prized *blanc de Chine*. The quality of the Fukien wares included the extremes from coarse, rough china to milk-pure, glossy, translucent porcelain indicative of the finest union between clay and glaze.[36] Quite possibly kilns in Fukien province as well as those at Ching-tê Chên supplied foreign demands. T'ang Ying, a profuse writer and the director of the imperial factory from 1736 to 1749 (or 1753), and Père d'Entrecolles, in his letter of 1712, both reported that potters from Ching-tê Chên were moving to Fukien in order to take advantage of the foreign trade out of Amoy, though their southern kilns apparently did not bring the added profit for which the potters had hoped.[37]

Less important were the communities north of Canton such as Swatow, where poorer-quality porcelain was made, although part of the products of these communities undoubtedly contributed to the supply for export.[38] At Shaouking, west of Canton, there were several factories producing wares the quality of which did not equal that of the porcelain made at Ching-tê Chên; but perhaps it was the Shaouking factories that produced the Canton blue-and-white pieces and a part of the plain ones that were decorated by the Canton enamelers. From these factories, too, may have come the mandarin wares also reputedly decorated at Canton.[39]

At the Yangtze River port of Nanking, wares made at Ching-tê Chên and sent to Canton by the sea route already described were transshipped from river junks to large sea-going junks (see map, Fig. 8). A porcelain of better quality than the usual Ching-tê Chên ware and with a distinctive underglaze blue decoration has acquired the name of Nanking or "Nankeen" ware from this place important in the shipping, rather than the making, of porcelain. The fact that its underglaze decoration had to be applied before the first firing of the porcelain means that the so-called Nanking ware had been decorated before it was ready for shipment from its place of manufacture, Ching-tê Chên.[40]

There is little information giving more than suggestions about the several sources of the export ware. Much more study is needed before a full story can be told. However, the remarks of a prominent American merchant in the China trade are revealing. Augustine Heard, of Boston, may have been generally correct concerning wares produced in the early nineteenth century when he remarked:

> All of the porcelain came from the north except the willow pattern and the "sister" ginger-pots in blue and white which were made in the south.[41]

Ching-tê Chên remains the best-known center of the foreign wares. Despite a general decline, porcelain production has continued there to modern times. By 1837 the population had been reduced by 50 per cent, and the number of kilns had fallen considerably.[42] In the period from 1853 to 1855 the town was sacked by the T'aip'ing rebels, a large part of the potter population massacred, the town burned, and almost all the ovens destroyed. In 1864 the kilns were rebuilt, and the town resumed porcelain-making operations.[43] The comments of a visitor to Ching-tê Chên in 1926 illustrate the continuity of the porcelain industry there. They also give a picture of the traditional methods of transaction between the Cantonese merchants and the porcelain manufacturers:

> I was last in Ching-te Chen in the spring of 1926. There were about 120 kilns working and the product went from the very finest to the very coarsest in all varieties. I hold that this must have been equally the case about 1800, when Ch'ien Lung had scarcely closed his eyes (he died in 1795) [actually, he died in 1799], and when there were still several thousand kilns active in Ching-te Chen. Then, as now, the merchants from all over the vast empire went there yearly and ordered the ware *according to the taste of their districts.* The Chinese merchant who orders porcelain exercises a rigorous examination on the spot, and accepts only the best. The rejected ware is sold by auction and finds ready buyers at greatly reduced prices.

Under such circumstances, the crafty Chinese becomes suddenly very lenient in his examination, and takes what he thinks at all saleable at Canton. The foreigner is not now as exacting as the Chinese buyer, and there is no reason to assume that he was more particular in the eighteenth century.

How orders were handled in China in the eighteenth century I cannot say. The procedure today would be to get in touch with a porcelain shop, say in Canton. The shopkeeper, who goes once a year to Ching-te Chen, or who, if his turnover is large, has a representative there, gladly takes any orders for sufficient quantities of porcelain. Delivery requires about eight months.[44]

Several orders for porcelain sets for Americans in the early years of trade took less than a month to be filled. This type of order required a far shorter time than that noted in the preceding account and referred to wares kept in stock at Canton and painted according to personal specification. Even this comparatively quick service was considered quite a wait. One American noted, in his observations concerning the trade at Canton in the 1790's:

If this Article [chinaware] is to be ship'd orders ought to be given the first thing after your business with the Hong merchant is fixed—as the Patterns are all painted after order & require three to four weeks to compleat.[45]

If, on the other hand, certain forms not in stock were desired, it was necessary to wait at least eight months to a year to have an order completed. In 1815 John R. Latimer, in Canton, wrote home to his mother:

To have china ware according to pattern as it respects shape it is necessary it should be engaged 12 months before wanted.[46]

# THE PROCESS OF PORCELAIN PRODUCTION

*Chinese Water Colors with Notations in English on Reverse*

*Ex Coll.* J. Kenneth Danby. *Courtesy of* Winterthur Museum.

*This group of Chinese water colors, on paper, approximately 10½ by 10 inches each, is believed to have been painted about 1800. On the back of each is an anonymous notation in English. The obvious inaccuracies of these notations (Figure 9, for example, is captioned "Digging the Ground for Porcelain") would make their reproduction here of dubious value. But these inaccuracies emphasize the fact that porcelain was made in areas of China from which all foreigners, including the author of the notations, were excluded. For a full description of porcelain manufacture, see Chapter V of the text.*

## DIGGING, PURIFYING, COMBINING, AND TRANSPORTING KAOLIN AND PETUNTSE

FIGURE 9

FIGURE 10

FIGURE 11

FIGURE 12

FIGURE 13

FIGURE 14

FIGURE 15

# FORMING, SMOOTHING, AND
# DRYING RAW CLAY OBJECTS

FIGURE 16

FIGURE 17

FIGURE 18

FIGURE 19

FIGURE 20

FIGURE 21

FIGURE 22

FIGURE 23

# REMOVING FINISHED PORCELAIN FROM KILNS, MIXING COLORS, APPLYING OVERGLAZE DECORATION, AND REFIRING

FIGURE 24

FIGURE 25

FIGURE 26

FIGURE 27

# PACKING, LABELING, AND DISTRIBUTING
## TUBS OF FINISHED PORCELAIN;
### GIVING A PLAY AT THE FACTORY

FIGURE 28

FIGURE 29

FIGURE 30

FIGURE 31

# VI

## The Exportation of Porcelain
## to America

AMERICA'S INDEPENDENT PURCHASE of Chinese export porcelain was in part simply a reflection of her Western heritage. The
taste for Oriental objects in the Near East and Europe dated from
early times. Arabia, Persia, and Turkey were long known as points of
import and entrepôts for chinaware.[1] During the late Middle Ages,
Genoa and Venice became the entry ports for wares which were either
kept and copied there or eventually passed on to the German states,
France, or England.[2] Between 1504 and 1532 Archbishop William
Warham presented New College, Oxford, with a pale-green celadon
bowl, handsomely mounted in silver. Two bowls given to Sir Thomas
Trenchard by Portuguese guests probably came to England as early as
1506.[3]

These pieces apparently predated the first European sea-borne commerce with China, begun by the Portuguese soon after 1517. By the end
of the next century, however, the Dutch had successfully challenged
Portugal's monopoly of the carrying trade from China. Both were
eventually outdone by England and to some extent by France in the
eighteenth century, the heyday of European interest in export porcelain.[4] Ships of these nations brought home quantities of tea, and by the
last quarter of the seventeenth century tea drinking was in high fashion

with the aristocracy. The demand to serve tea in appropriate native wares undoubtedly increased the desire for objects of porcelain.[5]

By the mid-eighteenth century China goods had stimulated the birth of an independent chinoiserie style in Europe, especially in France. But in the meantime the monarchs of the Continent and England set the fashion for purely imported wares. In the 1550's Charles V, the Holy Roman Emperor, reputedly had china that was decorated with his cipher and badge; and in France the china cabinets of Francis I and his son Henry II were famous for their displays of exquisite chinaware.[6] Shortly afterward a few wealthy Elizabethans owned excellent examples of late Ming blue-and-white ware mounted in silver or ormolu.[7] In 1724 Daniel Defoe, in his *Tour Through the Whole Island of Great Britain*, commented on the interest of Queen Mary (1662–1694) in Chinese porcelains and the wide influence of her taste:

> The Queen brought in the Custom or Humour, as I may call it, of furnishing Houses with *China*-Ware which increased to a strange degree afterwards, piling their *China* upon the Tops of Cabinets, Scrutores and every Chymney-Piece to the Tops of the Ceilings, and even setting up Shelves for their *China*-Ware, where they wanted such Places, till it became a grievance in the Expence of it and even injurious to their Families and Estates.[8]

Among many collections on the Continent, that of Augustus the Strong, Elector of Saxony, dating from the early eighteenth century, included pieces of exceptional quality. Unfortunately, this group of porcelains changed location several times at the expense of many objects of high value.[9] Louis XIV's courtiers, the Dauphin, and the Duke of Orleans followed a famous tradition when they built their elaborate collections, handsomely arranged at Versailles.[10] Americans, too, had the tradition of several centuries to guide them when the British East India Company first brought export porcelain to the colonies.

But chinaware came to North and South America almost two hundred years before the first English ship with porcelain arrived. Shards of the late Ming and early Ch'ing periods and Ch'ing enameled wares have been found in areas of the Western Hemisphere where Spanish traders imported wares from China. Spain had been established in the New World since 1521, and from that time exported a great quantity of silver to the Far East. In return, goods were shipped from China, Indo-China, Japan, and parts of Indonesia to Manila. From this center they went to Acapulco and then either to Peru or Chile or overland to Vera Cruz, where they were sent to Spain.[11] Some wares, of course, remained on this continent. The main goods included silks, metal objects, and porcelains. Thus for three hundred years, from 1521 to 1821, the Spanish carried on trade in these items through their colonies in America.

Though no whole pieces survive, fragments indicate the extent of Oriental porcelains in the New World, whether brought by the Spanish or by other Europeans, especially the English. In Florida shards have been discovered at the Spanish mission of San Francisco de Oconee, 26 miles southeast of Tallahassee, and at an Indian trading post on the Saint Johns River, south of Palatka. Since trading posts for the Seminoles existed only during the British occupation of Florida (1763–1784), the wares presumably were used there during that time. The fragments represent mainly blue-and-white pieces of the eighteenth-century type and a small group of Japanese blue-and-white, undoubtedly of the same period.[12] In 1945 three porcelain fragments were unearthed in "Merrimack Shores," Hampton, Virginia. They are late-eighteenth-century polychrome china with decoration in black pigment, reddish-orange and yellowish-green enamels, and gilt. Now in the United States National Museum are fragments of blue-and-white Chinese export porcelain cups and saucers dug near the site of a Marlborough, Virginia, house known to have been occupied between 1726 and 1768.[13]

Off the coast of Georgia, Fort Frederica on Saint Simon Island held the remains of a variety of wares. This fort, occupied from 1736 until about 1748, was an English settlement designed for defense against the Spanish in Florida, under the command of General James Oglethorpe. The largest number of pieces found there were of blue and white, 105 such fragments being discovered in one house. Another sort of ware seemed similar to the Japanese Arita type. Still another resembled Imari ware, with underglaze blue and overglaze red-and-gold decorations. The remainder were probably Chinese, decorated in underglaze blue and copper, in overglaze iron-red and pale watery-green enamels.[14] On the

Pacific Coast, in the area of Drake's Bay in Marin County, California, pieces of blue and white assigned to the late Ming dynasty have been uncovered.[15]

Beyond this evidence of porcelain in America before 1785, wills, inventories, and newspaper advertisements sharply illuminate the story. The inventory of Cornelis Steenwyck, mayor of New York from 1668 to 1670, who died in 1684, states that he had in his great chamber nineteen porcelain dishes, along with two flowered earthen pots. In 1696 Margharita Van Varick, widow of a Reformed Dutch minister of Long Island, left behind her:

> Three East India cups, three East India dishes, three Cheenie pots, one Cheenie pot bound in silver, two glassen cases with thirty-nine pieces of small china ware, eleven India babyes.

The inventory of her estate also lists 126 pieces of miscellaneous chinaware, including bowls, jugs, flowerpots, toys, and images. Other New York inventories indicate it was not unusual for a late-seventeenth-century New York burgher to own a hundred pieces of pottery and porcelain. These and other records of ownership of chinaware, sometimes in large quantities, by seventeenth-century Dutch families in New York are really not surprising when one considers the early entrance of the Dutch in the Eastern trade and the early and great admiration of the Dutch in Europe for Chinese porcelain (see p. 7); it seems quite likely that Dutch ships in the seventeenth century on trips from Holland to New Amsterdam would have filled at least some of the desire of the Dutch in America for this same ware.[16]

Eighteenth-century New York homes probably also had a generous number of individual porcelain pieces. The ledger kept by Philip Cuyler, a merchant of the city, from 1763 to 1794 listed several patrons' purchases of chinaware, with prices in shillings:[17]

Account of Abraham C. Cuyler of Albany
Dec. 11, 1765—with other purchases, 2 China Bowles 8/

Account of Capt Cortlandt Schuyler of 60th Regiment
Nov. 6, 1766—with sugar, materials (calico) & sundries,
      1 blew China Bowl 12/

# Exportation of Porcelain to America

Account of Peter Dewandler of Albany
Oct. 1, 1766–1 China Tea Pott 8/

Account of Mary Colleson of Albany
To 18 Stone Tea Potts 9/–Sept 13, 1770

Colonial chinaware was customarily shipped by British East India Company vessels from the Far East through England to America. *The New-York Gazette; and the Weekly Mercury* for July 14, 1777, carried the news of recently arrived "China Ware" (which may have been porcelain) for sale at Rhinelander's Store:

> China Ware just imported in the Hannah from London. A large and very general assortment among which are six complete blue and white table sets; bowls of all sizes, breakfast bowls and saucers, cups and saucers of different sizes and patterns, Looking-Glasses . . . to be sold at Rhinelander's Store, the corner of Burling's Slip.[18]

Through England, too, another type of Chinese porcelain may have reached America—that decorated with the arms, crests, or other symbols of English families some of whose members had gone to America. The plate pictured in Figure 32 (see p. 108) is an example of chinaware that could easily have found its way to the colonies long before America entered the China trade. Made before 1734, the plate, with border decoration picturing the harbor of Canton and the port of London, has as its central decoration an elaborate representation of the coat of arms of the Lees of Coton Hall, a Shropshire, England, family.[19] Colonel Richard Lee (1600–1664), of this family, emigrated to America in 1640, settled in York County, Virginia, and became an influential land owner and office holder; he was the first of the Lees of Virginia.[20] Though documentation is yet to be found for such porcelain in America, the Lees and other English families transplanted to America in the seventeenth or eighteenth century could credibly have brought family china with them or have had it sent from England in the days before orders were sent directly to China by American merchants.

Probably the bulk of chinaware brought to the colonies, however, arrived in New England. Newspaper notices and personal papers give evidence that chinaware was more prevalent in the North than in the South. As early as 1641 Thomas Knocker, of Boston, owned "I Chaynie Dish." Six years later the inventory of a wealthy widow, Martha Coteymore, listed "One parcel cheyney plates and saucers, £1." After the turn of the century the East India Company's increased activities brought additional quantities from the East Indies and China. In 1718 Isaac Caillowell's possessions included:

> Five China Dishes, One Doz. China Plates, Two China Muggs, a China Teapott, Two China Slopp Basons, Six China Saucers, Four China Cupps, and One China Spoon Dish.

Sales of privately owned porcelain were often announced in New England papers during the early eighteenth century; but public auctions, indicating a much larger amount of ware available than before, did not appear until the late 1730's. In September, 1737, spices, silks, and Negro slaves were sold on Scarlett's Wharf along with the following:

> A Rich Sortment of China Ware. A Parcel of fine large Enamel'd Dishes. Ditto of divers Sizes of Bowles burnt & Enamel'd. Ditto of all Sorts of Plates. Sundry Complete Setts of Furniture for the Tea Table. Blue & White Bowles; Blue & White Cups & Saucers. Several sorts of small Baskets, etc.[21]

Colonial Philadelphia doubtless had porcelain collections in proportion to her sizable population in the mid-eighteenth century. In 1764 the *Pennsylvania Journal* for December 13 carried the following advertisement:

> *Langdale, John, Junior, China,* Has just opened at Philip Benezets [*sic*] Store in Market Street, A very large Assortment of Enamelled, and blue and white China, which he will sell very low for cash or short credit.[22]

Colonists farther south are also known to have possessed porcelains, though in what quantities it is often hard to tell because of the losses in the South both in family effects and in records of them through Civil War damage, plundering, and vandalism. Even though a study of certain Maryland inventories does not produce much evidence of listing of chinaware until the late 1700's, the Chase family of Maryland used a large and elaborate dinner service illustrated by the polychrome soup plate in Figure 59.[23] Horatio Sharpe, Governor of Maryland from 1753 to 1769, and Lord Dunmore, Governor of Virginia from 1771 to 1775, both supposedly owned chinaware in the eighteenth century.[24] Sometime between 1783 and 1785. William Lee (1739–1795), a tobacco merchant in Virginia, wrote to General Nelson, in Williamsburg, about a box which he wished to send him "containing a dozen blue and White china Plates, a complete set of Nenkeen China, a fine enammelled 6 quart china punch bowl." [25] Patrick Henry's three bowls of export porcelain are now in the possession of a descendant in Lexington, Kentucky.[26] Although these and other pieces of porcelain are known to have been owned by southern families and although Civil War destruction of porcelain can only be estimated, it is reasonable to assume that, because of the earlier and greater commercial activity of New England and other northern ports and the urban development of the northern colonies, probably greater quantities of porcelain were bought and owned in the northern colonies than in the colonies to the south.

### QUANTITIES

It would be impossible to give an accurate account of the amount of porcelain exported to America from 1785 to 1835. If carefully studied, customs records of each port might give a partial idea; but for some cities these papers no longer exist, at least in certain periods.[27] Often, where they are available, their very bulk would require years of reading. Scattered sources, however, may suggest the quantity that arrived during the most active years of the China trade, the average amount carried by a single ship, and the common composition of a box of chinaware.

It was previously noted that the period after the War of 1812 saw a second boom in the America-China trade, with the peak number of forty-seven ships at Whampoa in the season 1818–1819. Benjamin Shreve, supercargo from Salem, estimated the approximate quantities of porcelain as well as other exports sent to America from 1815 to 1821. Unfortunately, he did not note the standard of measurement he used.

His figures may be quoted, however, to give a relative picture of the variations in the postwar trade in chinaware:

ESTIMATE OF ANNUAL EXPORTS FROM CHINA
TO THE UNITED STATES OF AMERICA
COMMENCING SEASON OF 1815–1816 *

| Season | China |
|--------|-------|
| 1815–16 | 5.935 |
| 1816–17 | 7.950 |
| 1817–18 | 12.487 |
| 1818–19 | 3.638 |
| 1819–20 | 2.872 |
| 1820–21 | .869 |

* Benjamin Shreve (Peabody Museum of Salem, MS, Brig *Comet*).

It is interesting to see that the largest quantity of porcelain was apparently sent out in 1817–1818, one year before the banner season of American voyages to China.

From these figures it might be said that chinaware enjoyed a popularity in this country, reaching a sharp climax shortly after the War of 1812 and then quickly declining. Chapter VIII deals directly with the falling off of the market, but the reasons for the porcelain's appeal may be noted here.

As seen before, the chinaware was already familiar to the colonists before the Revolution. They no doubt enjoyed the porcelain for its cleanliness and daintiness in contrast with pewter and wood utensils. Also, porcelain was probably less costly, more durable, and more fascinating because of its origin and decoration than was European pottery.

After American independence was won in 1783, the chinaware became even more appealing. Pewter still had to be bought from England, but porcelain could be independently purchased direct from China. In addition, Americans could glory in their own symbols, as Europeans had done, when they bought ware with national flags, family crests, or men in Western dress. Moreover, a dinner or tea service decorated with the owner's cipher announced his renewed feeling of individualism or gratified his growing pride in free enterprise. It is little wonder that export porcelain, being practically useful and at the same time expressive of the country's personality, was in such demand in America at the height of the China trade.

The number of tubs, chests, boxes, or piculs and tons carried by certain ships constantly varied. And comparisons between cargoes is complicated by the wide diversity of unit measurements, ranging from containers to actual weights. Special examples, however, may be chosen to illustrate typical shiploads. In 1785 the *Empress of China* brought home 962 piculs of chinaware in 137 chests.[28] The amount was second only to her black and green teas, with silks, nankeens, and cassia comprising the remainder.[29] The next year the *Grand Turk* returned to Salem with 75 boxes of porcelain.[30]

During the period from October 1, 1798, to June 30, 1799, Robert Waln recorded the return of five American ships and their chinaware cargoes. The ship *Neptune*, New York, which sailed out by way of the Falkland Islands, sold its 53,000 sealskins and bought tea, nankeens, silk, and 150 boxes of china to be sold in Boston. From Boston the *Thomas Russell* exchanged specie for tea, nankeens, and 400 boxes of china. The ship *Jean*, Philadelphia, sailed by way of Java with ginseng and specie and brought back 100 boxes of porcelain. For blackwood and specie, the ship *Pallas*, Portsmouth, New Hampshire, bought 177 boxes of china to be sold in Salem. The *Hope*, Boston, sailed direct to and from Canton, trading specie for 350 boxes of chinaware as well as other goods.[31]

Ten years later, in 1809, William Bell, of New York, noted various weights of twenty-two porcelain shipments destined for several ports along the East Coast. The range is somewhat remarkable, but may indicate the flexible nature of the market for chinaware according to the season and city. Captain Blakeman, of the ship *Trident*, New York, returned with 5,800 piculs, or about 385 tons, of porcelain. This amount almost outweighed the average tonnage of the small American craft and must be considered an unusual load. On the other hand, Captain Thomas W. Ward of the *Minerva*, Salem, carried only 2 piculs. The *Pacific*, headed for Philadelphia, sailed with 527 piculs; the *Hibernia* with 321, the *Susquehanna* with 291, the *Hunter* with 165, and the *Delaware* with 5 piculs, none of whose destinations were listed.[32] The median figure of those given (four were not recorded) was approximately 80 piculs of chinaware. The average was about 445 piculs. From these figures, and from the ones given by Robert Waln, it may be estimated that a typical vessel carried approximately 200 to 250 boxes of chinaware, weighing between 150 and 200 piculs. In passing, it may be noted that the quantity of porcelain carried by many ships was important as ballast. This fact may explain the large amounts brought back by single ships. The use of chinaware as ballast will be more fully discussed later in this chapter. In considering these calculations of an average shipload of porcelain, it must be emphasized that the great differences between individual shipments and between types of containers and measurements make these figures only hypothetical, but still they are useful as a rough gauge.

What might a typical box or chest of chinaware contain? An endless combination of different wares was often packed together; and, of course, private purchases varied from gross orders of porcelain for retail sale. In 1802 Captain Ichabod Smith, a Salem merchant, purchased two plain blue-and-white dinner services of 102 pieces each for a total of $58; a Nankeen blue-and-white stone china tea and coffee set, "with high gilt edges," of 115 pieces at $19.50; and blue-and-white dessert plates, washbowls and goblets, and chamber pots with covers, all for $86.[33]

Much larger amounts were shipped for dealers or shopkeepers. William Bell, supercargo for the ship *Eliza* in 1806, brought back a great quantity of porcelain for the New York merchant Peter McKinley. Eight boxes were filled with scalloped-edge tea sets, and nine contained ones with plain rims. Each box held, on the average, 600 pairs of teacups and saucers, 12 half-pint bowls and saucers, 18 pint bowls, 6 sugar dishes, 6 milk ewers, and 6 cake plates. An additional 100 boxes were "to contain a Tea Set of 46 p.[s] the patterns to be assorted and to consist of at least 10 diff.[t] ones, the price from 2 to 2 ¼ Dollars." Twenty small boxes were to hold "a Tea Sett of 26 pc[s] to consist of 5 Different patterns & to cost from 3 to 3 ½ D[rs]."[34] On the same shipment came a load very similar to McKinley's for Thomas Chrystie, another merchant, except that his tea sets were specified as bell-shaped instead of scalloped or plain.[35]

Three years later Bell again brought back a considerable consignment for John H. Titus, Thomas C. Pearsall, Peter Schermerhorn, and John J. Glover, all of New York. The total amount consisted of 548 boxes of tea and coffee sets at a price of $1,176.[36] In 1816 Albert Chrystie also employed Bell to bring back 98 boxes of tea sets, costing all together $16,451.80, as well as separate boxes filled with single types of pieces: butter boats, scalloped dishes, round pudding dishes, oval fruit baskets, square covered dishes, salad bowls, and custard cups.[37]

In 1816 John Jacob Astor also placed a huge order for porcelains, consisting of 265 boxes of blue-and-white tea and coffee sets, 600 boxes of tea china, and 102 boxes of assorted china, totaling $7,304.86.[38] At the height of the porcelain export to this country, in 1817–1818, Robert Waln and John C. and William H. Smith bought 3,000 boxes of chinaware brought by the *Caledonia*.[39] This shipload was undoubtedly an uncommonly large amount, but the others are representative cargoes of chinaware at the apex of the China trade in export porcelain. What happened to bulk shipments in the next few decades may be seen in Chapter VIII, where the eventual decline of American interest in porcelains from the Orient is considered.

QUALITIES

One may wonder about the quality of such quantities of export ware. The unrefined materials from which at least part of the foreign porcelains were made and their rigorous treatment during firing have been mentioned. As a result, an entire piece might warp or be badly sooted, and the glaze might not take well. If the glaze was too heavily coated, especially on larger pieces, it could crawl, bubble, and become pitted under kiln temperatures. These reactions produced either the curdled "potato soup" or "orange peel" surface.[40] In addition, the painting techniques of the Chinese did not always improve the appearance of export wares, at least to some Western eyes.

The Chinese never successfully mastered the European method of creating a three-dimensional scene. Despite the instructions of Italian and French artists at the imperial court in the late seventeenth and early eighteenth centuries, the art of producing isometric perspective through linear treatment and the use of cast shadows did not appeal to the Chinese, and was never used by artists in the provinces, such as the porcelain painters and the painters of local scenes. The peculiar style of the latter may be readily noted in the series of water colors that depict the porcelain manufacturing process (Figs. 9–31), as well as in many of the illustrated objects, notably the Declaration of Independence ware (Figs. 136 and 138). About 1820 Robert Waln observed the method of Chinese painting in general with some lack of appreciation:

> The character of Chinese Painting is totally different from the settled principle of the art in our country, and a landscape after their fashion appears one of the most incongruous things in the world: having no regard to perspective, the background is represented in a preposterous manner by placing it above the more advanced objects in the picture: the intermediate representations are arranged in the same way, according to their situation, all bearing the same tint. Variety of colors are seldom or ever used, and to the eye accustomed to the vivid beauties of a West or the proportioned excellence of a Trumbull, the whole appears a mass of black marks, representing nothing: no shading is used, and at the best it can be considered the bare outline of an unsuccessful attempt to imitate nature.[41]

Waln also commented on the originality of the Chinese artists:

> In execution, their progress is inconcievably [*sic*] rapid, if a beaten path is to be pursued;—if a new road is to be opened they become entangled in difficulties; & are slow, cautious & faulty; thus the first copy of a picture is liable to many errors, particularly if the original partakes of any quality or resemblance unknown to the Chinese artist.[42]

Not all the export porcelain shipped to America should be condemned, however, as scraps of the waste bin decorated by ignorant Chinese artists in a slipshod fashion. Individual pieces and large services of fine quality discount such a generalization. Perhaps they are in the minority among the great quantities of export porcelain that came here; nonetheless, they do show that Americans possessed porcelains of artistic merit. The *Grand Turk* punch bowl (Fig. 33), the Stephen Decatur and George Washington flagons (Figs. 115 and 109), a large bowl painted with the Canton hongs (Fig. 41), and others exhibit high skill in production and decoration. Though none of the wares equal the exquisite pieces reserved for imperial use, articles of excellent clay, dexterously painted in clear and lively enamels, may be found. The Oriental mind, trained to minute copying, could bring great care to the execution of detail.[43]

## Exportation of Porcelain to America

The differences between certain classes of porcelain were listed in the careful notes of Robert Waln, who derived his information from the French traveler De Guignes' *Voyages à Péking* published in Paris in 1808. Porcelain was, of course, distinct from either earthenware or stoneware by its finer composition, hardness, distinctive whiteness, sonority, and—in the best pieces—its translucency. Wares that might all be termed porcelains also varied according to the amount of kaolin and petuntse they contained. Of the first quality was stone china, according to Waln's memorandum, which had a better paste, was more carefully fired, and was smoother than other porcelains. It contained equal portions of kaolin and petuntse. Second-quality ware had six parts of petuntse to four of kaolin. The commonest china had one part of the former to three parts of the latter.[44] Types of decoration also changed the value of porcelains from the commonest sort of blue and white to those of better quality, especially the Nanking ware, and finally to the enameled wares. The variety of painted designs and the difference in their cost will be discussed later.

In judging the usual sort of chinaware that Americans received, it is revealing to read the letters of merchants and private individuals who specified the quality of ware they desired. They indicate that, unless one was particular, rather coarse porcelain might be sent. In 1815 Benjamin Shreve's employers directed him to bring back porcelain on board the *New Hazard:*

> Let the China be smooth, the cups & saucers in particular not thick & clumsy. Let the patterns of the Enamelled Tea Sets, Cups & Saucers & Bowls be delicate, of lively patterns and shades. Those of a thick heavy daub will not bring so good prices by a good deal & cost as much. The blue & white Dining sets should be of uniform shade & same pattern. They are often put up without attention to these particulars. The bottoms of Plates, Dishes etc. are apt to be very rough. Be very careful that none of the small old fashioned Sugars, Creamers, & Tea Pots are introduced into the Tea sets, they would be very injurious to the sale of them.[45]

The same year Joseph Minturn, in New York, wrote William Bell that he wanted his china to be "of the very finest quality & handsomest pattern." He further indicated that he would be willing to wait if it meant that he would finally receive the best sort:

> . . . would prefer waiting untill your return in preference to having them by the return of the Lion of inferior quality—at any rate will thank you not to send them by the Lion if you can find you can do better by waiting until you can have them made—as it is a rare thing that more or less of the china coming from Canton is not broken. Shall I beg your attention to having this packed in the very best manner—as to the pattern must leave that to your taste, merely observing that I think it handsomest when the white is principally covered by the Blue, and the Blue dark.[46]

In 1821 John Prince, Jr., of Salem, requested Benjamin Shreve to buy a list of Chinese goods for him, including a purple-and-gilt tea set, and added:

> With what money may be left after paying for the above please purchase me a dining-set of China dark-blue, with 2 or 3 extra 20 inch dishes—all free from knobs & specks.[47]

Enameled copperware was another article made especially for foreign export by the Chinese. It was and is often confused with porcelain, at least at first sight; but its metal foundation painted in enamel colors, with or without cloisons (partitions of bent wire fillets attached to the base), made it entirely different. Known as *fa-lang* (foreign) ware, it was glossy, bright, and pretty, but was considered by the Chinese to be of even lesser quality than export porcelain. The early-eighteenth-century director of the imperial factory, T'ang Ying, wrote about enameled copper in the following passage, but he might easily have included foreign chinaware:

> Foreign "porcelain" [enameled copper] and suchlike wares, though they are very gay and pretty, lack elegance, smoothness, and refinement. They are only fit for use on the ladies' dressing table. They are not the refined garniture of the scholar's study.[48]

# Exportation of Porcelain to America

## PRICES

As might be expected because of its usual quality, most of the export porcelain, except for elaborate special orders, was fairly inexpensive. Beyond specific examples, however, prices are as difficult to determine with accuracy as are quantities, especially since they, too, changed from period to period. Four major currencies make calculations of values even more confusing than the various containers and weight units make the calculation of amounts of porcelain imported. The Chinese used the tael, mace, candareen, and cash as standards of value. The English calculated on the basis of pounds, as did the Americans until they began to use dollars. Both used the trading medium most acceptable to the Chinese, the Spanish-American Carolus dollar, either whole or divided into pieces.

For the West, porcelain had perhaps always been a commodity of great value, but not of excessive cost. Marco Polo wrote of the wares of a city in Fukien:

> Here it is abundant and very cheap, insomuch that for a Venice groat you can buy three dishes so fine that you could not imagine better.[49]

Five centuries later an English sailor, who was captured by Chinese pirates but escaped and made his way to Canton with Chinese merchants, was reported as having visited an unnamed area of porcelain production. Traveling partly by land, but mainly by canals, he

> stopt a week in a part of the country where a great deal of China ware is made; [where] many farmers had little furnaces in some out-house, where they worked at leisure times, and made, some nothing but tea-cups, others nothing but saucers, etc., which they sold to country shop-keepers, who collected quantities for the merchants. The ware is there very cheap. He could have bought a dozen pretty cups and saucers for as much silver as is in an English half-crown.[50]

Probably the first chinaware taken home by the *Empress of China* cost comparatively little; at least, Samuel Shaw, in Canton for a second time in 1785–1786, noted a general price rise in all China goods from the year before.[51] The price of porcelain undoubtedly increased with a rising demand and reached a peak in the years 1817–1819. As chinaware gradually lost its appeal for Americans, it became cheaper. This assumption seems supported by the following figures. In 1785, 6 tea and coffee sets of 61 pieces each, that is, 366 pieces, could be purchased for a total of $30. In 1825, 1,000 coffee cups, painted and burnished, cost $40; at the same time an equal number of blue-and-white cups sold for $50. The average price for each item in 1785 was thus 8 cents. In 1825 it was half that price, or 4 cents.[52]

The quality of ware also determined the price. Hezekiah B. Pierrepont's notes give an excellent picture of the cost of the most popular types of export porcelain in the period from about 1794 to 1798:

> Tea cups & saucers of com: [common] quality & patterns to order at 5 or 6 Dollars p 100 Cups & Saucers which brings the half Chest of 600 C & S to 30 or 36 Dollars—Bkfrst Cups & Sau.ʳ of the same quality Costs from 7 to 9 Dollars p 100—The Bkfrst Cups & S of Nankeen blue & W. half Stone are 6 or 7 Dollars.
>
> Tea Setts of 51 pˢ enam.ᵈ & Painted to order at 2 or 2½ dollˢ a Sett & from that up to 3 & 4 doll.ʳˢ but higher will not do—those may be packed in Boxes of single Set to stow under the Beams.
>
> Table Setts of 172 pˢ Com: Ordinary blue & white Costs 22 Doll.ʳˢ The first quality Nankeen stone cost from 80 to 100 Dollars—painted or Enamell'd setts cost about the same—150 to 200 Dollars.
>
> This is [a] ready Money Article & payable in Dollars as soon as delivered.[53]

From this statement one can see that the most extravagant set was the last-mentioned enameled service, with each piece in the set costing about 87 cents (if there was a total of 172 articles in the set). The next most expensive was the Nankeen stone service of approximately 56 cents a piece. The cheapest sort was the common-quality teacup and saucer, each worth either 5 or 6 cents.

It is interesting to see the prices charged American traders in Canton by the Chinese merchants. In 1815 Powshong quoted the following costs for a series of nine breakfast and tea sets whose slight variations in composition and decoration notably altered their prices. The first set

served as a composition pattern for the others and consisted of fifty-nine
enameled pieces: twelve cups, twelve mugs, twenty-four saucers, one
teapot and stand, one sugar box, one bowl, and four flat cake plates, all
of which cost $3.25. Set No. 2 was similar, but had twelve bowls and
saucers instead of mugs, the price being $4. With only six instead of
twelve mugs, the cost decreased to $2.90; and with six bowls instead of
twelve, a set cost $2.25. Set No. 5, though identical in pieces with No. 1,
was nonetheless only $2.50 because of decoration in blue and white. The
remaining four sets, however, were all more expensive, not only because
they had white-and-gilt decoration, but also because an extra sprig, probably painted in a shield or mantling, was an optional added cost. For
example, No. 6 contained the same number and type of pieces as No. 1,
but cost $4.25 without a sprig; with one, the price was $4.75.[54]

Costs increased considerably from the purchase price at Canton
because of the profits charged by the merchants in this country and the
additional expenses of handling and shipping. In 1803 George Hodges,
supercargo of the ship *Union*, of Salem, brought four boxes of chinaware for Benjamin Pickman out of his total amount. The selling price of
the porcelain, with a quadrille box, was $463.22½. But of this amount
$319.38½ had to be deducted for import charges, wharfage, storage,
carriage, a proportion of the fees of entry, the cost at Canton ($264.70),
and Hodges' commission at 2½ per cent ($6.61½). The net profit for
Pickman was thus $143.84.[55]

Shipping duties also raised the final price; in 1796 the charge ad
valorem for imported chinaware of all sorts, European as well as Oriental, was 15 per cent for those carried in American vessels and 16½
per cent for wares packed in foreign ships.[56] This difference might well
have encouraged for a time the purchase of export porcelain in contrast
with European wares. By 1818 the duty had increased to 24 per cent.[57]

Fluctuations in price constantly changed cost levels. These were
caused not only by demand variations at home, but also by international
disturbances, such as the War of 1812, and by the state of supplies in
Canton. A letter to Stephen Girard written by business agents in Canton
in March, 1812, indicated the possible effects of reduced stores:

Tea, silks, china & Sugar are expected to be high at the early part of next
Season whether they will experience any depression in the latter part of

it will entirely depend on circumstances, quantities of Nankins & Cassia being on hand their prices will not much fluctuate from what they have heretofore been.[58]

Despite multiple charges above the first price in Canton and market changes from season to season, at least the commonest sort of ware was probably within the income of the middle-class householder; and, for all, there was equal protection from loss by breakage by a 2 per cent margin paid by the seller. In 1802 four patrons of Amos Porter, a Connecticut merchant, were reimbursed in the form of punch bowls for the "Brakage" of their wares. They received the following: [59]

| | |
|---|---|
| 2 Large Bowls first Chop | $2..00 |
| 4   "   2ᵈ Size AP   " | 3..00 |
| 4 Setts Blue Stone Bowls at $2⁵⁰ each Sett | 10  00  [*sic*] |
| | 15..00 |

USE AS BALLAST

En route to America, Chinese export porcelain customarily paid its way by serving as ballast for many vessels. This practice had long been employed by the English, who packed boxes of china in the holds of their ships. The boxes were stacked about 13 inches high in the leaky vessels to protect perishable teas and textiles.[60] Around the porcelain, in cracks and crevices, dunnage was wedged to prevent the cargo from shifting. This usually consisted of rattans, reeds, whangees (walking sticks of bamboo), sapan (a red dyewood), or anything else that could be used as stuffing.[61]

Americans probably followed this procedure for chinaware packing as soon as they entered the China trade. At least by 1788 they had the system well organized. One of Captain John Barry's officers, on board the ship *Asia*, from Philadelphia, anchored at Whampoa, wrote to Barry in Canton, September 25:

We received yesterday afternoon Sixty two Boxes of China and this morning gott them stoad away in the fore hold, from the Step of the fore

Mast to Midway of the Main Hatch way, from which to the step of the Mizen Mast will take, from forty to fifty Boxes more, but if we take flour with China, we shall be obligd to Discharge Four or five Boat loads, of Ballace more, not haveing any place to put it away with the China, and the whole China on board does not exceed ten Tons.[62]

Instructions for the supercargo of the *John Jay*, from Providence, in Canton in 1794, recommended that the pig iron, which served as ballast outward, should be replaced with china packed in strong boxes. This porcelain included:

30 to 40 Dining Setts of common blue and white China. 5 Setts of rather better Quality. 10 boxes Coffee Cups and Saucers. 20 Boxes Tea Setts. Some Pint and Quart Bowls. A few boxes of Nankeen blue Cups and Saucers.[63]

In the 1790's Americans were still learning from the English about the details of using chinaware as ballast. William Bell noted:

Ships generally floor off with this Article the English to save room have it packed in Sage [a starch prepared from the pith of an East Indian and Malaysian palm] instead of Straw—it wou'd be well to examine whether the Practice wo.<sup></sup> not be advantageous for Americans.[64]

When chinaware was slow on the market, cassia or sugar from China or Batavia might be substituted as ballast. When the chinaware became less popular, perhaps sugar succeeded to its use in the ship. In 1816 Benjamin Shreve on board the brig *Canton* was told:

Fill the lower hold with Sugar, in cases or Bags as you shall judge best, and perhaps more, as far up as a foot above the Beams—and on top of the Sugar stow the Nankins and on top of them the Cassia, enough to make her completely full.[65]

# VII

## *Porcelain Importation to America*

SHIPS FROM SIX MAJOR PORTS along the east coast brought home export porcelain from Canton. From Salem, Boston, and Providence in New England to as far south as Baltimore, vessels carried wares that were distributed in the port of entry, shipped to other cities, or dispersed to areas inland. Before the War of 1812 a few Connecticut towns, notably Stonington, joined these centers; but, after the financial difficulties of 1826, commerce with the Far East was concentrated in New York, Boston, and Philadelphia. The tendency toward control by a few large business houses instead of by many small firms and private individuals began before the war with England and progressed steadily after it. This change may be seen at each port, beginning geographically with one of the cities most celebrated in the China trade.

### SALEM

Salem was only one year behind New York in sending a vessel to Canton. In January, 1786, the *Grand Turk*, financed by Elias Hasket Derby, sailed as the third United States vessel in the China trade.[1] "King" Derby, son of the merchant Richard Derby, had never been to sea; but, from the profits of his shipping, he became one of America's earliest millionaires.[2] Before 1800 he fairly well monopolized the East India trade for Salem. Of fifteen United States vessels in Canton in 1789, five were from Salem and four of these were Derby's.[3] As the maritime leader of his community, Derby trained such men as Joseph Peabody, Nathaniel Silsbee, Stephen Phillips, Jacob and George Crowninshield, Benjamin Hodges, and Ichabod Nichols, who served him as captains and later became merchants on their own. The Crowninshields—George, Sr., George, Jr., Benjamin, Jacob, John, and Richard—were an especially active firm in the early nineteenth century.[4]

During the 1790's, however, few ships left Salem for the Far East. After 1790 the customhouse did not record another arrival from Canton until 1798. For the next few decades entries did not exceed one or two ships annually; and even in the peak years, 1818 and 1819, only three vessels each year came home from China.[5]

Salem's many shipping interests prevented concentrated commerce with China alone. By the turn of the century only twelve voyages had been made to Canton as opposed to fifty-four sailings to the Cape of Good Hope, Île de France, India, Rangoon, and Batavia.[6] At this last port and at other points on the Sumatra coast, Salem vessels loaded cargoes of pepper, which supplied the major part of America's demand for many years. Her ships also brought coffee and sugar from the Near East and Africa. The trade with China was thus only a branch of her total enterprise in Eastern seas.

Jefferson's Embargo Act of 1807 and the war with England five years later marked the end of Salem's prominence in the East Indies. Encounters with British vessels during the War of 1812 more than decimated the port's fleet, 57 ships remaining from an approximate 182 that had entered the conflict.[7] As a result, an increasing number of shippers followed the example of William Gray, who moved to Boston in 1808. Others waited longer, as did Abiel A. Low, who ultimately went to Brooklyn, in 1825, to continue in the China trade from there.[8]

Though Salem's first adventurers to Canton gradually gave up the enterprise, others succeeded them after 1815. Joseph Peabody took the lead in this "Indian summer" of the Salem trade and made a total of seventeen voyages to Canton. Almost all Salem-China trips, especially after 1826, were under his direction.[9] Peabody also maintained the highly profitable pepper trade. In 1830 his vessel, the *Friendship*, was attacked and captured near the village of Quallah-Battoo, on the west coast of Sumatra, where she had stopped to trade for pepper.[10] Although there were several vessels named *Friendship*, perhaps the plate shown in Figure 132 commemorates this tragic event.[11]

From the late 1820's until 1841 the Salem trade continued under Peabody's leadership. By that time only thirty-five ships had entered from Canton since the *Grand Turk* had sailed.[12] For all the fame that Salem has gained in connection with her China trade, this number seems quite small when compared with similar figures for Providence. Salem is thus more memorable because of her extensive contacts in the entire East Indies than in China alone, as is suggested by the seal of the city, *Divitis Indiae usque ad ultimum Sinum*, "To the farthest port of the rich East." [13]

Despite Salem's short-lived and sporadic trade with China, Oriental goods which still help furnish its historic houses tell of the difference her trade at Canton made to the city. The China shippers were highly interested in porcelain and gave special orders for distinctive services as well as requests for common blue-and-white or plain gilt pieces. In 1786 the captain and supercargo of the *Grand Turk* wrote to Elias Hasket Derby:

> We are now taking a Cargo for America on your Account Consisting of the following Articles. China Ware—Table sets Tea & Coffee ditto & Cups & Saucers the whole amounting to about 2000 dollars (sufficient to floor the ship) 30 or 40 pukle [picul] of Cassia Cinnamon at 24 dollars per pukle—300 large chests Bohea Tea amt[ing] to abt 15000 dollars—Hyson Singlo & Congo Teas to Compleat the Cargo, the whole of which will amount to abt 21000 dollars at Canton which place we hope to leave by 20th December.[14]

Along with the rest of the goods, the porcelain—packed in seventy-five boxes—helped yield a profit for Derby which may have been double his expense for the voyage.[15] The china was dispersed over a period of a year or more to local gentry or to dealers as far south as Baltimore and Charleston.[16]

The most notable piece of the entire chinaware cargo was a large punch bowl, presented by Pinqua, the hong merchant, to the ship's officers before they left Canton.[17] It bore the inscription *Ship Grand Turk at Canton, 1786* on two banners above and below a ship painting done in polychrome enamels (Fig. 33). The ship's design probably came from the engraving of the British ship *Hall*, which appears as a frontispiece in William Hutchinson's work on naval architecture, published in London in 1777.[18] The bowl does not appear to have been made particularly for Derby, but was merely presented as a souvenir to the captain and supercargo.

Derby, however, did receive a large order of chinaware from the total cargo of the *Grand Turk*. His purchases of blue-and-white dining, tea, and breakfast sets amounted to well over $200. He bought odd items like china figures and flowerpots as well.[19] In addition, a special group of porcelains in this order—a dining set of 171 pieces and a tea service of 101 pieces—were marked with his cipher *EHD*. Whether these wares were also painted with Derby's crest and motto *Spero*, as is the tureen in Figure 34, is an unconfirmed but likely possibility.

Later shipments of chinaware into Salem indicate the quantities of porcelain brought home. In 1802 the *Union*'s cargo of 71 boxes was divided among Ichabod Nichols, Benjamin Hodges, Clifford Crowninshield, and Nathan Pierce. The entire amount totaled $1,114.82½ after a 2 per cent deduction for breakage.[20] These orders were of such bulk and variety—chamber pots, washbasins, goblets, and patty pans (for pastries)—that they were undoubtedly resold at auction. Seven years later Thomas W. Ward brought back 11 boxes amounting to 1,407 pieces, mainly blue-and-white wares, at a net price of $284.70.[21] He also probably planned to sell this quantity wholesale.

What Salem buyers wanted or could afford in 1815 is indirectly indicated by instructions from the owners of the *New Hazard* to Benjamin Shreve, supercargo in Canton. He was told to decrease the planned shipment of chinaware and other goods in proportion to the increase in current freight rates, in case more profits might be gained by carrying other ships' cargoes. They wrote:

> If about $65 [per ton] can be obtained take half the bulk of China with one half of Teas, lessening chiefly of the large sized Boxes of China, bringing only *very few* (say ten) Dining Setts, as the small boxes of Breakfast Sets, large boxes Cups & Saucers etc. will pay the most profit.[22]

Shreve ultimately decreased the intended chinaware shipment by half and still had a heavy load to bring home:

> I have taken great pains to measure every article, which has gone on board, not excepting Whangees—and I believe we shall not stow in all more than 312 tons. . . . I am sorry to find the Brig will be as deep, or deeper than when we left Boston. I believe she will have but one of her bends out of water.[23]

Shreve's notebook for the *New Hazard* also records the order of a William Reed, of Marblehead, who wanted to invest one thousand specie dollars for a 406-piece table service and a set of breakfast and tea china of deep-blue Nankeen china "of the first quality, marked *R* in gilt cipher." Reed was desirous that special attention be given the dinner service:

> If it should be practicable in ordering the set of Dining China to have an R impressed in the Bottom, that is underside of each piece I should like it, this however must be done before the ware is baked. If there should be any difficulty or great expense in gilding the R on the Tea & Coffee set, that too may be omitted. As these articles form the entire set it is requested particular care should be given to the selection of fair and perfect articles and the packing of them, as the loss of a few pieces may cause much trouble in procuring them here, if at all practicable.[24]

Chinaware services ordered were not always so large. In contrast with Mr. Reed's order, for example, is the request of Catherine Elizabeth Peabody. One can easily imagine a restrained and precise New England lady from her quaintly phrased request. She asked Shreve to buy

> a handsome set of [tea] China rather diminuitive White with gilt figures —In a neat little Box to contain it, when not in use.[25]

It may have resembled the miniature tea pieces (Fig. 35) once belonging to the Lyles, of The Woodlands, in Philadelphia, Pennsylvania.

Benjamin Shreve's careful accounting of business transactions of both sides of the Salem-China trade, which he continued into the 1820's, gives an excellent picture of commercial details. It also indicates why he gained respect as a shrewd and highly capable supercargo. No matter how inconsequential, every order entrusted to Shreve received the same attention. In 1819 he made the following memorandum in his notebook for the *Governor Endicott*'s return cargo:

> D. L. Pickman wishes me to get a small dining set of ware for his Children to cost 3 or 4 Dolls small number of pieces—if it cannot be had for that then buy a few pieces small ware—they have a tea set.

Synchong estimated that such a dining set would cost $7.50. Although this figure was beyond Pickman's stipulated price, at least Shreve dealt with the best merchant and attempted to get the least expensive sort by asking for ware "painted in the cheapest Manner." [26]

BOSTON

Benjamin Shreve's directors occasionally, if not often, were Boston merchants, though their ships may have entered at Salem. Thus he illustrates the close connection between the two cities in the China trade. Even earlier, the ties between Salem and Boston were apparent when Thomas Handasyd Perkins went out in 1789–1790 as supercargo of the *Astrea*, one of Derby's ships.

In Canton, Perkins met the officers of the *Columbia* on its first voyage from the Northwest Coast, learned of the possibilities in the fur trade, and eventually planned large operations, including contacts in America, Asia, and Europe.[27] In 1792 Perkins formed with his brother James a partnership which developed into the most prominent firm in Canton in the early period. They fully exploited the Northwest fur trade; but they also carried on direct shipments to China, with these becoming their sole concern after the commerce in pelts declined.[28]

The Perkins enterprise included not only relatives but also other Boston merchants. Samuel Cabot, the Lambs, John P. Cushing, Ephraim Bumstead, Thomas T. and John M. and Robert B. Forbes, James P. Sturgis, and many others entered the company operations either in this country or in China. The firm perpetuated its interests by training nephews and cousins in its countinghouses and on its ships, thereby forming a regular dynasty of merchants to "take up the business as the older men laid it down." [29] Competing companies were not as strong—the Lymans, Dorr and Sons, J. Coolidge, Bass, J. Gray, Thomas Parish, and Hoy and Thorn. At least, surviving records indicate Perkins' unequaled leadership in the Boston-China trade and in the entire business at Canton for many years.

Concurrently, however, the firm of Russell and Company, directed by Samuel Russell, of Middletown, Connecticut, and several Rhode Island associates, was also operating. When Perkins finally ended his business in 1838, Russell took the lead among all American merchants at Canton. A former partner of Russell's, Augustine Heard, also was an important China shipper from Boston in the later years. He set up a separate house, which was carried on by his nephews until the Civil War.[30] These men thus were not permanently disturbed by the depression of 1826; and they extended operations, especially in tea imports, well into the middle of the century. By this time, however, many ships sent out from the home port were accustomed to entering at New York instead of Boston.[31]

There were several reasons for Boston's continued prosperity in the China trade. One of them stemmed from her early ventures on the Northwest Coast. After the *Columbia* established contact with the Indians in 1788, most of the profits from the sea-otter pelts went to Bostonians. Few vessels from other ports entered that region. In a later period Boston maintained her interest in the Canton trade because of a lucrative system of tramp shipping. Her ships made Boston almost synonymous with America in monopolizing the carrying trade in the East Indies after Salem's decline; and Boston was like Salem in that her China trade was only a part of her total enterprise in the Far East.[32]

Chinaware cargoes entering Boston probably did not greatly differ from those brought to other ports. They simply came in larger quantities and over a longer period of time, judging not only from the extended history of the city's trade, but also from the porcelain pieces that remain.[33]

Four particular items represented in Figures 36–39 indicate the variety of export ware entering Boston and also suggest the romance connected with the whole China adventure. The punch bowl inscribed

*Capt. Evans of the Charles Henry of Boston in America* proudly announces its owner's position and loyalty to his country (Fig. 36). Unfortunately, no history can be found in personal papers or ships' records for either the captain or his vessel. A cup (Fig. 37) with "penciled" decoration (in Chinese ware, done with a fine brush rather than a stylus), with the remnants of gilt trim still showing, illustrates a Chinese plowman at work. The owner supposedly was Fletcher Christian, mate on H.M.S. *Bounty* and leader of the mutiny on that ship in 1789.[34] A saucer and covered cup (Fig. 38) bearing the cipher of Oliver Smith, an early-nineteenth-century Boston doctor, also carry the rather plaintive motto *Memento*. Finally, a blue-and-white plate, whose underglaze decoration includes an unusual pagoda design in the center, belonged originally to a member of the Perkins family and now stands as a special symbol of that dynasty's enterprise in the Far East (Fig. 39).[35]

It is interesting to consider several written records of export ware that entered Boston. In January, 1800, William Ward, soon to return on the ship *Pallas*, wrote to his wife Nancy in Boston:

> I have on board for you a Dining Sett China two hundred & Ninty three pieces—one Tea Sett—same pattern of the Dining Set one other handsome Tea Sett—which was sent me as a present—one D° for our Sister Buebear —& one for Mrs. Clough.[36]

Four years later Ephraim Bumstead and a business friend received chinaware purchased of Exching and carried home by the *Rambler*, amounting to $210.50.[37] Later that year Bumstead purchased additional ware of penciled and gilt decoration and of blue and white amounting to well over $1,500.[38] About 1805 James and Thomas Handasyd Perkins bought 150 boxes of china, each containing a tea set at $2.50, thus totaling $375.[39] These large orders undoubtedly found their way to several Boston auctions.

Other invoice records of Perkins and Company which may be seen at the Massachusetts Historical Society indicate that quantities of porcelain entered Boston under the firm's name in the 1820's and probably until the company ended its affairs. These pieces consisted mainly of the commonest sort of ware—dining services of blue and white or with simple painted decorations. An average shipload, such as that of the *General Hamilton* on its arrival in 1826, included: [40]

```
100 Boxes each contg a Dining Sett of Blue & White China
        of 157 ps @ 15.25 p sett                              [$]1525
200 Boxes contg 20000 coffee cups @ 4.70                         940
  5 do ea    "    a Dining sett of Nankin stone china
        of 209 ps @ 72 p sett                                   360
 11 do  "    "    "    "  of ½ stone china
        of 157 ps @ 18.50                                       203.50
 12 do ea 200 S 2400 flatt 2ᵈ size half stone plates 8 cts      192
  5 do    200 " 1000 deep 2ᵈ size do do
        8 8/10                                                   88.
                                                               ————
                                                               3308.50
                              off 2%                              66.17
                                                               ————
                                                           [$]3242.33
```

The records of Russell and Company, many of which are at The Library of Congress, are not so rich in information about porcelain as are those of Perkins and Company. They are chiefly letters concerned with the formation of the firm and its most essential business. Russell, like other China shippers such as Stephen Girard, may not have imported porcelain, preferring heavier loads of more profitable goods, such as tea.

## PROVIDENCE

In Rhode Island, Providence stood far ahead of any other cities, such as Newport or Bristol, in the China trade. In 1787 she sent out the *General Washington* to inaugurate her contact at Canton. Because Rhode Island had a better supply of capital than did New York or Massachusetts at this time, her ships increased in number each year until 1803. Then, with the exception of 1810, they gradually decreased until after 1815. Following the War of 1812, Providence vessels contributed to the general rise in commerce to the Far East, with five ships registered from Canton in 1819. The next season, only one ship returned, but three vessels came home each year for the following two years. The depression of 1826 upset the Providence-China circuit from 1827 to 1831, and only six vessels returned before her trade closed in 1841.[41]

Even before the War of 1812, mercantile interests in Providence had begun to shift. The newborn spinning industry received increasingly more of the investments that had formerly supported the China trade. This trend was encouraged by the fact that Providence proved to be a poor distributing point for the China cargoes.[42] Nevertheless, it is interesting to note the extent of Providence's enterprise. With a span as long as Salem's, and with a contemporary decline, Providence yet had a much larger China trade than did her northern neighbor. A total of sixty-eight vessels, as compared with Salem's thirty-five, returned from Canton in the entire trading period.[43]

The names Brown and Carrington predominate among the Providence shippers. John Brown and his brothers Nicholas, Joseph, and Moses operated a flourishing partnership that lasted until 1774. Afterwards Nicholas and John continued separate trading ventures, but the second generation was the most active in the China trade. John Brown and John Francis sent the *General Washington* on her first voyage. Nicholas Brown, Jr., and Thomas B. Ives joined interests in 1796.[44] Their firm succeeded Brown, Benson, and Ives when George Benson died. The firm of Brown and Ives was noted as either shipping home the largest china cargoes or appearing high in the list of consignees from other shiploads. The company remained active, sharing the expenses of the *Hanover*, which made the next-to-the-last of the Providence-Canton trips, in 1838.[45]

Edward Carrington and Company also actively engaged in the China trade, almost monopolizing it in the years after 1815. Carrington's house, built in 1810–1811, still remains on Williams Street in Providence, hardly touched by the passage of more than a century. His double drawing room, decorated with Oriental wallpaper, is filled with furniture, paintings, and porcelain ornaments telling of his years in China. Three large services of blue-and-white enameled ware, and plain porcelain with a gold-star border may be seen in the first-floor pantry. Unpacked china is also stored in the house. The financial crisis of 1826 severely injured the activities of Carrington and small dealers associated with him. As a result, his ventures to the Far East were never so large afterward.[46]

When the *General Washington* arrived home in July, 1789, bringing Samuel Shaw back from his second trip, she carried in her hold $1,800 worth of chinaware, along with teas and silks.[47] A few years later the *Rising Sun*, sent out by Brown, Benson, and Ives, returned with a highly colorful cargo of taffetas, lacquered ware, hair ribbons, and the like, as well as "China, a great Variety."[48] Many other China cargoes followed these early shipments. The *John Jay*, launched in October, 1794, returned in 1796 with a huge quantity of teas and luxury items. In addition, her porcelain amounted to "138 boxes, 8 rolls, and 1 basket of China," plus "2 China pitchers."[49]

Providence probably exchanged china sets with nearby ports such as Newport when either was out of supply. Brown and Ives wrote to John Bennock, of Newport, in 1797:

> We are just favored with yours of the 6th Inst we do not expect any vessel ourselves from Canton this year but there is one ship Coming belonging to Messrs. Clark & Nightingale of this Town, looked for in a fortnight—we have yet on hand 4 or 5 blue & white dining setts of China & 5 boxes of Cups & Saucers assorted which we will sell you on good terms.[50]

In 1798 Brown and Ives built the ship *Ann and Hope*, named in honor of their wives and eventually famous as the "finest and fastest vessel in Providence."[51] Sailing for eight years, she made several trips to China and, according to documents now in the John Carter Brown Library, brought back quantities of chinaware. Her first voyage to Canton, in 1799, was supported by four major firms: Brown and Ives; Gibbs and Channings; John Innis Clark; Munro, Snow and Munro. All of them divided the total porcelain cargo of 302 boxes and 124 rolls, priced in Canton at $2,516.27. Most of it consisted of blue-and-white dining services with extra pitchers and cups. Brown and Ives bought the rest of the shipment for $1,048.45, a sum that exactly matched their investment. The others also received quantities in proportion to their subscriptions.[52]

In succeeding trips the *Ann and Hope* brought home for many merchants numerous orders, averaging from one to seven boxes. The type, amount, and price seem almost identical with those of her first voyage, so it may be assumed that most of them were of this sort.[53] The ship's china-importing days were ended, however, in 1806, when she ran aground on Block Island in a snowstorm and was lost with a valuable cargo aboard.[54]

Of the extant examples of export porcelain imported to Rhode Island, one of the finest and most interesting is the punch bowl shown in Figure 40a (with details, Figs. 40b-e). The bowl not only commemorates the years of service which the *George Washington*, built in 1793, gave to the China trade for its owners and for the State of Rhode Island (Figs. 40c, 40d), but it also prominently displays the name of Henry Smith, one of the ship's officers, who evidently obtained the bowl in Canton in 1794 (Fig. 40b).

### CONNECTICUT PORTS

Farther south and west from Providence, several ports in Connecticut engaged in the China trade; but there were no large firms, and activity was mainly concentrated in sealing voyages. Stonington, Hartford, New London, and New Haven each had a limited interest in this enterprise.[55] Porcelains brought to these ports may be seen in private houses and in historic collections such as those of the New Haven Colony Historical Society.

In 1802 Amos Porter, a merchant of Farmington, near Hartford, recorded purchases of thirteen boxes of chinaware, costing $154.51, from the ship *Penman*. At least one box, bought from Synchong at Canton, eventually was sold by Porter to a Luke Wadsworth.[56] Undoubtedly, many records of chinaware transactions exist which would describe more fully Connecticut's importation of export porcelains. But since so few ships engaged in the trade and then only until about 1817, we may assume that her purchases of porcelain by direct shipment were slight. She may have depended on supplies from Boston, Providence, or New York.

### NEW YORK

New York City's role in the America-China trade was unequaled by that of any other port. Her launching of the *Empress* in 1784 and her concentration on the China commerce in later years when other ports, such as Salem and Providence, had suffered setbacks made the city the unique leader of the whole exchange. Her course of trade followed the general pattern of a rise in 1805–1806, a decrease until the War of 1812, and an increase immediately after it. Following 1826, her ventures continued to increase.[57]

No single firms were outstanding in New York's early commerce as they were in Massachusetts and Rhode Island. John Jacob Astor was one of the first to begin shipping on a large scale, especially by way of the Northwest Coast; but after the massacre of the crew of his ship *Tonquin* in 1811, and following the War of 1812, his ventures in this area completely collapsed.[58] In the first years, Oliver Wolcott and Company and H. Fanning were also active.

Only after 1815 did large firms begin to dominate the trade.[59] One "spectacular plunger" was Thomas H. Smith, who quickly built up his business by extensive borrowing. In 1826, however, his shipping was seriously injured by the depression. By the following year, when there was a market glut in tea, he became bankrupt, owing the customhouse about $3,000,000.[60] Other big firms were more stable. N. L. & G. Griswold imported many Canton cargoes, in addition to their larger trade. The company directed by Daniel W. C. Olyphant even became famous for its philanthropy. Olyphant's policy prohibited the importation of opium into China; furthermore, he took over American missionaries free of charge. By such activities on Olyphant's part, his factory won the title of "Zion's Corner" at Canton.[61] Other firms included Grinnell, Minturn and Company; Minturn and Champlin; and Howland & Aspinwall. In the 1840's, the Low family—especially Seth, Abiel A., and William H. —directed an important concern at Canton.[62]

By the 1830's, however, more and more China-trade ships from Boston, Providence, and Philadelphia put into the New York port on their homeward voyages for quick disposal of their cargoes. Major profits still went to the owners in the other cities, but New York increasingly took over the commerce, at least as an entrepôt.[63] By 1860, although New York and Boston were on a par in the Far East trade in general, New York had the China trade securely in hand, with the highest tonnage in the commerce at Canton.[64] John R. Latimer, a Philadelphia merchant whose home was in Wilmington, Delaware, wrote to his brother from Canton in 1832:

I think that you must approve of my shipping to New York instead of Philadelphia. I did so for the purpose of preventing any hard thoughts on the part of my correspondents in Philadelphia and as New York is the market for Teas. Sales are there made promptly.[65]

Fortunately, the manifest for the cargo of the *Empress of China* on its 1784–1785 voyage still exists in the possession of a descendant of John Green, the captain on that first trip. From the manifest it can be seen, at least in part, how the 962 piculs of chinaware listed as part of the cargo were dispersed. The majority of the porcelains, according to remaining invoices, had been supplied by Synchong and Exching.[66] The bulk of the porcelain ware went to Constable Rucker and Company, of New York. A Dr. R. Johnson bought 17 chests, and Captain Green was third, taking 5 chests. Green's consignment contained all types and decorations of table china and one box of *chow chow* (miscellaneous) porcelain, including Chinese figures.[67] Unfortunately, none of his chinaware is known to be extant, but one tub in Green's order was filled with "4 Factory painted Bowles a 5½ p–$22," which were probably similar to the bowl shown in Figure 41.

Robert Morris, one of the financial backers of the *Empress*, also placed an order for china. A single case containing four small boxes of china images and a "marble" stone pagoda was sent to him in Philadelphia by the ship's clerk, Frederick Mollineux, and two packages were marked for Samuel Shaw. Whether the elaborate basket and stand illustrated in Figure 42 was part of this package or was brought back by Shaw on the *General Washington* on another voyage is not definitely known, but that it did belong to him is indicated by the cipher *SS*. The ship's carpenter, John Morgan, of Groton, Connecticut, sent home two punch bowls, shown in Figures 43 and 44. He died en route from Canton, but his executor, Thomas Blake, gunner and steward of the ship, delivered his effects to his father. The bowls thus survived.[68] The bulk of the cargo, however, undoubtedly was sold through retail shops or at auction. A little more than a month after the *Empress* docked, the *New-York Gazetteer and the Country Journal* carried the following advertisement:

Maria S. Morton Has on hand a neat assortment of Dry Goods, suitable to the season. . . . China arrived from Canton, in the ship Empress of

China. Table and tea table setts compleat, Blue and white and enamelled half pint basons and saucers. Blue and white and enamelled Breakfast and common cups and saucers. Blue and white and enamelled Bowls of different sizes.[69]

The next season the tiny sloop *Experiment*, Captain Stewart Dean, returned with twenty-six chests of teacups and saucers and five sets of breakfast china. These must have been sold for a tremendous profit if the plans of the ship's officers were realized. Calculations for the voyage (see Appendix I, p. 227) represent the typical manner in which most china shippers anticipated their returns. Of particular interest is the increase of 100 per cent in the price of porcelains from their cost at Canton to their sale in New York.

Surviving records show that New York imported the same kinds of porcelains as did the New England ports already listed. The extent of her trade no doubt meant that much more chinaware entered here than at other cities, even though it ultimately may have been shipped to various ports. Again, the shippers supplied both personal requests and large consignments.

In 1788 Samuel Fleming wrote to Captain Randall of the *Jay* in Canton:

> I gave you a small memorandum at New York 26th Dec[r] last which I now repeat with some addition. Be so good as purchase for me at Canton a compleat set of table china, with the desert: white ground and violet coloured border, as p the small specimen of Silk, affixed with ware to the border. The desert set ought to have four dozen of plates. Sometimes they only send two. Purchase also a child's tea set for my daughter, and a piece of best Nankeen black Sattin for Men's wear: one china jar of preserved Ginger: one ditto to match it; filled with Cassia buds: and charge to my Account.[70]

William Bell brought home two special orders in 1806. One was a forty-seven-piece tea set of "white w. Gilt Edge & Gilt Flower on one side & the Letter H on the other," for John H. Titus.[71] At the same time he purchased for William Bayard, of New York, a table set of Nanking china with the initial *B* in a shield with a mantling.[72]

Newspapers periodically announced the sales of common blue-and-white and painted wares which came into retail stores.[73] Merchants like Oliver Wolcott helped keep them in stock. A shipment originally purchased from Houqua was brought by the *Trident* in 1808 and was bought by Oliver Wolcott, Thomas Chrystie, Thomas Watterman, Isaac Bell, and others for a total of more than $9,000.[74] Two years later, the *Trident* again brought back boxes of Houqua's wares for Archibald Gracie (one of Wolcott's associates), Nehemiah Rogers, and Rufus King.[75]

Special single objects indicate the esteem in which many Americans in the early nineteenth century held export porcelains. One such piece is the large punch bowl pictured in Figure 45. As its border inscription tells, it was presented by General Jacob Morton to the Corporation of the City of New York, July 4, 1812. It was probably made about two years before. Beneath the border and around the outside are the seals of the United States and of the City of New York; a sea scene with a frigate, another ship with an American flag, and more vessels in the distance; and a scene of ships at anchor with boats under construction, and loading and unloading going on. Inside, the view "New York from Brooklyn, 1802," first drawn by William Birch and engraved by Samuel Seymour, appears in a careful copy. The inside border reads, *Drink Deep. You Will Preserve the City and Encourage Canals.* And the final inscription on the foot border tells its Chinese source, *This Bowl was Made by Syngchong in Canton Fungmanhi Pinx^T.* A bowl of such high quality with known sources and date rarely appears. A further novel feature is the bowl's size; it measures 21 inches in diameter, is 10 inches high, and holds 8 gallons of punch.[76]

In 1816 a Mr. Varick purchased a dinner and dessert set costing $323.40 from the porcelain cargo of the ship *William and John*, William Bell, supercargo. Whether Mr. Varick was Lieutenant-Colonel Richard Varick, one of Washington's former military aides, remains undetermined. If he was, he added to his chinaware collection, for he already owned a punch bowl decorated with the certificate of the Society of the Cincinnati, dated January 1, 1784 (Fig. 46). Undoubtedly, the bowl was made a few years after this date. Samuel Shaw may have arranged to bring it home on one of his early voyages.[77] Its fine quality and careful painting suggest that it may have come from Synchong's shop.

Through the height of the trade William Bell continued as a supercargo for many New York-China importers. In a later period men like John R. Latimer helped keep the exchange active. In 1825 Latimer shipped on board the *Washington* for Floyd S. Bailey, another New York merchant, three boxes of Nankeen stone chinaware with an undescribed landscape pattern.[78] Few additional orders appear in Latimer's remaining records after this date. The interest in chinaware was gradually drawing to a close. Scattered shipments probably continued, however, and New Yorkers made use of the wares already imported. In the inventory made in 1826 of the estate of the wealthy John C. Vanden Heuvel, appear two elaborate "East India dining sets," one plain white, another with a gold sprig, and both with gilt trim. Vanden Heuvel also owned a pagoda valued at $5.[79] Porcelain pagodas were quite popular in the Occidental market. For an elaborate example of the type that was imported into Europe, see Figure 47.

## PHILADELPHIA

Philadelphia's entry into the China trade, like that of New York, was partly due to the efforts of Robert Morris. In the spring of 1786, he sent out the ship *Canton*, Captain Thomas Truxtun, to inaugurate the commerce. The next year she sailed again and was joined by another Morris vessel, the *Alliance*. A third ship, the *Asia*, also went to Canton that year.[80]

A city which already was one of the richest in all the colonies, chiefly because of its large Quaker merchant plutocracy, Philadelphia soon had many shippers in the trade. Charles Wharton, Jones and Clark, Robert and Jesse Waln, Samuel Archer, and Stephen Girard were only a few of the entrepreneurs with business offices and warehouses near the Delaware River on Water Street and India Wharf.[81] In 1809 thirteen Philadelphia ships arrived from Canton; and in 1839 and 1840 seven different vessels were active in the trade. From the outset, therefore, Philadelphia had an excellent start in Far Eastern commerce, a lead which she maintained well into the later period. For many years she carried the heaviest tonnage of all the ports, and about one third of the entire trade in the busiest years before 1812.[82] During the 1830's, Philadelphia as well as Boston, however, eventually fell behind New York in the number of vessels in the China trade.[83]

One of the heaviest investors in the *Canton's* first voyage was Benjamin Fuller, a well-to-do merchant, who sent 1500 Spanish dollars in the care of Thomas Truxtun. According to Fuller's request, half of this sum was to be invested in chinaware:

> for every 100 Pair of Enameled Cups & Saucers there must be
> 16 Enameled pint Bowls
> 16     Do     3 pint     Do
> 8     Do     2 quart     Do
> 8     Do     Tea Potts
> 8 Enameled Sugar Dishes with Covers
> 8     Do     Cream Juggs

A cup of undescribed pattern was sent along since it was of the type "most in Esteem here at Present." [84] Mrs. Fuller also placed an order as part of her husband's request for "two genteel Rich China Punch Bowls one three Quarts the other four Quarts." [85]

What Fuller planned to do with part of this huge order is clear from a letter he wrote to Colonel John Mitchell, of Charleston, a few months before the *Canton's* return in 1787. He expected teas, pepper, mace, cassia, nutmegs, and striped Persians, black and colored taffetas, as well as sixty-six-piece sets of chinaware:

> The ship Canton Capt. Truxtun is expected from China in all June or beginning of July—I expect a Considerable Adventure by her in the following Articles. I desire to know if any of them would Sell with you about the time I mentioned & at what price Clear of Duty & other Charges.[86]

On the *Canton's* second voyage, Fuller was a more cautious investor, putting up only 700 Spanish dollars. Perhaps he had been discouraged both by losses due to breakage and by a poorer market than he had anticipated. He wrote to Truxtun:

> The China that I recd last Voyage was pack'd very badly, and I lost a Considerable part in Breakage; therefore have to request your Care in

haveing this 'now order'd packd in the most Carefull Manner—Inclos'd you have my Coat of Arms, which I request you to have put on every piece of China mention'd in the following List intended for Mrs. Fuller's own Use—Small or large in proportion to the size of the Piece of China— I most sincerely wish you a prosperous Voyage.[87]

Fuller further specified the painting for his wife's tea, coffee, and breakfast sets:

All this China of the most fashionable Kind and must have my Coat Armorial on each Piece—Small or large in proportion to the Size of the piece—The Best Nankeen China light Blue & White except the Coat of Arms which must be of the Colours there picturd. The Crest and Field to be a Silver Colour.[88]

The rest of the ware for this order was to be Fuller's own and in the latest vogue, which he believed was nearly square shaped. It included miscellaneous dining pieces plus a one-gallon punch bowl and a two-gallon bowl "Genteel & Elegant." In addition, he wanted Nankeen blue-and-white tea sets.[89]

There seems to be only one surviving object with Fuller's arms. A saucer with a Nanking border and a crest identical with the one which appears on Fuller's tombstone in the graveyard of Christ Church, Philadelphia, remains in a broken, but recognizable, state.[90]

Evidently, this shipment was more successful, for on the *Canton's* third voyage, in 1789, Fuller invested 1170 Spanish dollars. He again cautioned Captain Truxtun to take care that the chinaware be safely packed. It was an enormous quantity. After purchases of nankeens, teas, and other goods, the remainder of the funds was to buy enameled ware in sets of 300, with 10 teapots, 10 sugar dishes with stands and covers, 20 cream jugs with tops, and 20 pint bowls.[91]

Another china shipment worth considering closely was the cargo brought home by the *Asia*, Captain John Barry, on the 1787–1788 voyage. Many personal consignments from Philadelphians were entrusted to Barry on this early voyage. Hugh Doyle wanted "a set of table China composed of such pieces as your own judgment may point out." [92] Mrs. Hazlehurst, wife of a prosperous merchant, Isaac Hazlehurst, sent

$50 with Barry to be invested in a large dinner set according to an accompanying pattern, now lost. [93] Henry Gurney wrote:

> I will thank you to buy for me a very full dining set of Nankeen China likewise a double one of tea table of the same or any pattern of your choice.[94]

On the same date, John Nixon asked Barry:

> [to] bring 2 doz. Cups with handles & Covers Blue and White China agreeable to the Size of the patern Coffee Cup. A Coffee Pot Chocolate Pot tea Pot 2 Sugar dishes and 3 Slop Bowls of China of the same Colour as the Enclosed Cup.[95]

During one of his early trips, Barry ordered for himself porcelains that have been inherited by his descendants and may be admired today. One is a large punch bowl which commemorates the *Alliance* and exactly matches the *Grand Turk* bowl except for the few details already noted.[96] Figure 48 illustrates a garniture which once belonged to Barry, and a tea set which he brought home to his wife, Sarah, is shown in Figure 49. Patrick Hayes, Barry's nephew, who followed him in the China trade, may have had either a tea or a dinner service decorated as was the saucer in Figure 50, which shows his cipher enclosed by a conventional blue mantling.

Numerous ships carried home boxes of chinaware, according to shipping records which remain in several Philadelphia collections. The *Wooddrop Sims*, in 1797, and the *America*, in 1800, imported a large amount.[97] In 1801 the *Fame* brought in a substantial cargo of porcelain.[98] The records of Robert and Jesse Waln report many shiploads of chinaware and often mention merchants who received them. In 1805 Robert Waln wrote to Redwood Fisher in Canton requesting 110 Spanish dollars be spent on various items, plus a number of china pieces "to be blue & white of a landscape Pattern & of a good but common kind." A special tea set was to be ciphered *SS* in an oval with a neat dark-blue border and to cost not more than $10.[99]

Waln also noted the cycles of Philadelphia's interest in China goods. In a letter of 1811 to agents in Canton, he was not very optimistic about demands for porcelain:

Since you left us there has been considerable sales of China Goods. The young Hysons & Imperial Teas are nearly all sold, the former at 92 to 95 cents, the latter at 125 to 130 Cents. Skins have been sold at 53 cents & will not at present sell for a higher Price. Hyson Tea will not sell at any price, & Nankeens are a drug at 63 Cents. China is very dull.[100]

The Walns continued importing in the later years of the China trade; and their ship, the *Caledonia*, brought back two large shipments of porcelain in 1816 and 1819.[101] A blue-and-gold tray and covered sauce dish with the cipher *RPW* for Robert and Phoebe Waln, married in 1787, are shown in Figures 51a, 51b.

Stephen Girard is not to be forgotten in the Philadelphia-China trade. His ships, some of which were named for the French philosophers he particularly admired—*Voltaire*, *Rousseau*, and *Montesquieu*—brought back mainly teas in exchange for opium. He appears to have imported chinaware on only a minor scale. At Girard College, the exhibition room of Founder's Hall displays quantities of common blue-and-white Canton ware which his supercargoes undoubtedly brought home to their employer.[102]

Girard's household accounts include bills and receipts which list miscellaneous china bowls and saucers, teapots, chamber pots, and pieces of dinnerware. The limited extent of his interest in bulk porcelain cargoes, however, may be seen in the invoice made by his supercargo, Arthur Grelaud, of the *Voltaire*, in 1815. Only a single box of cups and saucers, bowls, and dessert plates amounting to a mere $69 was included in this shipment.[103] Girard undoubtedly concentrated on the money cargoes of tea and silk and was not bothered with an item of little account, as the porcelain increasingly became.

Besides the Barry and Waln pieces, other Philadelphia porcelains which represent the quantities which entered the port are shown in Figures 52–57. Perhaps the earliest of these is the plate showing a farmer and his cow in a pleasant pastoral setting; it represents a large dinner service which supposedly was designed by Mary Hollingsworth Morris, wife of Isaac Morris of Philadelphia. The Morrises were both Quakers. Mary's brother, Henry Hollingsworth, who was engaged in the China trade, took her pattern to Canton in the early 1800's and had two sets decorated, one for the Morrises and one for himself. Since Mary and her husband thought the extra gilt trim too elegant for their simple Quaker tastes, Henry eventually owned all the ware (Figs. 52–53).[104] Copies of this unusual pattern unfortunately have not preserved the precise painting of the originals, as can be seen in the teacup and saucer shown in Figure 54.

Three other porcelain objects which have remained in the possession of descendants of their original owners illustrate the variety in form and decoration of porcelains owned by early-nineteenth-century Philadelphians. A washbasin with pitcher bearing the cipher of Elizabeth Clifford Smith, who married Thomas W. Smith, a China merchant, in 1772, is shown in Figure 55. Pieces from a dinner service owned by William Phillips, son-in-law of the Smiths, indicate his ownership by a *P* surrounded by a mantling (Fig. 56). A monteith bearing the coat of arms of the Clements family represents a rather rare form among export porcelains (Fig. 57).[105]

Delaware, closely linked to Pennsylvania and especially to Philadelphia by historic, political, and economic ties, also received export porcelain as shown by the pieces remaining in private homes and in public institutions like the Historical Society of Delaware. The three pieces illustrated in Figure 58 are particularly well identified. On the left, the saucer bearing a black-painted decoration of a girl and dog, perhaps copied from an engraving of a painting by Jean-Baptiste Greuze (1725–1805), once belonged to Mary Hemphill Jones (1779–1834), daughter of William Hemphill and wife of Morgan Jones; her cipher appears in a shield on the upper border. In the center, a cream ewer with polychrome floral decoration, no doubt an earlier piece than the saucer, was part of a tea set owned by Jane Richardson McKinly, daughter of John and Ann Richardson, and wife of John McKinly, the first president of the State of Delaware. On the right, the chaste blue-and-gold-bordered dish with central dove decoration illustrates a service which Ann Spackman Richardson (1777–1845), wife of Joseph Richardson, once possessed.

BALTIMORE

In contrast with that of all the ports to the north, Baltimore's trade with the Orient was sharply limited. Even though as early as August, 1785,

Captain John O'Donnell brought in the ship *Pallas*, the second ship to arrive at a United States port with a cargo from Canton, no great movement toward the China shipping developed thereafter. O'Donnell himself did not continue in the trade after 1789, when the *Chesapeake* entered Baltimore as his last ship from Canton.[106] The ships which did participate later made only sporadic voyages, and in general the whole enterprise was a side issue.[107]

Reasons for this passive attitude toward the China trade are easily found. Baltimore's main market areas overseas were in Central and South America, as well as in Europe and the Mediterranean. To Venezuela, Brazil, Uruguay, Argentina, Peru, and Chile she sent foodstuffs, especially flour and tobacco, in exchange for coffee, sugar, hides, silver, copper, and platinum.[108] A few vessels did use these points to the south as stepping stones first to the Northwest Coast for sea-otter skins and eventually to China and India, returning by way of the Cape of Good Hope or following their outward course home; but Baltimore was a difficult place from which to distribute quantity cargoes of tea and spices. Thus, as a contemporary wrote in 1825:

> Some attempts were made at the China trade, but with such indifferent success, that they have seldom been repeated.[109]

A few remaining records give some information about the importation of porcelain into Baltimore, especially in the early period. According to its manifest, the *Pallas* arrived with 134 chests and 8 tubs of chinaware. A few bills of the 1790's, like those of Charles and Rebecca Ridgely, indicate that Baltimoreans were buying common blue-and-white tea and dinner sets, washbasins, and other useful items.[110] In addition, Baltimore inventories from 1797 to 1801 show widespread possession of "Chinia" or "Chaney," from a single plate or bowl to tea sets and dinner services. In 1797 the estate of George Hunter included a set of teacups and saucers, custard cups, and teapots, as well as 110 pieces consisting of plates, butter boats, and saucers.[111]

Because of Baltimore's limited China trade, it can be assumed that the major part of her porcelain imports came from ships of other ports. On July 1, 1808, the *Federal Gazette & Baltimore Daily Advertiser* announced the arrival of the *Stewart and Henry* from Canton by way of

Philadelphia with 241 boxes of chinaware, including complete dining sets with 180 and 228 pieces, as well as "Nanquin blue & gold, white and gilt, pencilled and enameled Tea Sets, with and without Coffee Pots." [112] Several similar advertisements reporting the arrival of Providence, New York, and Salem ships as well as Philadelphia vessels indicate that almost whole consignments of ware came to Baltimore in this manner.

The types of wares which were used may be seen from the city's many existing pieces once belonging to well-known Maryland families and now preserved at the Maryland Historical Society. The Chase service has been mentioned in connection with the pre-1784 porcelain commerce from England to the colonies. The dining set of about 258 pieces represented by the soup plate in Figure 59 was probably made for Jeremiah Townley Chase. Jeremiah's grandmother was Lady Margaret Townley, who married Richard Chase, of Annapolis, in 1714. The Townley coat of arms was adopted by the Chase family. Since the service was probably made for Jeremiah Chase and since its shield decoration is gaily rococo in style, the set can be dated about 1750–1760. It was designed for the English colonial market, however, and cannot be classified with porcelains made specifically for the American market.

The following pieces supposedly were made for Baltimore families after the Revolution. A double dinner service of 265 pieces was first owned by David M. Perine and thus bears a *P*. Part of the service is now at the Winterthur Museum; other pieces are at the Maryland Historical Society. Its grape-and-vine border, a standard pattern of the period of about 1800–1815, matches that of another service with the cipher *MDSF*, also in the Winterthur Museum (Fig. 60).

The lighthouse coffeepot in Figure 61 bears the crest of the John Nicholson family, and in the same illustration an elaborate punch bowl with four medallions, two of equestrian figures and two of small landscapes, was formerly owned by Samuel Sprigg, Governor of Maryland from 1819 to 1822. Allen Bowie, Jr., of the Hermitage, a country estate outside of Baltimore, supposedly owned the tea plates decorated with the American bald eagle shown in Figure 91. Now displayed at the Maryland Historical Society, a pair of apple-green porcelain vases or hearth jars, entirely Chinese in character, with raised white decoration, once belonged to Elizabeth Patterson, daughter of the China trader, William Patterson, and wife of Jerome Bonaparte. [113]

Chinese Export Porcelain

Concerning the activities of other southern ports—Norfolk, Charleston, Savannah, Mobile, and New Orleans—in the China trade, even less information is readily available than for Baltimore. A ship from Norfolk reputedly went to China in 1796; and a vessel from Charleston is known to have left for the East Indies, but it is uncertain whether or not it touched at Canton.[114] Some ships probably put into New Orleans en route to or from China.[115] Correspondence with libraries and museums in these areas has been uniformly unproductive of evidence of the South's trade with the Far East. Here again perhaps the destruction or removal of pertinent family or public records as a result of Civil War activities in these cities may account for some of the scarcity of materials that might shed light on direct sailings between southern cities and Canton.

Whether there were or were not such direct connections between southern American ports and the Far East, there was another way that the South received imports from China and many other countries. Probably most of the China goods received in this area came not from independent voyages, but through the coastwise trade with other ports. It was New York which undoubtedly supplied the South with most of its Oriental imports. Many years before the War of 1812, New York had gradually developed a profitable triangle trade between the southern states and Europe, carrying cotton to the Continent in return for manufactured wares. Often, all traffic passed both ways through the New York harbor.[116] After 1815 this connection rapidly grew. By 1822 cotton was the most valuable of New York's domestic exports.[117]

In this manner, the South became dependent on New York for a large part of its imported merchandise. Sloops, schooners, and other craft carried shiploads of wares down the coast; but private purchases were no doubt made in the city itself by Southerners who traveled there each year to place orders for the next season.[118] Possibly such purchases included chinaware, along with other Oriental products. New York's role in the later period of the China trade has already been noted.

Other ports besides New York also made profits from sending

chinaware to the South. However, the information is limited, and, in the absence of careful statistics for the coastal trade, only guesses can be made.[119] Single records relating to Charleston, however, are suggestive of a pattern of coastwise shipment. In 1787 the brig *Good Hope* left Salem for Charleston with three boxes of porcelain from the *Grand Turk*'s voyage, each containing a table set and the whole costing £49.10.[120] Four years later, Brown, Benson, and Ives, in Providence, informed Hazard and Robinson, of Charleston: "We are interested in a Ship just arriv'd from Canton & shall be glad to furnish you for sale on our Acco$^t$ with fine Teas & China."[121] Either this shipment or others apparently were made, because, two years afterward, Hazard and Robinson wrote in return:

> The China receiv'd in good Order, but am sorry to Inform thee the China is very much broke. but be assurd. we shall do the best in Our power for your Interest. . . . and the China, we think woud have brought a Satisfactory Price if it had been in good Order.[122]

Philadelphia also reshipped incoming porcelains to Charleston, according to one announcement in the *Columbian Herald* for July 2, 1794:

> *Lenox & Co., William*. China Ware. No. 120 Broad Street:
> Have received per the Alexander, Capt. Strong, from Philadelphia—
> An elegant Assortment of Enamelled and Gilt China, which will be sold for Cash, viz: Table sets complete. Tea and Coffee sets. China bowls from 1 to 6 quarts. Cups and saucers by the half dozen.[123]

Study of additional newspaper records and of yet undiscovered original records in southern ports may reveal more details about the transshipment of chinaware from the North. Baltimore's source material has not been exhausted by any means. Records of her packet ships, which established regular lines after 1825 with Charleston, Savannah, and New Orleans, may show reshipment of China cargoes as well as original shipments from her own voyages.[124] At this time, therefore, it may only be suggested that export porcelains found their way to ports south of Charleston.

From this brief account of the major ports, limited as it is, it can be seen that there was a widespread and uniform demand for export porcelain. Types of chinaware that entered the country at Salem differed very little or not at all from those sold in Philadelphia. Stock patterns, particularly the common blue-and-white wares, were popular in every city. This was certainly true if cargoes were interchangeable between ports. A particularly vivid reference to coastwise connections is the porcelain —an ash tray, a platter, and a sauceboat—painted with the steamboat *Philadelphia* of the Union Line (Fig. 62), which may have been made to commemorate her launching in 1816. Through the 1830's, the *Philadelphia* plied between the Chesapeake Bay and the Delaware River areas and may also have made runs between Philadelphia and New York.[125] The sale of export porcelain at many eastern seaports illustrates the unity and cooperation fostered among the newly formed states by the China trade.

FIGURE 32. *Plate decorated with the coat of arms of the Lees of Coton, in Shropshire, England, from which family came Colonel Richard Lee, the first of the Lees of Virginia. Border decoration pictures harbor of Canton and port of London. Probably before 1734. D. 11³⁄₁₆″. Courtesy of* The Metropolitan Museum of Art *(Gift of Mrs. Joseph V. McMullan, 1958. The Helena Woolworth McCann Collection.).*

FIGURE 33. *Inside center of the* Grand Turk *punch bowl with two banners bearing the inscriptions* Ship Grand Turk *and* At Canton 1786 *Courtesy of* Peabody Museum of Salem.

FIGURE 34. *Tureen with the crest and motto of Elias Hasket Derby. About 1786. H. 8½″, L. 11¾″.* Courtesy of *Winterthur Museum.*

FIGURE 35. *Pieces from a miniature tea set of twenty-two pieces with the Initial* L, *standing for the Lyles, an early-nineteenth-century family of The Woodlands, Philadelphia. About 1800–1810.* Courtesy of *Mrs. Joseph Carson, Bryn Mawr, Pennsylvania.*

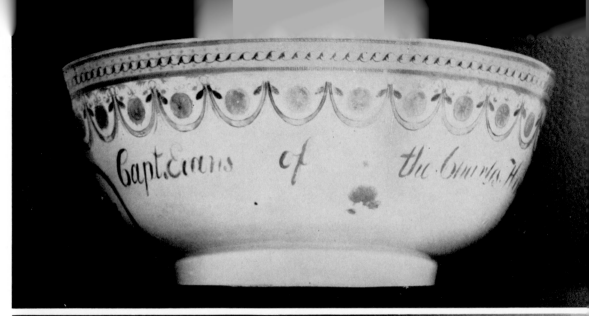

FIGURE 36a [top]. *Punch bowl reading* Capt. Evans of the Charles Henry of Boston in America. *About 1800–1810. H. 4¼″; D. (base) 5¼″, (top) 10″. Courtesy of Jeremiah Lee Mansion, Marblehead, Massachusetts.*

FIGURE 36b. *Opposite side of the Captain Evans punch bowl (Fig. 36a).*

FIGURE 37 [right]. *Penciled cup believed to have belonged to Fletcher Christian, leader of the mutiny on H.M.S. Bounty. About 1790–1800. H. 2½″; D. (base) 1¼″, (top) 2¼″. Courtesy of The Society for the Preservation of New England Antiquities.*

FIGURE 38 [above]. *Saucer and handleless covered cup with cipher of Oliver Smith, early-nineteenth-century Boston doctor. About 1800–1810. Saucer: D. 6³⁄₁₆″. Cup: H. 3½″; D. (base) 2³⁄₁₆″, (over-all) 4¾″. Courtesy of* Museum of Fine Arts, Boston *(Bequest of Miss Mary W. Stone).*

FIGURE 39 [below]. *Blue-and-white Fitzhugh-pattern plate originally belonging to a member of the Perkins family, of Boston. About 1810–1820. D. 7⅞″. Courtesy of* Museum of Fine Arts, Boston *(Gift of Mr. and Mrs. Samuel Cabot).*

FIGURE 40a. *Punch bowl made for Henry Smith, of Providence, Rhode Island, supercargo of the Ship George Washington. About 1794. H. 6½", D. 16". Courtesy of Winterthur Museum.*

FIGURE 40b [left]. *Inside center of the Smith bowl (Fig. 40a), with inscription* Henry Smith/Canton/1794.

FIGURE 40c [bottom left]. *One of four decorations on exterior of the Smith bowl, showing the Ship George Washington.*

FIGURE 40d [bottom center]. *Another exterior decoration on the Smith bowl, showing elements from the Rhode Island state seal.*

FIGURE 40e [bottom right]. *Another exterior decoration on the Smith bowl, showing the great seal of the United States.*

FIGURE 41a [top]. *Exterior view of punch bowl decorated with views of the foreign factories at Canton, with American and Swedish flags flying before them. About 1785–1800. H. 5⅜", D. 14⅜". Courtesy of Winterthur Museum.*

FIGURE 41b [middle]. *Second view of punch bowl (Fig. 41a), showing factories at Canton flying British and Dutch flags.*

FIGURE 41c [bottom]. *Third view of punch bowl (Fig. 41a), showing factories at Canton, with Danish flag flying in front of one of them.*

FIGURE 42 [left]. *Basket on stand with badge of the Society of the Cincinnati and the cipher of Samuel Shaw, supercargo on the first voyage of the* Empress of China *and, later, first American consul at Canton. About 1785–1790. H. 14½″, D. (base) 5½″, L. (basket) 7¾″, W. (basket) 6⅜″.* Courtesy of *Winterthur Museum*.

FIGURE 43 [middle]. *Punch bowl sent home on the* Empress of China *in 1785 by the ship's carpenter, John Morgan. H. 5″, D. 9″.* Courtesy of *Mystic Seaport, Mystic, Connecticut*.

FIGURE 44 [bottom]. *Punch bowl sent home on the* Empress of China *in 1785 by the ship's carpenter, John Morgan. H. 5″, D. 11 1/16″.* Courtesy of *Mystic Seaport, Mystic, Connecticut*.

FIGURE 45. *Punch bowl presented to the Corporation of the City of New York by General Jacob Morton, July 4, 1812. H. 10″, D. 21″. Courtesy of* The Metropolitan Museum of Art *(Lent by the City of New York, 1912).*

FIGURE 46. *Punch bowl decorated with the certificate of membership of Lieutenant Colonel Richard Varick in the Society of the Cincinnati. About 1786–1790. D. 18″. Courtesy of* The Washington Association of New Jersey, *Morristown, New Jersey.*

FIGURE 47 [right]. *Blue-and-white pagoda with gold trim and brass bells. About 1815–1830. H. 5′. Courtesy of* Winterthur Museum.

FIGURE 48. *Garniture originally owned by Captain John Barry, of Philadel-phia. About 1790–1800. H. 10″ and 11¼″.* Courtesy of *Mr. and Mrs. Barry H. Hepburn, Chestnut Hill, Pennsylvania.*

FIGURE 49. *Part of a tea set which Captain John Barry, of Philadelphia, had made for his wife Sarah, with her cipher SB in gilt. About 1790–1800.* Courtesy of *Mr. and Mrs. Barry H. Hepburn, Chestnut Hill, Pennsylvania.*

FIGURE 50. *Saucer with mantling and cipher of Patrick Hayes, of Philadelphia. About 1800–1810. D. 5½". Courtesy of* Mr. *and* Mrs. Barry H. Hepburn, *Chestnut Hill, Pennsylvania.*

FIGURE 51a [left]. *Blue-and-gold-decorated tray with initials* RPW *for Robert and Phoebe Waln, of Philadelphia. About 1785–1800. L. 7½", W. 5⅜". Courtesy of* Mrs. Joseph Carson, *Philadelphia, Pennsylvania.*

FIGURE 51b [right]. *Blue-and-gold-decorated covered sauce dish matching tray in Figure 51a. H. 4", L. 7¼", W. 4¾".*

FIGURE 52. *Part of a dinner service made for Isaac and Mary Morris, of Philadelphia. About 1810. Courtesy of Dr. and Mrs. John B. Carson, Newtown Square, Pennsylvania.*

FIGURE 53 [left]. *Plate from the dinner service of Isaac and Mary Morris, of Philadelphia. About 1810. D. 9⅛". Courtesy of Dr. and Mrs. John B. Carson, Newtown Square, Pennsylvania.*

FIGURE 54 [right]. *Saucer and teacup in a design derived from that of the dinner service of Isaac and Mary Morris (Figs. 52, 53). About 1815. Cup: H. 1¾", D. 3½". Saucer: H. 1⅜", D. 5½". Ex Coll. Arthur J. Sussel.*

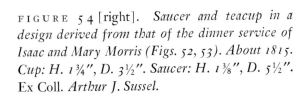

FIGURE 55. *Washbasin and pitcher with gilt cipher of Elizabeth Clifford Smith, wife of Thomas W. Smith, China merchant of Philadelphia. About 1805–1815. Basin: H. 5″, D. 13″. Pitcher: . 12½″. Courtesy of Mrs. Alfred Coxe Prime, Paoli, Pennsylvania.*

FIGURE 56 [right]. *Pieces from a dinner service made for William Phillips, of Philadelphia. About 1790–1805. Courtesy of Mrs. Alfred Coxe Prime, Paoli, Pennsylvania.*

FIGURE 57. *Monteith bearing the coat of arms of the Clements family, of Philadelphia. About 1790–1800. H. 4″, L. 10¼″, W. 6¼″. Courtesy of Mrs. Alfred Coxe Prime, Paoli, Pennsylvania.*

FIGURE 58. *Three pieces originally owned by early-nineteenth-century Delaware families. At left, a saucer (H. 1¼″, D. 5⅜″) with cipher of Mary Hemphill Jones, daughter of William Hemphill and wife of Morgan Jones. In center, a cream ewer (H. 5½″, D. 2½″) from tea set of Jane Richardson McKinly, daughter of John Richardson and wife of John McKinly, first President of the State of Delaware. At right, blue-and-gold-bordered dish (H. 1⅜″, D. 7⅞″) from a dinner service of Ann Spackman Richardson, wife of Joseph Richardson. Courtesy of Historical Society of Delaware (saucer presented by Mrs. Charles P. MacArthur; cream ewer and dish presented by estate of Mrs. Samuel Bancroft, Jr.).*

FIGURE 59. *Soup plate from the dinner service of Jeremiah Townley Chase,
of Annapolis, Maryland, bearing the coat of arms of the family of his grandmother,
Lady Margaret Townley, wife of Richard Chase. The Chase family adopted the
Townley coat of arms. About 1750–1760. D. 9".* Courtesy of *Maryland Historical
Society.*

FIGURE 60. *Three platters and a vegetable dish with grape-and-leaf border.
Cipher* MDSF *in gilt. About 1800–1815.* Courtesy of *Winterthur Museum.*

FIGURE 61. *Lighthouse coffeepot with crest of the John Nicholson family, of Maryland. Punch bowl originally owned by Samuel Sprigg, Governor of Maryland from 1819 to 1822. Coffeepot: H. 9¾″, D. (base) 4¹³⁄₁₆″. Punch bowl: H. 6⁹⁄₁₆″; D. (base) 8⁶⁄₁₆″, (top) 16″.* Courtesy of *Maryland Historical Society.*

FIGURE 62. *Ash tray, platter, and sauceboat with picture of Steamboat* Philadelphia *and inscription* Philadelphia/Union Line. *About 1817–1830. Ash tray: L. 7⅝″, W. 6″, H. 1½″. Platter: L. 18¼″, W. 15¾″, H. 2″. Sauceboat: L. 7¼″, W. 3½″, H. 3⅛″.* Courtesy of *Winterthur Museum.*

# VIII

## *The Decline of the Export Porcelain Trade to America*

ABOUT 1820 Robert Waln, Jr., wrote an enlightening account of the importance to America of its China trade during the previous forty years. It is interesting to find that he mentioned several facts which have been noted earlier, especially the widespread use of porcelains because of their popular price:

The Trade from China to the United States has been a prolific source of emolument to our merchants and revenue to the government. The articles of which it is composed have now become more incorporated with the necessaries, in actual use, an importance almost equivalent to that of bread: there are few families in our country, however humble their situation, which would not be greatly inconvenienced by a deprivation of this exhilerating beverage [tea]; the various species of the Tea Plate fortunately afford a corresponding variety of qualities, so that, notwithstanding the enormous import-duties, certain kinds are procurable at a low rate by the poorer classes of society.

This universal consumption of the principal article of import, increasing with the growth of the country and progress of the trade, afforded ample encouragement to those adventurers who first embarked in their long and hazardous voyages: the state of Europe at peculiar periods also furnished an additional impetus, and the trading community was beneficially employed in supplying the continent with the products of China, not only by re-exportations from America, but direct transportation from Canton; the consumption of silks & nankins was gradually extended, and the importation materially encouraged by the demand for Europe & the West India Islands: the Porcelain of China, displaced the English Ware hitherto in use, & became exclusively employed by the higher & middle ranks; even the poorest families could boast at least a limited proportion of China Ware, and although it should require the united exertions of the family to effect the object, few young girls, at the present day, enter into the marriage state, without contributing their respective China Ware Tea Setts to the general concern.[1]

Waln's comments referred to the earlier period of commerce; but the next two decades saw a mild revolution in the nature of the China trade. Not only did smaller shippers give way to bigger firms,[2] but outward cargoes increasingly carried manufactured products, especially coarse white and printed cotton, instead of raw materials.[3] The clipper-ship era, beginning in the 1840's, well marked these changes.[4] When the clipper *Rainbow* made her first Canton voyage in 1845, Philip Hone, the well-known observer of New York's commercial affairs, remarked:

The same articles which we formerly imported from China, and for which nothing but dollars would pay, are now manufactured here at one third the cost, and sent out to pay for teas. [Cottons had replaced nankeens.] The difficulty now is to find sufficient returns for the American cargoes. We do not send them specie—not a dollar.[5]

In addition, the Treaty of Wanghia in 1844 gave America five more ports of commerce in China as well as equal trading terms with the Chinese.[6] It established the Americans as a trading nation worthy of respect and just treatment within China's boundaries.[7] Consequently, for almost twenty years before the Civil War. America enjoyed a reversal of her former position in commercial and diplomatic relations in the Far East. The China trade continued until the War, but did not resume afterwards, partly because of the growing interest in westward migration.[8]

As far as imports were concerned, change was also evident. Though tea remained high and became even higher in demand, silks and nankeens had fallen off a great deal by the 1840's. As has been suggested, chinaware cargoes appeared to have shrunk considerably since the mid-1820's; in the season 1833–1834, only 1,322 boxes of chinaware left Canton for America.[9] This quantity could easily have been handled by four or five ships, only a fraction of the total number of forty-three vessels registered in China that year.[10] It is easy to understand why remaining business papers contain infrequent references to chinaware after about 1825.

Again, Americans followed a pattern set by the English. The British East India Company stopped importing porcelain in 1801, partly because of an overstocked market and a decrease in the appeal of Chinese things, but also because of the increased activities of English ceramic industries and the beginning of high tariffs to protect them.[11]

Perhaps another influence on the British was the fact that the wares of Ching-tê Chên began a gradual, but steady, decline in quality in the late eighteenth century. By the reign of Chia-ch'ing (1796–1821), copies of older porcelains became the main production, indicating a breakdown in the inspiration of the potters. Even for objects destined for domestic use, the clays were poorer than in the fine porcelains of the mid-eighteenth century. In addition, the drawing became less creative and more mechanical. In the reign of the succeeding emperor, Tao Kuang (1821–1850), this deterioration was even more apparent, though imitation could still be executed with great skill.[12] One may imagine that, if this were true of the best porcelains, the foreign wares were even more poorly made.

These factors also combined to explain America's decreased interest in export porcelains. As discussed previously, chinaware was often too coarse, rough, and poorly painted for buyers in this country. In 1822 John Latimer noted this latter fact in a letter to his brother Henry in connection with porcelain for his fiancée:

> I shall have the China-Ware done and take it home with me . . . I know not how your lady will like my disobeying orders but I have got the China Ware of the same pattern as my own. I could not find in the Celestial Empire a Lanscape [*sic*] pattern that pleased me.[13]

Other buyers continued to be displeased with careless packing. In 1827 Matthew Ralston, a Philadelphia merchant, objected to losses because of breakage, as Benjamin Fuller had forty years before. He also indicated the type of ware then being imported:

> Some Blue & White China plates might answer of all the different sizes—both flat & deep, they must be packed differently—more straw, & not so many put into a Box—as the breakage is very great, in the present mode,—the quality has been much complained of lately.[14]

With this state of affairs in regard to Chinese export ware, the potteries and porcelains of Europe became increasingly popular in American markets. From England, the factories of Wedgwood, Worcester, Staffordshire, and Liverpool sold products to this country. Their wares had been imported simultaneously with export porcelains, but, after 1810, gradually replaced them.[15] Such pieces, with a smooth body and precise transfer printings in the Western style, had greater appeal than the Chinese wares; and their blue-and-white decoration undoubtedly satisfied a taste for such paintings first stimulated by the export porcelains. From France, wares from centers like Sèvres and Limoges, with a light body and careful decoration, also rose in demand.[16] This development was a natural one, for European ceramics had always been highly regarded by Americans and, in fact, mainly determined the form and decorations of many export wares (Chaps. IX and X).

As had the Europeans, the Americans finally succeeded in making wares for their own market. The Philadelphia firm of Bonnin and Morris reportedly made porcelain in the early 1770's, but the business was not a financial success and was short-lived.[17] Thirty and forty years later there were also abortive attempts in New York and New Jersey to produce chinaware equal to that made in Europe. Not until William Ellis Tucker began his firm in 1826 did any amount of native porcelain supply the American demand; even then, the amount of ware probably satisfied only local customers. Tucker's firm, which had several series of associates, finally was discontinued in 1838.[18] It was not until after 1843, when the factories in Bennington, Vermont, first made porcelain figures, commonly known as Parian ware, that the United States again produced porcelain comparable to that of Europe.[19]

However, Tucker ware undoubtedly attracted many Americans who might otherwise have placed orders for export porcelain. The fact that the period of Tucker ware manufacture and that of the decrease in chinaware imports coincided and the fact that the fashions particularly reflected by Tucker ware were those of France, rather than of the Orient, would suggest that America now wished to satisfy its own tastes, based on those of Europe, independent of Oriental features.

Chinese export porcelain, suffering from breakage, poor quality, and competition, thus had been fairly well superseded by European wares by 1841.[20] As if in a final statement, one commentator wrote in 1844:

At the present day only a fancy set [china] occasionally comes to this country.[21]

# IX

## The Forms of Export Porcelain Made for America

IN DISCUSSING various forms of export ware, it seems best to consider first the most predominant types and their customary shapes and then the rarer items and their function. Possible sources for a few of these forms are suggested in Chapter XI.

By far the greatest amount of porcelain imported by this country consisted of services for the table.[1] In countless invoices and letters of order, there are listings of breakfast, dinner, dessert, and evening services as well as tea and coffee sets.[2] What pieces composed these services may be seen from the notebook of an anonymous trader from Providence, Rhode Island, listing prices current at Canton in 1797 (see Appendix II, p. 228). His account shows combinations of pieces which remained fairly standard throughout the period of trade, except for special orders.

His records and those of others show that a breakfast service consisted usually of twelve cups and saucers, a sugar dish and stand, a milk pot, a teapot, a slop bowl, and a plate. Extra pieces might include a cake plate and a coffeepot, or a butter boat and stand.[3] Tea and coffee sets varied only slightly from this pattern except perhaps for the addition of a tea canister. They might contain from forty to seventy items, although the usual services had approximately forty-nine pieces.[4] A long or double tea set contained about 101 objects.[5] One such service of 103 pieces of the best quality porcelain with white-and-gilt decoration was ordered in 1802 by Daniel Hopkins, of Farmington, Connecticut, who also wanted his cipher painted in gilt.[6] Usually twenty-four cups (twelve for tea and twelve for coffee) were combined in sets, with only twelve saucers to divide between the two types of cups.[7]

Dinner services, of course, were much more extensive. Although several sets numbering pieces in the 200's and a few having over 400 pieces have already been discussed, the average set contained about 171 or 172 articles.[8] The standard service was composed of plates and platters of a great variety of sizes, ranging from 6 to 18 inches, some specified as "flat" and some "deep"; soup, entree, salad, or dessert plates; vegetable, pudding, and pie dishes; salad bowls; soup and pickle tureens; sauce and butter boats; fruit dishes or baskets, all with stands; and salts.

Often the set also included special dishes for serving meat or fish. In 1815 William Law brought home a service of blue-and-white Nanking stone china which contained "3 Beef steak Water dishes [with a] place for gravy" of three sizes and a "Fish Dish & Strainer." [9] The former piece was probably a large platter with a depression at one end for the gravy, combined with a hollow base and openings at the rim for hot water. Hot-water dishes, not specified for use with meat, were also included in the service Law imported. They had openings similar to those of the orange Fitzhugh dish with sepia eagle in Figure 63. The fish dish which Law referred to was undoubtedly long and narrow, following the customary outline of its intended contents.[10]

Separate dishes for gravy were also part of dinner services. In 1815 J. W. Rogers, of Boston, asked Benjamin Shreve to buy him a 253-piece service to include "1 Beef Steak Dish, 1 Gravy Dish (18 Inches), and 1 Fish do (18 Inches)." [11]

Fruit baskets frequently were included in dinner or dessert services. Many of them were pierced, exhibiting the ability of the Chinese to execute difficult punchwork, sometimes called "openwork" (see Appendix II, p. 228). Examples of typical forms may be seen in Figure 64. Fruit shells are also listed in some invoices. It is difficult to learn what their exact form was; however, they may have resembled the left rear dish in Figure 52. A special sort of fruit compote was ordered in a dinner service by Mrs. Joseph Peabody, of Salem, in 1815. She sent with Benjamin Shreve a pattern, unfortunately missing from the existing records, but of a French design, and, besides the usual sorts of ware, desired "Round Scollop'd dishes like Mrs. Tucker's [Mrs. Gideon Tucker]" and "4 Oval Fruit dishes 10 inches long 2½ deep at the side rising a little towards the ends. . . ." [12] These fruit containers may have resembled the compote pictured in Figure 65, although they may have had a more intricate border decoration.

Curry dishes sometimes were brought to America and are particularly interesting as an indication of Far Eastern influence on Western tastes. In 1817 Benjamin Shreve bought from Hupsong four curry dishes along with beefsteak, pudding, pie, and "Hot water Cover'd Dishes." [13]

Punch bowls were not actually part of a dinner service; but, judging from the number of orders for them, they were used extensively, probably before or after the evening meal and for special gatherings. Several punch bowls have already been reviewed (Chap. VII) and others with a variety of decorations will be considered. They were particularly suitable as presentation pieces. One such bowl, now preserved by the Philadelphia Armory, shows signs of frequent use since its first use by the members of the Gloucester Fox Hunting Club of Philadelphia in the late eighteenth century. It was a gift to Samuel Morris, president of the club, who was also captain of the Philadelphia Troop of Light Horse from 1776 to 1786. A descendant, Effingham B. Morris, presented the Armory with the bowl encased in silver and with a carved wooden stand.

Specific items had interesting variations. Plates often are mentioned in invoices as square, round, or oval, with plain, fluted, ribbed, or scalloped edges. In the original records consulted, the plain and scalloped edges appear most often in large consignments, but it would be difficult to determine which type was the most popular at a particular time. Probably the more elaborate dishes, such as the plate in Figure 67, were made in the period beginning after the War of 1812. Of course, one style might be preferred continually above others, according to the purchaser's taste. Mr. Christie's order for eighteen boxes of tea sets in 1816 specified that they all "be rib'd if possible & of as clear a white as can be." [14]

Cups also had a range of form all their own. A good number, like the pair in Figure 66, resembled Oriental tea or rice vessels; but a large percentage of the cups seem inspired by European models, or at least are a combination of designs from East and West. Tea and coffee cups, coffee mugs or cans, and custard cups were the three main types. Although the first two types were often used interchangeably, certain features usually distinguished them. Teacups might be completely handleless, with a rounded base and wide brim, and raised on a small foot; or they might have single or double handles attached to sides which were essentially vertical in contrast with the former type (cf. Figs. 66, 81, 82). Coffee cups, on the other hand, usually were cylindrical mugs with handles and without a foot (Figs. 84a, 98). Custard cups were usually smaller than either of the foregoing types, were pear shaped, and each had a cover (Fig. 64).

Goblets were also ordered, though only rarely in comparison with the cups.[15] Figure 68 shows two goblets decorated with American eagles. They are similar to, but not identical with, the standing cup, which had a larger bowl above its stem and also had a top.[16] Egg cups appear to have been another unusual form. In 1806 John H. Titus ordered eighteen egg cups in a tea service of fine blue-and-white china.[17]

Several forms were characteristic of tea, coffee, or chocolate pots, as well as of pitchers, flagons, or jugs. The drum teapot and the lighthouse coffeepot shown in Figure 116 are easily differentiated forms. On the other hand, the pear-shaped pot with pistol handle seen in Figure 69 may have been used for either coffee or chocolate. Milk or cream pots were also distinctive. The helmet pitcher in Figure 116 is quite different from the milk pot of an earlier eighteenth-century shape. The cream pitcher, of course, was an entirely different form from the flagons or jugs, such as those shown in Figures 99 and 100 and in many other illustrations.

Less important in quantity and practicality than the tablewares were a number of decorative forms. Mantel garnitures (see Fig. 48) and pistol-handled urns (see Fig. 127) were the two forms which were probably the most popular porcelain forms used for interior decoration, rather than for serving food. Garnitures were in great vogue in 1806, when John H. Titus requested:

> To be very handsome Deep blue Nankin, with the Edge Gilt 2/8 of an inch, one Sett (of 5 p) Chimney Jars the most fashionable.[18]

The anonymous Providence trader whose notebook is quoted in Appendix II noted in 1797, "Jars and Tumblers for ornaments to a Chimney, 6 to 18 inches high, 5 to a sett." In addition, his list included "Large Urns or flower Jars, richly gilt, 2 to 3 feet high." This reference might pertain to urns of the pistol-handled variety, which usually vary from 1 to 3 feet in height, and which may have been used as flower jars; but it is more likely that it referred to large hearth jars placed on either side of a fireplace opening. In 1806 Thomas C. Pearsall, of New York, ordered nine boxes containing, among other items, two such jars, for which he paid a total of $20; the jars came in the same shipment on the ship *Eliza* from which John H. Titus received his garniture.[19] Other purely luxury pieces included pagodas, such as that seen in Figure 47, as well as china figures. William Law purchased from Manchong in 1816 fifty "Small Images of China Men and Women with painted Costumes"; he paid $1.25 for the lot.[20]

Flowerpots might be considered semidecorative wares since they were functional pieces with a decorative purpose. Many references to these containers appear scattered through shipping records of almost every port. The pots differ widely in form. The large, round, double-handled pieces like those in Figure 70, resembling French forms, were perhaps most popular. An entirely different form, the low square flower container illustrated in Figure 71 shows Oriental form in its feet and its use of lions; it also shows the typical Chinese representation of Occidental people, making them appear strangely Oriental, despite their Western dress. This pot was probably made for the European market, or at most for the English colonial market in the eighteenth century, and not specifically for American buyers. Its decoration, however, is interesting in comparison with the figures painted on the Declaration of Independence ware (see Figs. 136, 138). All types of flowerpots were undoubtedly in demand because of their reasonable price. In the 1784–1785 cargo of the *Empress of China*, there were "10 Sett Flower Potts 5 p$^r$ Sett a 3$^{doll}$," totaling $30, or 60 cents apiece.[21]

Other useful porcelains of a semiluxurious nature were included in the previously mentioned shipment which William Law purchased from Manchong in 1816. He bought two garden seats for $4 each and four pairs of cuspidors for $3. He paid the generous amount of $20 for a pair of candlesticks, but six white stone paper holders cost only $3.[22] The fact that candlesticks are so infrequently mentioned in the records consulted makes it difficult to judge how the porcelain candlesticks in Figure 72, with their stark lines and chaste decoration, would have compared in price with those purchased by William Law.

Law's garden seats may not have been so purely Chinese in character as the one illustrated in Figure 73, but that such fine types of porcelain pieces found their way to America is evident from remaining examples, some of which have a traceable history, as do the hearth jars which once belonged to Elizabeth Patterson Bonaparte, of Baltimore (see p. 105). One should be careful not to confuse these pieces with the chinaware made especially for Americans.

Chamber pots and covers also appear frequently in listings of ships' papers or in personal invoices. They were only one item among several types of bedchamber porcelains. Others included shaving bowls, washbasins and pitchers, and special tubs. Bathing bowls approximately 3 feet in diameter, with blue-and-white decoration, were often raised above the floor in teakwood stands.

Another type of porcelain object known, through remaining examples with traceable history, to have come to America is seen in tureens formed in the shapes of heads of animals or in the form of geese, ducks, and fish. A pair of huge, white goose tureens with fine incised decoration, shown in Figure 74, were presented to the East India Marine Society, of Salem, by Captain Ward Blackler in 1803.[23] The Society, founded in 1799, undoubtedly used them at its annual banquets after their presentation.[24]

There are several polychrome goose tureens in the Winterthur Museum, smaller than the white ones in Salem. Also at Winterthur are a tureen in the shape of the head of a water buffalo and another in the form of a boar's head, both with large teeth set in hideously gaping mouths. All these animal pieces seem to be of fine, if heavy, porcelain and are quite well painted. None of them, however, are known definitely to have been made for the American market. They may have been made for Europeans in the eighteenth century and brought to the United States more recently.

FIGURE 63. *Orange Fitzhugh-pattern hot-water dish with sepia eagle. Early nineteenth century. H. 2⁵⁄₁₆″, L. 14″, W. 9¾″.* Courtesy of *Mr. and Mrs. Charles K. Davis, Fairfield, Connecticut.*

FIGURE 64 [below]. *Part of a dinner service. Two fruit baskets and stands, sauce and pickle tureens, a custard cup, a salt dish, and a mustard pot. About 1800–1812.* Courtesy of *Winterthur Museum.*

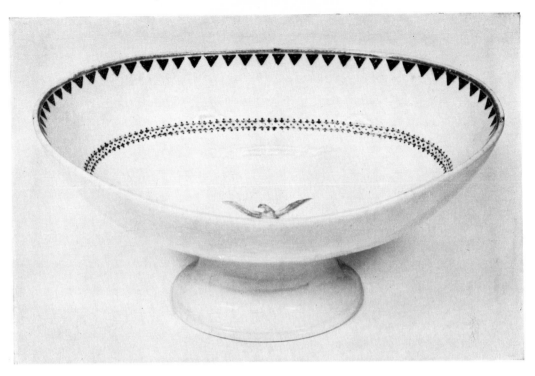

FIGURE 65. *Fruit compote with eagle design and saw-tooth border. About 1810–1820. H. 4½″, L. 10¾″, W. 7½″.* Courtesy of *Mr. and Mrs. Alfred E. Bissell, Wilmington, Delaware.*

FIGURE 66. *Teacup, with no handles, a rounded base, a wide brim, and a small foot. A typical form. About 1795–1810. D. 3⅜″.* Courtesy of *Peabody Museum of Salem.*

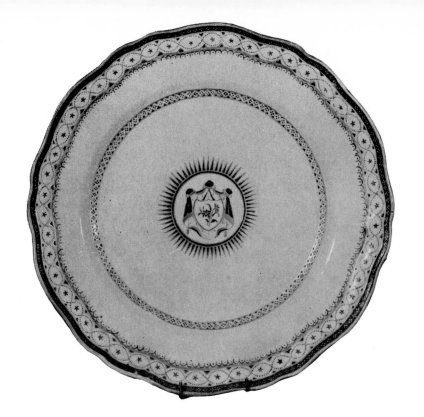

FIGURE 67. *Scallop-edged, blue-and-gold-bordered plate. About 1810–1820. D. 9¾″. Ex Coll.* Arthur J. Sussel.

FIGURE 68. *Pair of goblets with American-eagle decoration. About 1795–1815. H. 5½″; D. (base) 2⁷⁄₁₆″, (top) 3″. Courtesy of* Museum of Art, Rhode Island School of Design.

FIGURE 69 [right]. *Pear-shaped coffeepot or chocolate pot with pistol-handle arm. About 1790–1800. H. 9″. Courtesy of Mr. and Mrs. Alfred E. Bissell, Wilmington, Delaware.*

FIGURE 70. *Part of a dinner service, with two flowerpots in back row. About 1800–1810.* Courtesy of *Winterthur Museum.*

FIGURE 71. *Flower container showing Chinese conceptions of European taste. Eighteenth century. H. 8″, L. 13″, W. 13″.* Courtesy of *Winterthur Museum.*

FIGURE 72 [left]. *Pair of white porcelain candlesticks with borders of red-orange and green. About 1750–1825. H. 10¼".* Courtesy of *Winterthur Museum.*

FIGURE 73 [below]. *Pale-green Chinese garden seat with raised white decoration. H. 18½", D. 12".* Courtesy of *Winterthur Museum.*

FIGURE 74. *Pair of white goose tureens presented to the East India Marine Society, of Salem, Massachusetts, in 1803 by Captain Ward Blackler. L. 22".* Courtesy of *Peabody Museum of Salem.*

# X

## The Decorations on Export Porcelain Made for America

THE REAL BASIS for identification of Chinese export wares made particularly for America lies in their decoration. Forms are helpful to indicate European or Oriental influences and to date objects; but American symbols on export porcelain alone signify pieces intended for the American market. The drawings vary greatly in design and color, and not all of them can be considered, even if all types were known. Only the more common and the particularly significant examples will be cited.

### COMMON WARES

Certainly, the blue-and-white porcelain far outnumbers any other type of decorated ware in the export trade. Endless orders, bills of lading, and invoices list both Canton and Nanking blue-and-white wares, and these wares appear to have been popular throughout the period of trade. Blue-and-white Fitzhugh-pattern pieces are less frequently listed as such, but perhaps they were not specified in some records except for the color.[1]

Figure 80 illustrates a particularly fine example of the quantity of blue-and-white ware imported in a single set. This view shows only a portion of a complete double dinner service imported for Sally Fiske Ropes at the time of her marriage to her cousin, Joseph Orne, in 1817.

[ *139* ]

The chinaware may now be seen in the Ropes Mansion in Salem, Massachusetts.[2]

The differences between Canton ware and Nanking ware decorations lie not so much in their central design—often similarly painted with islands, trees, bridges, boats, and perhaps figures (Figs. 75, 76)—but in their outer borders. Canton ware customarily has a dark-blue lattice or network border on a solid light-blue ground with a wavy or scalloped line above. The Nanking border consists of a closer network with a small ornament in each mesh of the net. Instead of the scalloped line of the Canton ware, it has a spearhead border.[3] These differences may be seen in Figures 77 and 78.

The blue-and-white Canton and Nanking wares were noted not only because of the color, but also for the charm of their central patterns. The usual decoration, consisting of a river scene with an island from which there generally sprang a willow tree, gave this pottery its alternative name of "willow ware." This motif was a traditional one among Chinese potters, but it was never rigidly standardized, and the details might vary from set to set, although they were generally consistent within any one set. In China it was always considered only as a decorative pattern, never as an illustration of any particular tale or legend. However, in eighteenth-century England, about 1780, an English designer at Caughley, probably Thomas Turner, produced a European version of the Chinese pattern, introducing a number of specific details to make a story, thereafter known as the "Legend of the Willow Pattern Plate."[4] There is no such "legend" in the Chinese tradition, and one may look in vain on the porcelain actually painted in China for all the details required by the English story, even though some of them, such as a bridge with people crossing it, may happen to be shown.[5] Even though the Canton and Nanking porcelains did not actually illustrate a story, the pictures on them had a certain exotic charm.

Why did Americans, as well as Europeans, find the Canton and Nanking porcelains so appealing? The standard types bore no familiar Western symbols; in fact, they seem to contradict the thesis that Occidental tastes were imposed on the export porcelains. However, on closer examination it may be seen that, no matter what the decorations represented, the objects themselves were generally copies of European forms, from dinner services to toilet articles. Second, the decoration was enjoyed not as an expression of Oriental aesthetics, but mainly as a quaint —though fabricated—story about a distant and strange people. For the most part, Americans were fleetingly curious, rather than profoundly scholarly, about the culture of the Chinese. Perhaps the prevention by the Chinese of cultural exchange in the early period kept Western appreciation of the Oriental arts at a minimum, except in the case of a few students. Third, and perhaps most significantly, the blue-and-white ware was among the least expensive of the porcelains (see Chap. VI). Thus the great popularity of Canton and Nanking porcelains in America can be understood.

A third type of blue-and-white chinaware was known, for some reason not yet explained, as "Fitzhugh." [6] The complete Fitzhugh pattern was entirely different from the other two. It consisted of a circular medallion at the center (sometimes replaced by another device, such as the eagle, as shown on the plate in Figure 90a), four panels of floral design, and a wide border broken into several areas filled with diaper patterns, of which the only recognizable symbols were four butterflies (see Fig. 79).[7]

The total pattern, as here described, was not always used together. Not only was the central medallion sometimes replaced by another motif; on other examples, the characteristic Fitzhugh border was replaced by the familiar Nanking one, while in other cases the Fitzhugh border was used to ornament a piece with the usual Canton willow-tree island in the center. The Fitzhugh pattern appeared not only in blue and white, but also in red or orange, and in green. The plate illustrated in Figure 90a has the pattern predominantly in green, with a sepia eagle. Sometimes elements in the pattern were outlined in gold.

Despite their differences, however, all the blue-and-white wares— Canton, Nanking, and Fitzhugh—were alike in being decorated under the glaze at Ching-tê Chên or at other possible sources of production.[8] A separate set of Chinese specialists evidently worked on this type of painting alone.[9] The pieces, first having been dried, were painted with a blue slip made from a cobalt-bearing manganese ore. A transparent glaze was then applied, and the pieces were fired to set the glaze.[10] The glaze had to be applied before the firing; otherwise, the blue pigment employed would become black in the kiln; and, of course, if the color was applied over the glaze, it soon wore off.[11] Often the red and green

Fitzhugh patterns were applied before glazing, although some were painted in overglaze enamels. Eagles and ciphers, when used with the Fitzhugh pattern, were added by painting over the glaze.[12]

Underglaze red and penciled decorations were probably less popular in the West than the blue, even though they sometimes appear in records of large shipments. The imperfect color of the red ware mainly prevented the growth of a demand for it. By the time of the export porcelain period, iron had generally replaced copper as the source for underglaze red, its advantages being that it was cheaper and easier to work.[13] However, the iron compounds did not always retain their original color after firing and sometimes became a red-orange, and underglaze reds did not achieve the brilliance and liveliness of the blue pigments.[14] Overglaze red did not suffer from this difficulty. The penciled wares bore a black or brown line decoration like that appearing on the cup in Figure 37. Without the appeal of color and often with sketchy painting, these wares were also less popular than the blue-and-white porcelain.[15]

A large amount of several sorts of common ware came to New York under William Law's supervision in 1815. One may note the predominance of blue-and-white wares in the shipment: [16]

4 Boxes—1200 pair black penciled Tea cups & saucers  
                              $5^{75}$ pr 100 pr. is         $ 69  
50 Boxes—15000 Do Red enameled do        562.50  
12   "   —3600 Do blue & White do       207 —  
8   "   —1600 Do  Do Coffee Cups & saucers  
                              $7^{25}$ pr. 100 pr. is      116 —  
10   "   —3000 Blue & White $2^{d}$ size plates  
                              $6^{50}$ pr 100 pr. is      195 —  
10   "   —3000 Do          3 Do  
                              $5^{50}$             165  
15   "      30 sets enameled Tea cups & saucers  
        48 pieces each at $2            60  
              [Total]           1674.50

The last-mentioned item, enameled wares, also figured largely in various other shipments. These were porcelains which were painted over the glaze with enamels that required an extra firing in separate ovens after the decoration had been applied. As with the blue-and-white ware, the enameled porcelains were produced only by a specially trained group in their own establishments, known as "Red shops." [17]

Wares of this sort might be of polychrome pigments or of a solid color. The punch bowls which John Morgan sent home on board the *Empress* (Figs. 43, 44) have already been mentioned, but simpler types were also popular. In 1821 Benjamin Shreve brought back to Salem two such orders. A dining set "of a handsome dark blue" was bought by John Chadwick, and an extensive tea set was purchased by John Prince, Jr., who had requested that it be "light purple and gilt—the edges about ¼ inch & the handles; with any pretty device other than a mere sprig." [18]

Earlier in the trade, *famille rose* services had gratified American tastes for multicolored wares with a floral design. They are never mentioned by name in the records, but the quantity existing today suggests their former popularity, though perhaps before the 1780's and 1790's. At the turn of the century, however, pieces with dainty bouquets scattered all over or placed in the center, borders with swags and festoons, landscapes in sepia or polychrome, and special patterns were more in style. Then, by the later period of the trade, mandarin wares which were painted in almost the entire range of enamels made their appearance.[19] As early as 1817 Benjamin Shreve bought a box of mandarin cups and saucers of an unknown quantity for $10 in a miscellaneous shipment.[20]

THE UNITED STATES SEAL ON EXPORT PORCELAIN

The great seal of the United States was used almost as often as the American flag to distinguish wares made for this country. Officially adopted June 20, 1782, the seal was current on coinage even before the Constitution was ratified; and in the 1780's it was one of the chief decorations on government gold, silver, and copper pieces.[21] An eagle with drooping wings and without a sunburst appeared on the Massachusetts copper cent and half-cent pieces of 1787–1788. The sunburst did not appear above the eagle until 1796, when it was first used on United States two-and-a-half-dollar gold pieces.[22] No doubt Americans carried these coins with them as design patterns for the Canton enamelers. The cup and saucer in Figure 81 show the eagle with shield and banner like that on the double-handled cup in Figure 82, but the starry heavens above and the shields in front of them are quite different, indicating the wide variety of this pattern.

Sources for the eagle design also extend to official documents which bore the great seal, such as consular papers or business records which used the emblem as a decorative motif. One paper of the latter variety was a certificate of ownership used by the ship *Elizabeth* of New York in 1804 (Fig. 83). The document was cf a standard sort and must have been current for most contemporary New York ships, if not for those of other ports as well. Perhaps the eagle with the doleful eye on the two mugs and flagon in Figure 84a is so precisely executed because its design source was from a record of this type. Certainly the comparison of details shows very few differences, except perhaps for the placement of the stars, which number fifteen in both illustrations (cf. Figs. 83 and 84b).[23]

The plate in Figure 85a bears an eagle design (Fig. 85b) similar to, but not so precisely drawn as, the bird just considered. This chubby eagle with reduced head and neck looks more like a plump chicken than a symbol of the nation's strength. The heavens above, falling closely about its head, follow the line of the lowered wings, both contributing to the confined nature of the drawing. The cipher *FP* above the bird may stand for Franklin Pierce, for whom the tea service is believed to have been made. Many other sets bear this particular eagle, making it one of the most common types represented.

Many variants of the eagle appear. Sometimes the wings are spread high, and sometimes they are lowered; the shields are striped and colored, or filled with a monogram, or painted with a floral motif. Generally, the eagles are reddish brown or sepia against a sunburst pattern touched with gold. The right talon clutches a twig of laurel or an olive branch, signifying peace; the left grasps a bunch of arrows, indicating defense. Often the bird resembles nothing more than a scrawny sparrow with toothpicklike arrows and leafless branches.[24] Yet others, like those described below, are rather robust specimens.

The independent birds on the two ovoid garniture pieces in Figure 86 stand unadorned by the shield and by the banner reading *E Pluribus Unum* seen on pieces already cited (Figs. 81–83). The eagle pattern in Figure 87, though quite similar to the eagle on the garniture pieces, is an enlarged detail of the decoration on one of the most extensive dinner services known. The set, consisting today of 416 pieces, belonged to the John Jacob Ridgway family, of Philadelphia.

Other eagle designs probably were derived from documents which did not follow the seal or coins closely, but merely used the bird in a decorative manner. An eagle which appears on the heading of the National Insurance Company's policies for New York ships in the second decade of the nineteenth century swoops down below his widespread wings to grasp two banners, one reading *E Pluribus Unum* and the other, *National Insurance* (Fig. 88).[25] Although this design is different from that of the rampant eagle on the saucer in Figure 89, the similarity of the two does indicate that documents of this sort were used for patterns at Canton. The decoration on the plate in Figure 90a combines the same type of broad-winged bird in sepia, grasping the usual symbols, with the intricate Fitzhugh pattern in green.

The eagle design of Figure 91 shows a bald bird, with white-barred wings, casting a wary eye behind him as he looks to his left. This posture seems similar to that of the eagle which appears on the United States quarter-eagle minted in 1792.[26] It has been mentioned in Chapter VII that the family of Allen Bowie, Jr., living near Baltimore, owned a service with this decoration painted in sepia.

A flying eagle with pinions extended (Figs. 92a, 92b) varies from the others already seen. It grasps a trumpet of fame in its talons, and its beak holds a banner reading *In God We Hope*, on top of which lies a shield with anchor. Above the eagle's head was once a crown of gilt stars. Several services of this sort humorously show the problem which arose between two peoples who did not know each other's language, for the banners sometimes read *I E Coe W E Hope*. Although this design has often been considered peculiar to Rhode Island because of its anchor, there seems to be little evidence to support such a belief.[27]

MARINE SCENES

Perhaps as prevalent as the eagle designs are the paintings of ships proudly carrying the Stars and Stripes and symbolizing the country's new wealth from commerce. Countless numbers of vessels appear on all sorts of tea, coffee, and dinner services, and on punch bowls, as illustrated in Figures 93 and 96, but rarely are there ships on garnitures, flowerpots, and other decorative porcelains. Perhaps the design was too masculine for such pieces.

Certainly the paintings differ, but very few distinguish the ship for which they might have been made. Most resemble the cumbersome vessels of the sixteenth and seventeenth centuries, used as patterns by the porcelain painters throughout the eighteenth century. Even the *Grand Turk's* punch bowl was not done according to the ship's actual design, but from a print of an English ship (see Chap. VII).

Actually, the main sources for the ship designs undoubtedly were printed patterns which appeared on business papers. The bill of lading of the ship *Lion*, shown in Figure 95, shows a vessel resembling many of the ships in the previous illustrations. From such stock sources, perhaps supplemented by portraits of ships done from the actual vessels by some of the Chinese artists, great quantities were undoubtedly made up, and an American flag added when an American order was placed.

A range in quality of clays and painting, however, provides some variation in the marine wares. The borderless plate in Figure 94 shows the results of poor porcelain combined with bad glazing; but these defects are perhaps compensated for by the unique drawing in a primitive style which shows the silhouettes of sailors on deck and in a rowboat to the left. In addition, the American flag, almost sail size, flies over the stern. The mug in Figure 97 is painted with the "Sailor's Farewell and Return," a popular subject of eighteenth-century prints in England as well as in America.

Another common pattern is illustrated by the mug in Figure 98. The stern of a ship with an American flag is visible, the rest of the ship hidden from view by a large pedestal on which stands a bird; above the bird is a banner reading *America*. This design, however, is not especially American, as many similar ones appear with European, and especially English, flags and without the bird and banner. The cipher *SG* on this particular mug may signify Stephen Girard, of Philadelphia, though there is no documentary evidence that he actually owned this piece.

A few special marine views have been preserved which indicate that not all the patterns were derived from the stereotyped designs of commercial papers. A "Foul Weather and Fair" flagon shows, on the one side, a vessel with full sails under perfect sailing conditions, while on the other the ship is tossed to one side by the wind and by waves that are quite Oriental in style (Figs. 99a, 99b). The design is painted with a freer brush than most ship pictures. Unfortunately, the prototype for this design is not known, and only a few such flagons still exist.[28]

A direct source for the decorations on the flagon pictured in Figure 100 appears to have been an undated print published in New York by J. Tiebout as an American school sheet.[29] Entitled "American Naval Victories," the sheet of line engravings by A. Anderson of drawings by W. B. Morgan has at the center top a large oval drawing of the Battle of Lake Erie; down each side, three smaller pictures of naval engagements in the War of 1812; and, at the center between the two bottom views, a vignette of a sailor holding a banner reading *Don't Give Up The Ship*. The inscriptions on the engravings, which do not appear on the flagon, identify the encounter pictured in Figure 100a as "U.S. Frigate *United States*, Commodore Decatur, capturing H.B.M. Frigate *Macedonian*, Capt. Carden. Octob. 25$^{th}$ 1812" and the one on the opposite side of the flagon (Fig. 100b) as "U.S. Brig *Enterprize*, Lieut. Com$^t$ Burrows capturing H.B.M. Brig *Boxer*, Capt. Blyth. Sept. 4$^{th}$ 1813." [30] Below the spout (Fig. 100c) is a sailor vignette matching the sailor vignette of the print. The monogram *WC* above the sailor is the only difference between the flagon pictured here and one in the Peabody Museum of Salem. The initials *IMBS*, which appear faintly on the Salem example, are explained by the history of the purchase of the flagon by Isaac Smith as a wedding gift for his wife, Margaret Van der Bogert.[31]

The two views of the punch bowl shown in Figure 101 serve as a final reminder of the importance of shipping to the new nation, not only in the China trade, but also in overseas and interstate commerce. The vivid design of the eagle grasping a trophy of war suggests a strong defense of the nation's freedom of the seas; and the bold lines of the ship's hull (Fig. 101b) denote that the "Strength & Wealth of the Nation" stemmed from the very foundations of the shipping trade.

STATE COATS OF ARMS

An emblem as significant to New York as the great seal is to the United States is that state's coat of arms. The earliest known engraving of this design (Fig. 102) was adopted by the colonial legislature on March 16, 1778. Liberty and Justice are dressed in the Dutch costume of colonial days, and Liberty steps cautiously on the British crown.[32] New York copper cents, or tokens, of 1786 and 1787 also carried this design. They show the same central cartouche of a sun rising above three mountains with an eagle above, perched on half the globe; but the dresses worn by Liberty and Justice have tighter bodices and fuller skirts than those in the print.

Many discrepancies between the official arms and the arms which appear on quantities of porcelain suggest that the decoration was made up in stock sets for ready purchase, as were the eagle and ship designs, waiting only for a monogram or an initial to be added.[33] Such a procedure is not surprising since New York was the first state to enter the China trade and was also the leader in a later period. No doubt many state papers were thus available for the Chinese copyists.[34] On some services, two striped United States shields appear below the central cartouche, and often the cartouche is filled with a floral sprig or a monogram instead of the scene depicted on the seal. The decoration of the cup and saucer shown in Figure 103 represents as close an approximation of the 1778 seal of New York as any of the paintings on porcelain.

The Pennsylvania state arms are an extremely rare pattern on export porcelain. The finely painted cup and tray in Figure 104 show two steeds rearing up to support an oval medallion. Inside the medallion is a ship, and on top of the medallion sits a spread-winged eagle. The banner below reads *Virtue, Liberty, Independence*.[35] Unfortunately, very few pieces like these are extant.

The only other examples currently known of export porcelain with patterns of states' arms reproduced with as great exactness as in the case of the New York and Pennsylvania examples are those bearing the arms of the State of New Jersey.[36] A design of a classic female holding an anchor in her right hand and resting her left elbow on a shield has often been thought to represent the arms of Rhode Island. This consists of an anchor, the symbol of stability, and a cable added in 1664 with the word *Hope*. However, because similar figures probably personifying Commerce in general appear in both British and American naval motifs, the design cannot be reserved for Rhode Island alone.[37]

# Decorations on Export Porcelain for America

An outstanding indication of the classical tastes and Francophile attitudes of American leaders just after the Revolution was manifested in the Society of the Cincinnati. Its origin stemmed from the efforts of Major-General Henry Knox, who successfully proposed an association of American and French officers to perpetuate the friendships made during the Revolution. Knox and his former aide-de-camp, Samuel Shaw, probably worked together in designing the Society's emblem. They were inspired by the legendary Roman patriot, Lucius Quinctius Cincinnatus, who in the fifth century B.C. left his farm for the battlefront, but returned to his farm when his military duty was done.[38]

The medal is of gold, suspended by a blue ribbon about 2 inches wide, edged with white "descriptive of the Union of America and France." [39] The obverse view shows Cincinnatus receiving a sword and other military symbols from three senators. In the background, his wife stands at the cottage door, while nearby are implements of agriculture. The encircling motto reads: *Omnia Relinquit Servare Rempublicam.* The reverse view pictures a rising sun, the open gates of a city, and vessels in port. In the foreground, a figure of Fame is crowning Cincinnatus with a wreath inscribed *Virtutis Proemium.* Below him, joined hands support a heart with the message *Esto Perpetua.* The whole is enclosed with *Societas Cincinnatorum Instituta A.D. 1783.*[40]

French influences appeared not only in the color of the ribbon, but also in a major way through the work of Major Pierre Charles L'Enfant, who was commissioned to execute the insignia. It was he who suggested the bald-eagle form. This bird, distinguished by its white head and tail, is peculiar to America. The Society's emblem was to be applied to the front and back of the gold eagle. L'Enfant suggested that it be highlighted by silver or enamel or even diamonds set in its head and tail. He further recommended the addition of laurel and oak leaves above its head.[41]

Although reproductions of the badge on export porcelain are hardly as precise as the badge itself, they did become highly popular with the members of the Society in the first years of the China trade. Samuel

Shaw was the first to investigate its possibilities on chinaware. On his first voyage to Canton, as supercargo of the *Empress of China,* he wanted a special set made, but was not very well pleased by what the Canton enamelers produced:

> There are many painters in Canton, but I was informed that not one of them possesses a genius for design. I wished to have something emblematic of the institution of the order of the Cincinnati executed upon a set of porcelain. My idea was to have the American Cincinnatus, under the conduct of Minerva, regarding Fame, who, having received from them the emblems of the order, was proclaiming it to the world. For this purpose I procured two separate engravings of the goddesses, an elegant figure of a military man, and furnished the painter with a copy of the emblems, which I had in my possession. He was allowed to be the most eminent of his profession, but, after repeated trials, was unable to combine the figures with the least propriety; though there was not one of them which singly he could not copy with the greatest exactness. I could therefore have my wishes gratified only in part. The best of his essays I preserved, as a specimen of Chinese excellence in design, and it is difficult to regard it without smiling. It is a general remark, that the Chinese, though they can imitate most of the fine arts, do not possess any large portion of original genius.[42]

On either his first or his second trip to Canton, Shaw had a service decorated with the Cincinnati insignia and his cipher made for himself. The cup and saucer in Figure 105 are from this set, the saucer showing the obverse of the badge and the cup the reverse. Shaw's basket-and-stand with the emblem of the Cincinnati on the stand (Fig. 42), possibly purchased about the same time, was discussed in Chapter VII.

Although Shaw, as quoted above, was not pleased with the results of his first order for a figure of Fame to be painted with the badge, such a figure is represented on a blue-and-white Fitzhugh service purchased by George Washington (see Frontispiece). This set, or part of it, may have been brought home by Thomas Randall in the *Pallas,* which arrived, with John O'Donnell as captain, in Baltimore on August 12, 1785. The cargo of chinaware, along with other Oriental imports, was announced in the *Baltimore Advertiser* as due to be sold October 1. Several qualities of porcelain were advertised, including "Evening blue and white Stone

Cups and Saucers; Ditto painted; Ditto with the Arms of the Cincinnati." On August 17, 1785, five days after the arrival of the *Pallas*, Washington wrote Colonel Tench Tilghman, of Baltimore, that he would like several chinaware pieces decorated with the Cincinnati insignia. "If great bargains are to be had," he wrote, "I would supply myself agreeably to an enclosed list." Part of that list was as follows:

A sett of the best Nankin Table China
Ditto—best Evening Cups & Saucers
* A sett of large blue & white China Dishes say half a dozen more or less
* 1 Doz small bowls blue & white
* 6 Wash hand Guglets & basons
6 Large Mugs or 3 mugs & 3 jugs

* With the badge of the Society of the Cincinnati if to be had.[43]

Tilghman died early the following year, evidently without doing anything about Washington's request.

Perhaps Washington thus delayed until the next summer to buy his set. On July 3, 1786, Colonel Henry ("Light Horse Harry") Lee, a delegate to the Continental Congress then sitting in New York, wrote that chinaware numbering about 306 pieces, decorated with the Cincinnati eagle, could be had for the equivalent of $150. Ledger B of Washington's accounts shows that he paid £45.5 for a set of chinaware. Later, Washington wrote Lee that "the china came to hand without much damage." Perhaps the Cincinnati pieces brought home by the *Pallas* were sent up to New York because of slow sales, were reduced in price, and thus were finally purchased by Washington.[44]

Many officers in the Society—including General Benjamin Lincoln, first president of the Massachusetts Society, and Henry Jackson, first treasurer of the national Society—had separate dinner services made with the emblem.[45] A saucer (Fig. 106) of more fanciful design than usual, with twin figures of Fame holding the bow of the emblem's ribbon, is from a set originally owned by William Eustis, who served as a vice-president of the Society from 1786 to 1810 and again in 1820. Eustis was the Governor of Massachusetts for a year before his death in 1825.[46]

Still another Cincinnati medal appears on the inside rim of a punch bowl with Washington's bust in the center (Fig. 107). The possible design source for the chain of states framing the President is an Amos Doolittle print which was first done in 1787 (Fig. 108).[47] In turn, Doolittle may have derived his pattern from the first United States copper cent, initially minted the same year.[48] The Doolittle print also shows the shield of each state, with shapes reminiscent of those which appear on the cups in Figure 66.

### PORCELAINS RELATING TO GEORGE AND MARTHA WASHINGTON

The enormous popularity which this country's first President enjoyed is certainly evident in porcelain decorations which he inspired. Already mentioned is his portrait combined with the Cincinnati emblem (Fig. 107). Another bust portrait, done from an engraving of one of Gilbert Stuart's portraits, appears on the barrel-shaped flagon in Figure 109.[49] Four such flagons are known to have been ordered by Benjamin Chew Wilcocks, a Philadelphia merchant in China from 1800 until 1829, and American consul at Canton from 1811 until 1818. The one of the four flagons which Wilcocks ordered for himself bears the cipher *BCW* opposite the Washington bust; the one illustrated (Fig. 109) was made for his nephew, Edward Tilghman, a distinguished Philadelphia lawyer, and bears the cipher *ET*. It is not known where the other two flagons, made for close friends of Wilcocks, now are.[50] The practiced hand of the Chinese imitator is especially evident in this painting; the lines and the dots of the original engraving are rendered almost as exactly as in a transfer print.

Washington's death, in 1799, occasioned a period of mourning, recorded in the country's decorative arts to an extent perhaps unequaled until after Lincoln's death. Like the paintings on glass, the wax figures, and the prints which recorded his passing were the decorations on export porcelain such as appear on the pieces in Figure 110. Even in later years, Washington was not forgotten. His home, Mount Vernon, seems to have inspired chinaware decoration in the latter part of the China trade, as is illustrated by the saucer in Figure 111. Its floral border pattern indi-

cates a date in the period after the War of 1812. The setting and build-
ing closely resemble the print *Mount Vernon, the Seat of the late Genl.
G. Washington,* done in 1804 by Samuel Seymour after a painting by
William Birch.[51]

Martha Washington's chinaware has been almost as famous as her
husband's. A tea service, brought to her by A. E. Van Braam Houckgeest, is represented by the cake plate in Figure 112. Mr. Van Braam
Houckgeest, a Dutch merchant with many years' experience in China,
had recently become an American citizen and perhaps expressed his
American sympathies and his admiration for President Washington by
presenting this unique set to Mrs. Washington. In April, 1796, he returned from China to Philadelphia aboard the *Lady Louisa.* A last item
attached to the ship's manifest read, "A Box of China for Lady Washington." [52] In Mrs. Washington's will, a "set of tea China that was given me
by Mr. Vanbram [*sic*] every piece MW on it" was bequeathed to her
grandson, George Washington Parke Custis.[53]

The design for the tea set is as full of nationalistic symbols as is the
Cincinnati insignia. From behind the circle of interlaced initials, the
rising sun of the Republic extends its rays toward a chain composed of
fifteen links, each with the name of a state, including Vermont and Kentucky. Around the inner circle with cipher is a wreath of olive and
laurel leaves symbolizing peace. Below the wreath, a motto on a ribbon
refers to the Union: *Decus Et Tutamen Ab Illo,* "Honor and defense
come from it." A serpent, biting its tail, surrounds the chain of states and
symbolizes eternity. A gold band finishes the outer edge.[54]

PERSONAL DECORATIONS

Special orders of export porcelain were often individualized by the crest
or cipher of the purchaser, and more rarely by his portrait. The services
of Elias Hasket Derby and Benjamin Fuller as well as the porcelains
which Captain John Barry brought home have been discussed (Chap.
VII). The following objects further indicate the importance attached
to personalized wares, perhaps as a result of the renewed spirit of individualism after the Revolution.

Decorations of this sort divide themselves into two groups, those painted according to a special family coat of arms, called armorial, and those made to suit buyers who did not have a family coat of arms, but who desired the prestige which one might bring. This second type of decoration, called pseudoarmorial, often took the form of the buyer's cipher painted in gilt within the stock pattern of a gilt-trimmed shield against a mantling with ermine lining, as in the case of the Hayes and Phillips sets (Figs. 50 and 56). Others used similar standard patterns, such as the grape-and-ivy border and the New York state-arms design to surround a monogram.

A few families with historic arms, however, ordered unique and colorful pieces. A mug which depicts the Hancock coat of arms, probably made for John Hancock, is pictured in Figure 113.[55] A dinner service supposedly made for Thomas Jefferson is represented by the plate seen in Figure 114. Its wide outer border is matched by an inner rim of deep-blue diaper, trimmed with a spearhead pattern in gold. In the center, a shield, the blue border of which carries thirteen stars, bears the gold letter *J*.[56] One may imagine that the severe classical design, completed by a blue-and-gold helmet with visor shut above the shield, pleased Jefferson's taste for the Roman style, a preference also indicated by the architecture of Monticello, his home in Virginia, where the few remaining pieces of this service are now on display. About the same time that these wares were made, John Quincy Adams received a mug decorated with his family coat of arms.[57]

The bust of Stephen Decatur, whose naval victory has already been considered, decorates a flagon pictured in Figure 115. The medallion portrait of Decatur from a picture by Saint-Mémin also appears on a punch bowl designed for the Commodore about 1800.[58] The flagon, no doubt, was made about the same time. The bouquet on either side of the medallion and the full border in red-orange make the flagon an exceptionally rich piece.

Less prepossessing is the decoration on a tea set (Fig. 116) with a history of having been owned by Isaac Hull, Decatur's compatriot. Bearing the cipher *IH* within a shield, the service stands as another reminder of one of the most famous heroes of the War of 1812 and as an additional sign of early-nineteenth-century self-expression.[59]

A unique example of personal arms combined with historic symbolism appears on a tea service made for John Stark, of Londonderry,

New Hampshire. As commander of the militia from his state during the Revolution, he was victorious over the British in the Battle of Bennington, August 14–16, 1777. This encounter prepared for the American success at Saratoga later that summer. The teapot from the Stark service (Fig. 117) illustrates the unusual decoration of the set—two shields, one on each side of the piece. The design within one shield is the Stark family bearings; that within the other commemorates Stark's achievements at Bennington, with the time and place of the battle suggested by the sun rising over the Green Mountains.[60]

In the Winterthur Museum collection are a platter and a basin originally belonging to De Witt Clinton and his wife, Maria Franklin Clinton, and bearing their cipher, in gilt, on a border of polychrome Chinese figures. As seen in the illustration of the platter (Fig. 118), the central landscape, also polychrome, is as Oriental in style as the border; without the monogram, the platter would have nothing to identify it as having been made for the American market.

## MISCELLANEOUS DECORATIONS

Patterns which appear less frequently on export porcelain, yet not less importantly, include those with mythological, religious, and genre subjects, historic buildings, landscapes, and Masonic motifs.

Reproductions of mythological or religious scenes, typical of many porcelains made for Europe in the eighteenth century, do not often appear on distinctively American wares.[61] The cup and saucer in Figure 119, originally belonging to Deborah Fairfax Anderson and showing Minerva and Cupid as well as the cipher *DFA*, may be considered rather unusual pieces.[62] Perhaps such designs, and particularly religious ones (of which very few examples with American associations are extant) were unpopular with Americans after the Revolution because of the influence of liberal philosophical views. Both Deism and Unitarianism were leading movements in the late eighteenth and early nineteenth centuries. Not until the second Great Awakening in the 1830's was orthodox religion revived to any great degree.[63]

Few genre scenes are known to have appeared on chinaware. The example of the farmer and his cow as decoration on the dinner service made for Isaac and Mary Morris in the early nineteenth century is unusual both for the occurrence of the pattern and for the copies and variations that have survived (Figs. 52–54). Probably the "Sailor's Farewell and Return" was as popular in America for several years after the China trade began as it had been in Europe and in the American colonies before the Revolution (Fig. 97).

An architectural and landscape decoration which surpasses the Mount Vernon design already seen (Fig. 111) is the painting of the Pennsylvania Hospital on a punch bowl presented to the Hospital early in the nineteenth century (Fig. 120). Not only does the reproduction of the Hospital follow the actual structure more closely than does the Mount Vernon view follow Mount Vernon, but also it is in bright enamels instead of sepia and is much better executed. A probable design source was a sketch done about 1800 by George I. Parkyns, an English artist temporarily living in Philadelphia. In March, 1801, the Hospital Board of Managers sent his drawing to England to be engraved, since Parkyns had left the city and could not do it himself. Under the supervision of Benjamin West, a line engraving was made by W. Cooke and finished by October.[64] There is some question as to how a print from the engraving reached Canton from London to serve as a model for the punch bowl painting. Correspondence shows that the Hospital Board wished to have the design reproduced on a service of Staffordshire pottery. Their agent in England reported that his efforts in this regard were generally unsuccessful.[65] The Board thus may have sent the print to Canton by a ship which stopped at London en route, hoping to have the print appear on Chinese export porcelain.

However the print was sent, the vessel which brought back the bowl was the ship *Dispatch*, whose supercargo, William Redwood, Jr., was a cousin of the donor of the bowl. The *Dispatch* had left Philadelphia for Canton in March, 1801, at the same time that Parkyns' drawing was sent to London to be engraved. When the *Dispatch* returned to Philadelphia in early April, 1802, it carried the finished punch bowl, which was then presented by Joseph S. Lewis to the Hospital Board on April 26, 1802.[66] The view of the Hospital and a view of the Delaware River on the opposite side of the bowl are both in polychrome, while two unidentified English views, between the two, are in sepia.

Other landscape patterns are rarely as large and as ambitious as those on the Hospital bowl. A notable exception is the presentation piece made for the Corporation of the City of New York (Fig. 45). Average-sized wares appeared with vignettes such as the one shown on the flagon at the left in Figure 122; these two identically decorated flagons (pictured facing each other to show both sides) once belonged to the Beech family, of Farmington, Connecticut. A rather whimsical view on a lighthouse coffeepot shows unidentified buildings behind three silhouetted gentlemen whose broad hats punctuate the scene (Fig. 121).

Porcelains showing Masonic emblems were undoubtedly more popular in the earlier era of the China trade than later. At the turn of the nineteenth century, many sorts of furniture, glass, silver, and other metals, embroidered or woven fabrics, as well as pottery, carried the mystic symbols of the fraternity. Most frequently seen are the arch, plumbline, square, compasses, calipers, trowel, the sun and the moon, and Solomon's seal. Evidence that Masonic porcelains came to this country may be seen in the Providence trader's notebook quoted in Appendix II, p. 228. At least one tea set is known which has the United States arms framed by the calipers and square.[67]

At the end of the eighteenth and beginning of the nineteenth centuries, chinaware with classical forms and motifs was constantly in demand as opposed to the "old-fashioned" ware of rococo form sometimes decorated with classical motifs (Fig. 69). A very well preserved pair of covered urns (Fig. 123) seem to include all the characteristics of this "new" style: i.e., bold, simple outlines; precise, controlled decoration, including medallions with a bust of a classical male figure. Joseph Bonaparte, the Emperor Napoleon's brother, once owned the urns. In 1816 Joseph purchased "Point Breeze," a mansion near Bordentown, New Jersey, and two years later came there to live. When the house was destroyed by fire three years later, he rebuilt it and furnished it with European imports.[68] Quite possibly, the urns were thus not made for the American, but rather for the European market. However, they could well have exerted an influence on the taste of those who visited "Point Breeze."

FIGURE 75. _Blue-and-white leaf-shaped stand with Canton border. (For detail of border in color, see Fig. 77.) About 1785–1820. L. 7¼", W. 5¼". Courtesy of_ Winterthur Museum.

FIGURE 76. _Blue-and-white ice pail with Nanking border and gilt trim. (For detail of border in color, see Fig. 78.) About 1790–1812. H. 9½", D. (at rim of lid) 7". Courtesy of_ Winterthur Museum.

FIGURE 77. *Detail of Canton border of blue-and-white leaf-shaped stand (Fig. 75). Courtesy of Winterthur Museum.*

FIGURE 78 [above]. *Detail of Nanking border of blue-and-white ice pail (Fig. 76).*

FIGURE 79 [below]. *Detail from border of plate from Fitzhugh-pattern dinner service in blue and white. (See Frontispiece for tureen and platter from the service.) Courtesy of Winterthur Museum.*

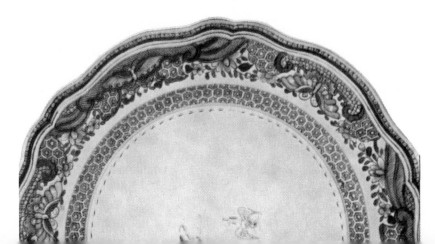

FIGURE 80. *Part of a double dinner service of blue-and-white china imported for Sally Fiske Ropes, of Salem, at the time of her marriage in 1817.* Courtesy of *The Trustees of the Ropes Memorial, Salem, Massachusetts.*

FIGURE 81. *Saucer and cup with eagle design derived from the great seal of the United States. About 1795–1810. Saucer: D. 5⅝″. Cup: H. 2¾″, D. 2¾″. Courtesy of* Winterthur Museum.

FIGURE 82 [above]. *Double-handled cup with eagle design derived from the great seal of the United States. About 1795–1810. H. 2¹¹⁄₁₆″, D. 2¾″. Courtesy of* Mr. and Mrs. Samuel Schwartz, Paterson, New Jersey.

FIGURE 83 [left]. *Eagle design on the certificate of ownership of the Ship* Elizabeth, *New York, February 4, 1804. Courtesy of* The New York Public Library, Manuscript Division (William Law Mercantile Papers).

FIGURE 84a. *Two mugs and a flagon with eagle design (shown in detail in Fig. 84b). About 1795–1812. Mugs: H. 4″, D. 2⅞″. Flagon: H. 10″, D. 4¼″. Courtesy of Winterthur Museum.*

FIGURE 84b [right]. *Detail of eagle on mugs and flagon in Figure 84a.*

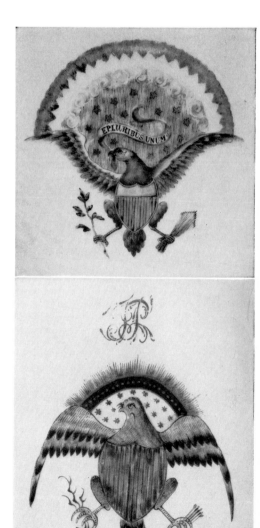

FIGURE 85a. *Plate from a tea service with eagle design and the cipher FP, believed to stand for Franklin Pierce. About 1810–1835. D. 7½″. Courtesy of Winterthur Museum (Gift of Charles K. Davis).*

FIGURE 85b [right]. *Detail of eagle from plate in Figure 85a.*

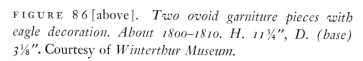

FIGURE 86 [above]. *Two ovoid garniture pieces with eagle decoration. About 1800–1810. H. 11¾″, D. (base) 3⅛″. Courtesy of Winterthur Museum.*

FIGURE 87 [right]. *Eagle detail from a plate in the 416-piece dinner service of the John Jacob Ridgway family, of Philadelphia. Early nineteenth century. Eagle similar to, but not identical with, that of garniture pieces in Figure 86. Courtesy of Winterthur Museum.*

FIGURE 88 [below]. *Eagle from the National Insurance Company policy for the Ship* Lion, *New York, March 30, 1816. Courtesy of The New York Public Library, Manuscript Division (William Law Mercantile Papers).*

FIGURE 89. *Saucer with eagle design and floral border. About 1815–1825. D. 5⅜″. Courtesy of Mr. and Mrs. Samuel Schwartz, Paterson, New Jersey.*

FIGURE 90a. *Green Fitzhugh-pattern plate with eagle design in sepia. Initial M on shield. About 1815–1830. D. 9⅝″. Courtesy of Winterthur Museum.*

FIGURE 90b. *Detail of eagle on green Fitzhugh-pattern plate in Figure 90a.*

FIGURE 91. *Detail of eagle design on a plate originally owned by the Allen Bowie, Jr., family, of Prince George's County, Maryland. Courtesy of Maryland Historical Society.*

FIGURE 92a. *Part of a tea service showing an eagle design with a banner reading* In God We Hope. *About 1800. Courtesy of Winterthur Museum.*

FIGURE 92b. *Detail of eagle design on tea service shown in Figure 92a.*

FIGURE 93. *Pieces from tea and coffee sets decorated with ships flying the American flag. About 1790–1810.* Courtesy of Peabody Museum of Salem.

FIGURE 94. *Plate showing rough clay and poor glazing, but rather unusual ship with crew visible. About 1800–1840. D. 7¾".* Courtesy of Peabody Museum of Salem.

*Shipped* in good order and well-conditioned, by *William Law* on board the *Ship* called the *Lion* whereof is Master, for this present voyage, *Adam Champlin* now lying in the port of *Canton* and bound for *New York* To say,

TCB *N° 1 a 311* . . . . *Three hundred & Eleven Boxes China Ware*

" *N° 1 a 361* . . . . *Three hundred & Sixty one Chests Young Hyson Tea*

" *N° 1 a 362* . . . . *Three hundred & Sixty Two Chests of Hyson Tea*

" *N° 1 a 1242 & 1244 a 3894* . . *Three Thousand Eight hundred & Ninety three Chests of Hyson Skin Tea*

" *no N°* . . . . *Seventeen hundred & forty Two, Ten Catty Boxes of Hyson Tea*

" *d°* . . . . *Fourteen hundred & four, Ten Catty Boxes Young Hyson Tea*

" *d°* . . . . *Three hundred & seventy seven, Ten Catty Boxes Imperial Tea*

" *N° A* . . . . *Four hundred & Twenty four, Twenty five Catty Boxes Souchong Tea*

" *N° B* . . . . *Four hundred & Seventeen, Twenty five Catty Boxes Souchong Tea*

*S 1 a 10 & TCB 11 a 208.* *Two hundred & Eight Boxes White powdered Suga*

*A* . . . . *Nine hundred & fourteen small Mats of Cassia*

*B* . . . *Three Thousand & forty nine, small Mats of Cassia*

*Three hundred & Eight small Mats of Cassia*

*Forty four pieces of Rattans for dunnage &*

*C Five hundred & Seventy, small Mats of Cassia, being for the sole Account & Risk of, & Consigned to M° Tho° C. Butler, a Citizen of the United States of America and Resident Merchant Blanchard at New York*

being marked and numbered as in the margin, and are to be delivered in the like good order and well-conditioned at the aforesaid port of *New York* (the danger of the seas only excepted) unto *M° Tho° C. Butler* or to *his* assigns, he or they paying freight for the said *goods, nothing being*

*Owners property*

with primage and average accustomed. In Witness whereof, the Master of the said vessel hath affirmed to *Four* Bills of Lading, all of this tenor and date; the one of which Bills being accomplished, the other to stand void. Dated in *Canton* the *22* day of *Nov° 1816* *Adam Champlin*

FIGURE 95. *Bill of lading for Ship* Lion, *order of Thomas C. Butler, November 22, 1816.* Courtesy of *The New York Public Library, Manuscript Division (William Law Mercantile Papers).*

FIGURE 96. *Three punch bowls showing ships flying the American flag. About 1790–1810. (Left): H. 4½"; D. (base) 5⅜", (top) 10⅜". (Center): H. 6"; D. (base) 7½", (top) 14½". (Right): H. 4⅞"; D. (base) 6⅞", (top) 11¼". Cour-tesy of* Peabody Museum of Salem.

FIGURE 97. *Mug bearing decoration of the "Sailor's Farewell and Return." About 1800–1810. H. 7³⁄₁₆", D. 5⅛".* Courtesy of *Peabody Museum of Salem.*

FIGURE 98. *Mug with ship decoration and banner reading* America. *Initials* SG *possibly for Stephen Girard. H. 4", D. 3".* Courtesy of *Mr. and Mrs. Rafi Mottahedeh, New York City.*

FIGURE 99a. *Fair-weather view of a "Foul Weather and Fair" flagon. About 1805–1820. H. 11½".*

FIGURE 99b. *Foul-weather view of flagon in Figure 99a.* Courtesy of *Peabody Museum of Salem.*

FIGURE 100a [left]. *Flagon decorated with view of encounter of the Frigate* United States *and the Frigate* Macedonian *on October 25, 1812. H. 11″, D. (base) 4⁹⁄₁₆″. Courtesy of* Winterthur Museum *(Ex Coll. J. Kenneth Danby).*

FIGURE 100b [center]. *Opposite side of flagon (Fig. 100a) showing the encounter of the Brig* Enterprise *and the Brig* Boxer *on September 5, 1813.*

FIGURE 100c [right]. *Spout side of flagon (Fig. 100a), showing sailor with banner reading* Don't Give Up the Ship. *Monogram WC. Sailor vignette and battle views on sides are from an engraving by A. Anderson of a drawing by W. B. Morgan.*

FIGURE 101a. *Punch bowl decorated with eagle grasping a trophy of war. H. 4½″, D. 11⅜″. Courtesy of* Winterthur Museum.

FIGURE 101b. *Opposite side of punch bowl in Figure 101a, decorated with design of a ship under construction.*

FIGURE 102. *Coat of arms of the State of New York, shown within the initial of a commission from Governor Clinton to Theobald Baker, August 21, 1778. From an original commission in the New York State Library at Albany. Courtesy of* New York State Library.

FIGURE 103. *Cup and saucer with the coat of arms of the State of New York, shields, and floral-sprig border. About 1790–1815. Cup: H. 1⅞″, D. 3½″. Saucer: D. 5½″. Courtesy of* Winterthur Museum.

FIGURE 104. *Tray and cup showing the coat of arms of the State of Pennsylvania. About 1800. Tray: L. 4¾″, W. (at center) 3½″, H. ⅝″. Cup: H. 2½″; D. (base) 1⅛″, (top) 2½″. Courtesy of* The New-York Historical Society, New York City.

FIGURE 105 [left]. *Saucer and cup bearing the badge of the Society of the Cincinnati and the cipher of Samuel Shaw. About 1785–1795. Saucer: H. 1¼″, D. 5½″. Cup: H. 2⅝″, D. 2⅝″.* Courtesy of *Winterthur Museum* (Ex Coll. *Edmund Quincy*).

FIGURE 106 [right]. *Saucer with twin figures of Fame holding a bow from which is suspended a Society of the Cincinnati medal. About 1785–1795. D. 5½″. From set originally owned by William Eustis.* Courtesy of *Winterthur Museum* (Gift of *Charles K. Davis*).

FIGURE 107. *Punch bowl with Cincinnati medal on inside rim, bust portrait of Washington in center. About 1798–1805. H. 4¹¹⁄₁₆″; D. (base) 5½″, (top) 11⁵⁄₁₆″.* Courtesy of *The Historical Society of Pennsylvania.*

FIGURE 108. *Print by Amos Doolittle, 1787. Possible design source for punch bowl in Figure 107. Illustrated in* Charles H. Hart's Catalogue of the Engraved Portraits of Washington *(New York, 1904), p. 354. Courtesy of* The Grolier Club.

FIGURE 109. *Flagon with black-and-white painting from a stipple-and-line engraving of Washington by David Edwin based on a portrait by Gilbert Stuart. About 1810–1820. H. 11", D. (base) 4⁹⁄₁₆". Courtesy of Winterthur Museum.*

FIGURE 110 [below]. *Plate, platter, and custard cup from a dinner service with tomb inscribed* Washington, *a weeping willow, and a hovering eagle. About 1800–1810. Plate: D. 7½". Custard cup: H. 3¼", D. 2½". Platter: L. 4⅝", W. 11⅞". Courtesy of Winterthur Museum.*

FIGURE 111 [left]. *Saucer showing Mount Vernon, probably taken from an 1803 print by Samuel Seymour, based on a painting by William Birch. Wide floral border. About 1805–1820. D. 5⁷⁄₁₆".* Courtesy of *Winterthur Museum.*

FIGURE 112. *Cake plate from a tea service presented to Martha Washington by A. E. Van Braam Houckgeest. About 1796. D. 13". Courtesy of Winterthur Museum.*

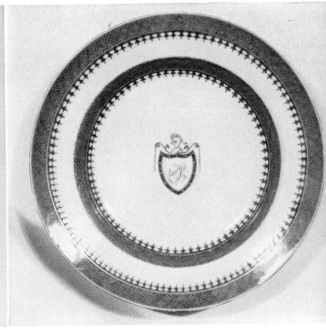

FIGURE 113. *Mug bearing the Hancock coat of arms. Probably made for John Hancock. About 1780–1790. H. 4¾", D. 3⅞". Courtesy of Winterthur Museum.*

FIGURE 114. *Plate from a dinner service believed to have been made for Thomas Jefferson. About 1790–1800. D. 9½". Courtesy of The Thomas Jefferson Memorial Foundation, Charlottesville, Virginia.*

FIGURE 117. *Teapot from a tea service made for John Stark, of London-derry, New Hampshire. About 1785–1800. H. 5⅛", D. (base) 5³⁄₁₆". Courtesy of The Bennington Museum, Hall Park McCullough Collection, Bennington, Vermont.*

FIGURE 118. *Platter with cipher of DeWitt Clinton and his wife, Maria Franklin Clinton. The Clintons were married in 1796. About 1796–1810. L. 15¼", W. 13". Courtesy of Winterthur Museum.*

FIGURE 119. *Saucer and cup from a service made for Deborah Fairfax Anderson, of Salem, with her cipher in gilt. Brought from China on the Ship* Grand Turk, *1786. Saucer: D. 6⅛″, H. 1⅜″. Cup: H. 2¼″; D. (base) 2¹⁄₁₆″, (top) 4⅜″. Courtesy of* Essex Institute.

FIGURE 120. *Punch bowl with view of the Pennsylvania Hospital. Presented to the Hospital on April 26, 1802. Courtesy of* Mr. John Lewis Evans, Haverford, Pennsylvania.

FIGURE 121. *Lighthouse coffeepot with landscape view, drapery border. About 1810–1820. H. 9½", D. (base) 5". Courtesy of* Winterthur Museum.

FIGURE 122. *Flagons with identical decorations, pictured facing each other to show landscape on one side, a standard ship design on the other. About 1800–1810. Flagon on left: H. 11½"; D. (over-all) 6", (base) 4⅞". Flagon on right: H. 10"; D. (over-all) 5", (base) 4⅜". Courtesy of* Winterthur Museum.

FIGURE 123. *Pair of pistol-handled covered urns once belonging to Joseph Bonaparte, of Bordentown, New Jersey. Urns show classical motifs, including medallion with classical male figure. About 1795–1820. H. 26½″, D. 11″; base 6⅞/₁₆″ square. Ex Coll. Mrs. Francis B. Crowninshield. Courtesy of Winterthur Museum (Gift of Mr. Franklin Benkard in memory of Mrs. Crowninshield).*

# XI

## *The Dating of Export Porcelain Made for America*

SEVERAL FACTORS complicate the problem of assigning even approximate dates to the wares imported to this country. In the first place, the American market did not continue so long as the European market. Within Europe's century of trade, definite changes in form and decoration occurred which permit a student to observe the steady progression of style and style variations. For America, the trade in chinaware lasted hardly fifty years, within which period production standards at the porcelain factories at Ching-tê Chên were on the decline. Consequently there are fewer noticeable mutations in form and decoration in the porcelain made for the United States than in that made for the European market.

Secondly, the documents and records studied rarely give specific information as to definite shapes. No actual drawings of porcelains have been found, but only rude sketches of pitchers, sugar bowls, and light-house coffeepots, and these almost always without indication of design source. Thirdly, except in the cases of personal orders, instructions regarding decoration are usually presented in a very general manner. For example, the most detailed specification for large consignments often reads simply "best Nankeen stone China Ware." Fourthly, such forms as plate shapes and such decorations as border patterns introduced at an early period continued to be used year after year throughout the trade.

Pieces of porcelain exist, however, for which approximate dates are known. There are others for which design and decorative sources may be discovered in Western pottery or in paintings and prints. Such pieces serve as standards of form, general decoration, and border designs in any consideration of the evolution of styles in Chinese export wares.

The porcelains made during the fifty years which saw the most activity in the America-China trade seem to fall into three main periods: 1785–1795, 1795–1812, 1815–1835. These will serve as arbitrary, but convenient and flexible, guides. In the first two periods most of the forms and paintings follow those of European ceramics; certainly this is true of the decorations.[1] By the latter part of the third period, however, Oriental forms are increasingly evident.

The first period, 1785–1795, includes the earliest porcelains, which differ only slightly from many English wares of the same time. Essentially, these initial American pieces represent the end of an era of European trade. Ships painted on porcelains of this period may bear this country's flag, or eagles may appear on dinner services, but the pseudo-armorial mantlings and the chaste classical borders remain similar to those on wares of ten years before. Examples of several such types have been used in the discussion of particular ports (Chap. VII) and of porcelain forms (Chap. IX). The sample plate in Figure 124 shows four border patterns which may be assigned to this early period because of their restrained and precise style. Central motifs also exhibit this economical and cautious decoration. The dishes which bear the place and date inscription *Canton in China 24ᵗʰ Janʸ 1791* (Fig. 125b) show on the opposite side (Fig. 125a) symmetrical shields, similar to those on Jefferson's dinner service (Fig. 114). These are typical of the armorial designs of this time as contrasted with the flourishing rococo escutcheon of the coat of arms on the Chase dinner service (Fig. 59).[2]

Toward the end of this first period changes were evident. It may be noted that, when Benjamin Fuller, of Philadelphia, placed his order in 1789, he specified that he did not want "old-fashioned" ware. The Providence trader's price-current list of 1797 (Appendix II, p. 228) also distinguished "old-fashioned" pieces. Probably both of them referred to rococo shapes such as mid-eighteenth-century teapots and coffeepots.

These pear-shaped pieces, often with molded embellishments on their spouts, probably did not suit new tastes, best represented by the Isaac Hull tea service (Fig. 116). The newer forms had cleaner and more geometric lines than the earlier wares, corresponding to the fashion for styles of ancient Greece and Rome. A probable design source for the cylinder form like that of the drum teapot may be found in similar pieces made at Worcester from about 1765 to 1770.[3] Additional new touches were the interlaced strap handles ending in leaf ferns, also shown in Hull's tea service and other pieces, which were inspired by Leedsware.[4]

In the second period, 1795–1812, classical motifs such as the dainty floral swags on Mrs. Barry's tea service (Fig. 49) became fuller and more naturalistic. Blossoms opened out and leaves began to turn; vines started to grow. Their arrangement, however, continued to be studied. A border of intertwined floral swags and ribbons, almost identical with that of the Decatur flagon (Fig. 115) appears on the inside of the Pennsylvania Hospital punch bowl (Fig. 120), dated about the same time; and it also decorates a dinner service originally made for Henri Chanopin Belin, one-time Governor of Guadaloupe, illustrated in Figures 128a and 128b.[5] Such designs closely follow those of French porcelains, as can be seen by comparing them with the Chantilly plate shown in Figure 129, which dates from the third or the fourth quarter of the eighteenth century.

English patterns were also still influential. The Malcolm Bull Smith tureen in Figure 126 follows in outline and in almost every detail a pattern first published in Wedgwood's catalogue in 1774 and reissued in 1817.[6] The only ways in which the Smith tureen differs from its Wedgwood model are in the absence of Wedgwood's bed of fallen leaves on the lid at the base of the handle, an open flower on a short stem, and in the use of intertwined strap handles on the body of the tureen in place of the plain handles of the original design. Despite the early date of the first appearance of the Wedgwood pattern, the influence of the form on European export porcelain did not become evident for another two decades.[7] In American ware this model probably was most popular beginning in the late 1790's.

In the last seven years of this second period—that is, from 1805 to

1812—styles seem to have remained fairly stable. The inspiration continued to be chiefly European, with Derby, Worcester, and French porcelains predominating.[8] Perhaps about this time, or even earlier, the pistol-handled urn, with the cipher of Mary Alexander Duane, shown in Figure 127 was made. Although its probable design source first appeared about 1775 in a flint-porcelain urn made at Marieburg, Sweden, doubtless other such urns of later make were available as models at this time.[9] The grape-and-vine border in dark blue and gilt used around the oval medallion, the neck, and the lid help to date the urn in this second period of more highly elaborate wares.

In the third period, beginning after the War of 1812 and lasting until the end of the trade in export porcelain, three major features seem apparent. One is the general dependence on French, rather than English, forms and designs as models. This was probably a minor reflection of American antagonism toward England which had developed during the War. In April, 1815, Gideon Tucker, of Salem, asked Benjamin Shreve to purchase for Mrs. Tucker a set of china with coffeepots and teapots similar to those of Mrs. Peabody, whose order was mentioned in Chapter IX. Shreve evidently took with him a draft of the particular pattern Tucker desired, for he wrote Tucker almost seven months later:

> The small things you requested me to procure for you I have purchased, as well as those for Mr. Peabody, J. Goodhue, & Dr. Readwell, but I am very much displeased that I could not get the China to my mind—and I fear it will not be very satisfactory to you. The Chinese have been called good at imitating but they have made a poor fist of it in attempting to give me ware like Mrs. P's [Peabody's] *French* pattern. [10] [Italics added.]

The French influence is also clearly seen in a red-orange tea service (Fig. 130) made for an early-nineteenth-century Philadelphia family and brought to Philadelphia in 1817. The style of this set seems very much like that of the covered cup and saucer in Figure 131, which were made in Paris about 1775–1793 and which are also painted in red.[11] The creamer in the 1817 service (Fig. 130) follows the form of French porcelain jugs of the Empire style made at factories such as Caen in the early nineteenth century.[12]

In 1822 Shreve again bought porcelains painted in the French manner. An invoice for 143 pieces purchased of Cumshong included:

```
5 Doz Tea Cups & Saucers with handles French pattern
        hair colour'd      [sepia or light brown]
        Gilt edge   a       $4                                    $20.00
```

The total amount of the invoice—which also included two teapots and a coffeepot, their stands, cake plates, ewers, and quart and pint bowls—was $30.43.[13]

A second feature of the wares of this later period is the increased decoration and the heaviness of the border designs. The plate in Figure 132, bearing the inscription *Friendship Salem*, was made about 1820. Its elaborate border, painted in polychrome and gold, of scenes symbolic of health, wealth, and happiness is similar in ornateness to that used on mandarin wares, although the reserve medallions are very much like earlier *famille rose* patterns.[14] Among other borders of this period was one with a pattern of conch shells and intertwined seaweed, a design known to have been used in combination with central motifs of ships or other subjects inspired by early American commerce.[15]

By the 1830's the trend toward more complex painting styles was quite apparent in the memorial punch bowl presented to Henry Eckford, the American naval architect, by the Turkish government (Fig. 133). Eckford had served as director of naval construction in Turkey, beginning in the 1830's. Two flagons with matching decoration were included in the gift. The wide intricate borders of the bowl hang heavily above two medallions. In one are the initials *HE* in gold. In the other appears a big East Indiaman under construction. There are large Chinese carp on the inner sides. The painting and body of the bowl are excellent, thus indicating that even at this late date wares of some merit were being made.

Another contemporary piece of equal quality is a punch bowl now exhibited at the State House in Boston. Its inscription reads, "Presented to Dwight Boyden, proprietor of the Tremont House, Boston, in 1832, by the Officers of the US ship Peacock."[16] Its wide border is brightly painted in polychrome enamels.

A further aspect of porcelain in this later period is the appearance, in both forms and decorations, of more Chinese elements in contrast with Western patterns.[17] Whether they predominated over the European models may be a question, but they do seem more prevalent than the occasional lion finials and meander patterns of the earlier wares.

From the beginning of the trade with the West, of course, at least a few Oriental shapes and motifs had indicated the Chinese nature of the export porcelain, although, when forms of Chinese origin—such as the teacup—were used, they were generally modified to conform to European taste. Conversely, when European models (such as animal heads, geese, or fish) were used as the form for tureens (see Chap. IX), the product frequently has an Oriental appearance as the result of the Chinese artist's interpretation of an animal not native to China and therefore not familiar to him.[18] A pair of goose tureens (Fig. 74), already mentioned, are known to have come to Salem, Massachusetts, as early as the first decade of the nineteenth century.

Then later in the nineteenth century, when orders from America became scarce and those from Europe ceased altogether, there was no longer the constant demand for Chinese wares in foreign patterns, and Chinese potters reverted more and more to native designs. The goglet (guglet) in Figure 134 represents the results of such a development. Its form is Oriental, especially with the elephant-head handles, and may be compared with a shape made in the Yung-chêng period (1723–1735).[19] The eagle decorating it is similar to earlier birds of the same design, yet has forsaken its laurel branches or olive leaves for the Chinese flag bearing the imperial dragon. A dish with an identical eagle with two flags, but with an elaborate border of purple, blue, and pink roses is at the Winterthur Museum, a good example of the blending of European and Chinese influences with American symbols.

The plates in Figure 135 show both the fuller decoration and the Oriental influence typical of ware in the later period. At the right, a red-orange-and-gold pattern of birds, butterflies, and flowers covers the entire surface except for a central medallion, which bears the superimposed cipher of Malcolm Bull Smith. Probably the service represented by this plate was made after the War of 1812, although there are earlier examples which are almost identical.[20] The Fitzhugh-pattern plate on the left, perhaps earlier, represents another service also made for Smith and bearing the same cipher.

A particularly interesting group of pieces at the Winterthur Museum bears pictures of the signing of the Declaration of Independence. Though they vary in quality of clay and painting, their forms and decorations date them probably after the War of 1812. The small four-legged covered box in Figure 136 has the familiar form of a Chinese censer, one of which is illustrated in Figure 137.[21] One may compare the relative proportions of the two pieces and the sharpness of the modeling. Perhaps the greatest contrast is between the two lion finials. The one on the true censer is fiercely performing his function as an imperial guard, while the other one, on the export piece, is lost in inexact carving and masses of glaze. Another Oriental form decorated with the signing of the Declaration of Independence is found in the table screen pictured in Figure 138; its porcelain slabs have the same decoration as the container (Fig. 136). Other wares with this pattern are more European in form, but nonetheless all show the signers as oddly Oriental gentlemen, again indicating the influence of the Chinese style.

The design source for the decoration on all these was probably John Trumbull's *The Declaration of Independence*, now in the Yale University Art Gallery. Asher B. Durand's engraving of Trumbull's painting and several copies by Edward Hicks, probably about 1840–1845, may have been used as patterns by the Chinese painter.[22] The reproductions on the porcelain show different groupings from the original, and the perspective is quite disrupted; but the door arrangements and the furniture are similar.

Besides their Oriental touches, the Declaration of Independence pieces also show the decline in the porcelain in both clay and painting. Earlier wares also included pieces of poor material, inexpertly decorated; therefore, the standard of quality alone cannot be used for dating. However, the later pieces, and especially the Canton blue-and-white wares, often are thick and clumsy, with rough bottoms and edges, and are very sketchily painted. In addition, their glaze is unevenly applied and is often splotchy.

Three broad periods of Chinese export ware made for America have been traced. None of them is entirely exclusive. Despite this fact, the period when various pieces were made can often be estimated on the basis of known characteristics of pieces dated by extant records or family histories; on knowledge of innovations resulting from change in fashion; on the presence of border patterns which are known to have run their course within a certain period; and finally, at least partially, on judgment of the quality of the wares.[23]

FIGURE 124. *Sample plate with four different border patterns and a pseudo-armorial mantling typical of the period 1785–1795 and still used into the early 1800's. D. 10". Courtesy of Winterthur Museum.*

FIGURE 125a. *Pieces with shield similar to Thomas Jefferson's; on reverse, place and date inscription* Canton in China 24th Jan.y 1791. Courtesy of *Winterthur Museum.*

FIGURE 125b. *Reverse of three of the pieces in Figure 125a, showing place and date inscriptions.*

FIGURE 126. *Tureen similar in shape to one appearing in Wedgwood's catalogue for 1774. Cipher of Malcolm Bull Smith, of Smithtown, Long Island. About 1800–1820. H. 11″, L. 10″, W. 7″. Courtesy of Mrs. Dunham Higgins, Chestnut Hill, Pennsylvania.*

FIGURE 127. *Pistol-handled urn with cipher of Mary Alexander Duane, wife of James Duane, Mayor of New York City; floral border in blue and gold. About 1790–1812. H. 17″, D. (mouth) 4″. Courtesy of Ginsburg and Levy, Inc., New York City.*

FIGURE 128a. *Dinner service originally made for Henri Chanopin Belin, at one time Governor of Guadaloupe. About 1800–1810.* Courtesy of *Mr. and Mrs. Alfred E. Bissell, Wilmington, Delaware.*

FIGURE 128b. *Platter from Belin service (Fig. 128a), with border of inter-twined floral swags and ribbons. L. 16″, W. 13½″.*

FIGURE 129. *French porcelain plate from Chantilly, last half of eighteenth century. D. 9¼″.* Courtesy of *Victoria & Albert Museum, Crown Copyright.*

FIGURE 130. *Part of a 139-piece tea and coffee service made for an early-nineteenth-century Philadelphia family. Purchased in 1817.* Courtesy of *Mrs. Benjamin Rush, Sr., Chestnut Hill, Pennsylvania.*

FIGURE 131. *Saucer and covered cup of a style made in Paris about 1775–1793. H. (cup) 4⅞".* Courtesy of *Victoria & Albert Museum, Crown Copyright.*

FIGURE 132. *Plate with inscription* Friendship Salem *and with American ship firing a broadside. Border similar to that of mandarin wares. About 1820. D. 9*$^{15}$/$_{16}$*''. Courtesy of* Peabody Museum of Salem.

FIGURE 133. *Punch bowl presented to Henry Eckford, American naval architect, by the Turkish Government. About 1830–1835. Courtesy of* Miss Elizabeth I. Richardson, Providence, Rhode Island.

FIGURE 134. *Goglet of a Chinese form, with eagle decoration. In bird's talons, Chinese and American flags. About 1815–1830. H. 12½", D. (base) 4³⁄₁₆". Courtesy of Winterthur Museum.*

FIGURE 135. *Two plates from services made for Malcolm Bull Smith, of Smithtown, Long Island. About 1815–1825. D. (left) 8", (right) 9½". Courtesy of Mrs. Dunham Higgins, Chestnut Hill, Pennsylvania.*

FIGURE 136 [left]. *Four-legged decorative container in the form of a Chinese censer (compare Fig. 137). Decorated with Declaration of Independence pattern. About 1825–1850. H. 3³⁄₁₆″, W. 2⅛″, D. 1⅝″. Courtesy of* Winterthur Museum.

FIGURE 137 [right]. *Chinese censer (derived from a bronze form), made of porcelain, covered with turquoise-blue glaze. Made during reign of Ch'ien-lung, 1736–1795. H. 5⅝″, W. 3¼″. Courtesy of* Victoria & Albert Museum *(The Salting Collection), Crown Copyright.*

FIGURE 138. *Table screen with porcelain slabs decorated with the Declaration of Independence pattern. About 1825–1850. H. 14⅜″, W. (each panel) 7⅜″. Courtesy of Winterthur Museum.*

# NOTES

## Key to Abbreviations

In the notes to each chapter, the full name of a library or museum is used in the first reference to material in that institution. In all other references in the chapter the name of the institution is used in abbreviated form as follows:

| | |
|---|---|
| The John Carter Brown Library, Brown University | JCBL |
| Essex Institute | EI |
| Girard College Library | GCL |
| Haverford College Library | HCL |
| The Historical Society of Pennsylvania | HSP |
| The Library of Congress, Manuscript Division | LC |
| The Library Company of Philadelphia | LCP |
| Maryland Hall of Records | MHR |
| Maryland Historical Society | MdHS |
| Massachusetts Historical Society | MHS |
| The New-York Historical Society | N-YHS |
| The New York Public Library, Manuscript Division | NYPL |
| Peabody Museum of Salem | PMS |
| University of Delaware, Memorial Library | UD |
| Winterthur Museum, Joseph Downs Manuscript Library | WM |

# NOTES

## to Chapter I

1. *Pennsylvania Packet, and Daily Advertiser*, May 16, 1785, p. 2. See also Samuel Shaw, *The Journals of Major Samuel Shaw, the First American Consul at Canton*, edited with a life of the author by Josiah Quincy (Boston, 1847), pp. 211–13. The 32,458 nautical miles recorded by Shaw (18,248 miles on the trip from New York to Canton and 14,210 miles on the return trip) would be approximately 37,400 statute miles. In telling of the departure of the *Empress* on its first voyage to Canton, a more recent account states, "When all was at last in order the *Empress of China* set forth on its 13,000-mile voyage" (see Foster Rhea Dulles, *The Old China Trade* [Boston, 1930], p. 8).

2. Samuel W. Woodhouse, Jr., "The Voyage of the *Empress of China*," *The Pennsylvania Magazine of History and Biography*, LXIII (January, 1939), 30. A picul is a commercial weight varying in different countries and for different commodities. In China, Japan, and Sumatra it is equivalent to 133⅓ lbs. Nankeen was a brownish-yellow cloth of firm texture and great durability used, for example, in making trousers. Cassia is the bark of a tree of the same genus as, but a different species from, the cinnamon tree. Resembling cinnamon in appearance, smell, and taste, cassia was used as a substitute for it.

3. The Roman trade with India and China is authoritatively reviewed by Sir Robert Eric Mortimer Wheeler, *Rome Beyond the Imperial Frontiers* (New York, 1954), pp. 115–76. The embassy purported to have come from Marcus Aurelius Antoninus is mentioned on page 174.

4. L. Carrington Goodrich, *A Short History of the Chinese People* (3d ed.; New York, 1959), pp. 45–46, 58.

5. Hosea Ballou Morse and Harley Farnsworth MacNair, *Far Eastern International Relations* (Boston, 1931), pp. 15–17.

6. Goodrich, pp. 137–38.

7. A full account of the international trade through Ch'üan Chou, by a Chinese official who helped to supervise it, has been translated into English by Friedrich Hirth and W. W. Rockhill: *Chau Ju-Kua: His Work on the Chinese and Arab Trade in the Twelfth and Thirteenth Centuries* (St. Petersburg, 1911).

8. Morse and MacNair, p. 19.

9. *Ibid.*

10. Marco Polo, *The Description of the World*, trans. and annotated by A. C. Moule and Paul Pelliot (London, 1938), p. 156.

11. Some of the previous European travelers in Far Asia are discussed in Leonardo Olschki, *Marco Polo's Precursors* (Baltimore, 1943).

12. Morse and MacNair, p. 20.

13. Goodrich, pp. 192–94.

14. *Ibid.*, p. 195. See also Morse and MacNair, p. 20.

15. Carlton J. H. Hayes, Marshall Whitehead Baldwin, and Charles Woolsey Cole, *History of Europe* (New York, 1949), pp. 431–41.

16. Kenneth Scott Latourette, *The Chinese, Their History and Culture* (3d ed.; New York, 1957), p. 296. See also Morse and MacNair, pp. 21–22, and Goodrich, p. 196.

17. Morse and MacNair, pp. 22–23.

18. *Ibid.*, pp. 23–24. See also John Goldsmith Phillips, *China-Trade Porcelain; an Account of Its Historical Background, Manufacture, and Decoration and a Study of the Helena Woolworth McCann Collection* (Cambridge, Mass., 1956), p. 29. See also Hosea Ballou Morse, *The Trade and Administration of the Chinese Empire* (London, 1908), pp. 16, 271–72.

19. Morse and MacNair, pp. 43–44. See also Goodrich, p. 196.

20. Morse and MacNair, pp. 43–44.

21. Gertrude Z. Thomas, "Cane, a Tropical Transplant," *Antiques*, LXXIX (January, 1961), 92.

22. Latourette, p. 296. See also Morse and MacNair, pp. 45–46; Goodrich, p. 196; and Phillips, pp. 22, 24.

23. Phillips, p. 28. See also Morse and MacNair, p. 48.

24. Phillips, pp. 28–29. See also Morse and MacNair, p. 48; and J. A. Lloyd Hyde, *Oriental Lowestoft, Chinese Export Porcelain, Porcelaine de la C$^{ie}$ des Indes; with Special Reference to the Trade with China and the Porcelain Decorated for the American Market* (Newport, Monmouthshire, 1954), p. 8.

25. Phillips, p. 29.

26. Morse and MacNair, p. 64.

27. *Ibid.*, pp. 49–51. See also Goodrich, p. 220.

28. J. K. Fairbank and S. Y. Teng, "On the Ch'ing Tributary System," *Harvard Journal of Asiatic Studies*, VI, No. 2 (June, 1941), pp. 135ff., especially pp. 177–82, 201–2, 204–5.

29. *Ibid.*, p. 172. See also Morse and MacNair, p. 59.

30. Schuyler Cammann, "The Interchange of East and West," *Asia in Perspective* (Philadelphia, 1959), pp. 3–5, and especially p. 21.

31. Dulles, pp. 9–10, 129–30.

32. Tyler Dennett, *Americans in Eastern Asia; a Critical Study of the Policy of the United States with Reference to China, Japan, and Korea in the 19th Century* (New York, 1922), p. 54. See also Shaw, pp. 168–71; Morse and MacNair, p. 46; and Goodrich, p. 220.

33. Dulles, pp. 115–17. See also Morse and MacNair, pp. 69, 76.

34. Phillips, p. 32. See also Shaw, p. 183; and George H. Danton, *The Culture*

*Contacts of the United States and China; the Earliest Sino-American Culture Contacts, 1784–1844* (New York, 1931), p. 17.

35. For example, see Dulles, pp. 130–35.
36. *Ibid.*, pp. 130–31, 139.
37. The war is described in *ibid.*, pp. 139–74; also in Morse and MacNair, pp. 113–26.
38. Morse and MacNair, pp. 127–45. See also Dulles, 193–207.

# NOTES

## to Chapter II

1. This is the period division used by Kenneth Scott Latourette in "The History of Early Relations Between the United States and China, 1784–1844," *Transactions of the Connecticut Academy of Arts and Sciences*, XXII (August, 1917), 3, 8, 10–84.
2. Edmund Burke, *Speeches and Letters on American Affairs* ("Everyman's Library," ed. Ernest Rhys; London, 1908), pp. 88–89. See also Frances Little, "America's East Indiamen and the China Trade," *Antiques*, XV (January, 1929), 27.
3. Paul Maxwell Zeis, *American Shipping Policy* (Princeton, N. J., 1938), pp. 2–3.
4. Tyler Dennett, *Americans in Eastern Asia; a Critical Study of the Policy of the United States with Reference to China, Japan, and Korea in the 19th Century* (New York, 1922), p. 6.
5. Latourette, p. 10.
6. Samuel Eliot Morison, *The Maritime History of Massachusetts, 1783–1860* (Boston, 1921), p. 96.
7. Latourette, p. 12.
8. *Ibid.*, p. 13.
9. Samuel Shaw, *The Journals of Major Samuel Shaw, the First American Consul at Canton*, edited with a life of the author by Josiah Quincy (Boston, 1847), pp. 133, 218.
10. *Ibid.*, p. 210.
11. Maryland Historical Society, copy of Bond for Ship *Pallas*, August 15, 1785; and miscellaneous notes on the *Pallas* in files of the Society. See also Shaw, pp. 200, 218; Foster Rhea Dulles, *The Old China Trade* (Boston, 1930), p. 11; and Latourette, p. 15.
12. Shaw, p. 218. It was only 25 per cent of the original investment.

13. *Ibid.*, pp. 114, 219. The United States consular post was a highly ambiguous one in the years before the Treaty of Wanghia. Although the consul was a Government appointee, he was not a salaried official, nor was he given much authority from home. The Chinese regarded him merely as chief supercargo for the Americans. His income depended on his own trading arrangements. After Shaw, the post was filled by Samuel Snow (1799–1804), Edward Carrington (1806–1808), Benjamin Chew Wilcocks (1815–1822), and Peter W. Snow (1835). See also Dennett, pp. 62–63.

14. Shaw, p. 233.

15. Latourette, pp. 16–17.

16. *Ibid.*, pp. 16–18. See also Shaw, pp. 295–304.

17. James D. Phillips, "East India Voyages of Salem Vessels Before 1800," *The Essex Institute Historical Collections*, LXXIX (April, 1943), 117.

18. Dulles, p. 210. Dulles appears to have used the best available statistics for making a chart of the China trade from 1784 to 1844. He used contemporary official foreign and domestic documents, as well as Kenneth Scott Latourette's "Voyages of American Ships to China, 1784–1844," *Transactions of the Connecticut Academy of Arts and Sciences*, XXVIII (April, 1927), 237–71.

19. Dulles, p. 49.

20. Zeis, p. 3.

21. Dennett, p. 8.

22. Morison, p. 184.

23. *Ibid.*, p. 186.

24. *Ibid.*, pp. 174–75.

25. Zeis, p. 5.

26. The Library Company of Philadelphia (hereafter cited as LCP), Waln Papers, Letter Book of Robert Waln (September 24, 1784, to February 23, 1808), Robert Waln, Philadelphia, to Bainbridge, Ansley and Company, London, March 6, 1799.

27. Massachusetts Historical Society (hereafter cited as MHS), Thomas H. Perkins MSS, Ephraim Bumstead, Canton, to James and Thomas H. Perkins, Boston, June 9, 1804.

28. Peabody Museum of Salem (hereafter cited as PMS), Benjamin Shreve MSS, Accounts for Ship *China*, Circular Letter, Benjamin Chew Wilcocks, Canton, July 1, 1817.

29. Dulles, p. 210.

30. Latourette, "History of Early Relations," p. 52.

31. Dulles, p. 210.

32. *Ibid.*, p. 211.

33. Dennett, p. 75.

34. *Ibid.*, p. 3.

35. *Ibid.*, p. 19. See also Robert E. Peabody, *The Log of the Grand Turks* (Boston, 1926), pp. 63–64, for invoice of merchandise on board the *Grand Turk* as it was outward bound from Salem in December, 1785.

36. Dennett, p. 19.

37. *Ibid.*, p. 20.

38. *Ibid.*, p. 21.

39. Morison, pp. 59–60.

40. Dennett, p. 24. See also Robert Greenhalgh Albion, *The Rise of New York Port (1815–1860)* (New York, 1939), p. 202.

41. See Schuyler Cammann, *China's Dragon Robes* (New York, 1952), pp. 56–57, for fur-lined, fur-trimmed robes; pp. 143, 148 for specific mention of otter skins for imperial robes. The otter skins replaced sable skins, which had been used previously, but were becoming scarce (*ibid.*, pp. 137–38).

42. Raymond A. Rydell, *Cape Horn to the Pacific; the Rise and Decline of an Ocean Highway* (Berkeley, Cal., 1952), p. 28.

43. Latourette, "History of Early Relations," pp. 54–55.

44. PMS, Benjamin Shreve MSS, Accounts for Brig *New Hazard*, Benjamin Shreve, Canton, to Lammer and Snyder, New York, October 28, 1815.

45. Rydell, pp. 29–30.

46. *Ibid.*

47. *Ibid.*, p. 34. See also Morison, p. 61; and Latourette, "History of Early Relations," p. 39.

48. Rydell, p. 36.

49. Timothy Pitkin, *A Statistical View of the Commerce of the United States of America . . .* (2d ed.; New York, 1817), p. 249.

50. Latourette, "History of Early Relations," pp. 42–43. John Jacob Astor, of New York, sent many furs from the interior of eastern North America to Canton before he began his ventures on the Northwest Coast. Unfortunately, his scheme to use Astoria as a center for exporting furs eventually failed, with great financial losses.

51. Dennett, p. 41.

52. Rydell, pp. 39–40. See also Latourette, "History of Early Relations," p. 43; Dulles, p. 95.

53. LCP, Waln Papers, Alexander McNeilledge, "Notes on the China Trade, May 1, 1818," p. 36.

54. University of Delaware, Memorial Library (hereafter cited as UD), Latimer Papers, "Statement of the American Trade with the Port of Canton During the Season of 1833–34, Ending June 30th, 1834."

55. PMS, Benjamin Shreve MSS, Accounts for Brig *New Hazard*, Joseph Peabody, William Ropes and Company, Salem, to Benjamin Shreve, Canton, May 8, 1816.

56. The balance of trade was in favor of China for many years; but, since the exchange at Canton was part of America's total foreign commerce, this country could make up the deficit through sales in Europe and elsewhere. Adam Seybert, *Statistical Annals . . .* (Philadelphia, 1818), pp. 276–89.

57. Pitkin, p. 247.

58. It is interesting to note the importance of tea as a reason for the continuation of the America-China trade. During the period 1790–1800, the average consumption per year equaled 2,545,504 lbs. In the next twelve years that figure jumped to 3,771,194 lbs. (Pitkin, pp. 247–48). As other Chinese products declined in popularity, tea won their place. From 1822 to 1840 the proportion of tea to other exports increased from 36 per cent to 81 per cent. This

change also involved an increasing amount of the better grades of tea, the green instead of the black, which indicated a rise in American purchasing power as well as knowledge of and taste for the better teas, as pointed out by Latourette, "History of Early Relations," pp. 76–77.

59. LCP, Waln Papers, McNeilledge, p. 29.
60. UD, Latimer Papers, "Statement of the American Trade with the Port of Canton During the Season 1833–34, Ending June 30ᵗʰ, 1834."

# NOTES

## to Chapter III

1. Kenneth Scott Latourette, "The History of Early Relations Between the United States and China, 1784–1844," *Transactions of the Connecticut Academy of Arts and Sciences*, XXII (August, 1917), 139–44.
2. William C. Hunter, *The Fan Kwae at Canton Before Treaty Days, 1825–1844* (Hong Kong, 1911), p. 81.
3. Even there, as Samuel Shaw discovered, women were rare and much appreciated. (Samuel Shaw, *The Journals of Major Samuel Shaw, the First American Consul at Canton*, edited with a life of the author by Joseph Quincy [Boston, 1847], pp. 173, 242–43.) Later, Harriet Low, in Macao for five years, 1829–1834, to be a companion to her aunt, the wife of William H. Low, remarked about the dearth of English-speaking women and consequently her many beaux. (Arthur W. Hummel, "The Journal of Harriet Low," *The Library of Congress Quarterly Journal*, II [June, 1945], 47–48.) She wrote her sister in Salem engaging descriptions of the gala social season of plays, operas, grand dinners, and balls, as well as endless games in evening gatherings. For a proper New England young lady, Macao's sophistication was an artificial adventure, but a great deal of fun. (Hummel, p. 50.) With its diversions the island provided a needed outlet from the circumscribed life of commerce at Canton.
4. The Historical Society of Pennsylvania (hereafter cited as HSP), Ship *China Packet* MS, "Diary of Chas. Graff of Phila., 1804–1805." Charles Graff described the forts in 1804–1805: "They are situated exactly at the Mouth of the River one on each side of the entrance, the fort on the right hand in going up the river is built close to the Waters edge on the Main the other on the left is built on a small Island handsomely covered with Trees. The distance between them is 3 or 400 Yards."
5. Hunter, p. 14.

6. Hosea Ballou Morse, *The Gilds of China, with an Account of the Gild Merchant or Co-hong of Canton* (London, 1909), pp. 87–88.
7. Shaw, pp. 176–77.
8. Hunter, p. 54.
9. *Ibid.*, p. 102.
10. Peabody Museum of Salem, Ship *Minerva* Papers, Thomas W. Ward, Notebook, Canton, 1809.
11. Shaw, pp. 173–74.
12. HSP, Hepburn Collection, Barry Papers, John Barry, "Memorandum relating to the Trade at Canton, 1787–1788."
13. Hunter, p. 50.
14. *Ibid.*, p. 51.
15. Shaw, pp. 177–78.
16. Hunter, p. 101. A document with the grand chop (seal) is illustrated in Robert E. Peabody, *The Log of the Grand Turks* (Boston, 1926), facing p. 96.
17. Hunter, p. 20.
18. Shaw, p. 178.
19. Hosea Ballou Morse and Harley Farnsworth MacNair, *Far Eastern International Relations* (Boston, 1931), p. 61.
20. Hunter, p. 24.
21. HSP, Hepburn Collection, Barry, "Memorandum . . . , 1787–1788."
22. Hunter, p. 23.
23. Morse, *The Gilds of China*, pp. 80–83.
24. The Library Company of Philadelphia, Waln Papers, Alexander McNeilledge, "Notes on the China Trade, May 1, 1818," p. 30.
25. PMS, Benjamin Shreve MSS, Accounts for Brig *New Hazard*, Benjamin Shreve, Notebook, 1815. "Qua" as a suffix denotes "Mr." or "Sir" (see Hunter, p. 34).
26. Alan Priest, "A Note on Houqua," *Bulletin of the Metropolitan Museum of Art*, XXXVI (September, 1941), 191. There were several Houquas; but the most famous one to whom the Americans referred was named Wu-Ping Chien (1764–1843).
27. PMS, Ship *Minerva* Papers, Ward, Notebook, Canton, 1809.
28. LCP, Waln Papers, Robert Waln, Memo Book, September, 1819, to January, 1820.
29. Hunter, p. 35.
30. LCP, Waln Papers, Robert Waln, Memo Book, 1820.
31. LCP, McNeilledge, "Notes," pp. 28–29.
32. Essex Institute (hereafter cited as EI), MS Account Book of Elias Hasket Derby, 1785–1796, Ship *Grand Turk* Invoice No. 15, December, 1786, and March, 1787.
33. The New York Public Library (hereafter cited as NYPL), Constable-Pierrepont Collection, Hezekiah B. Pierrepont, "Notes on the Trade of China, taken chiefly from Observations made at Canton in the Season of 1796 & corrected in London, June 1798," 2d copy.
34. PMS, Ship *Minerva* Papers, Ward, Notebook, Canton, 1809.
35. Gertrude S. Kimball, "The East-India Trade of Providence from 1787–1807,"

*Papers from the Historical Seminary of Brown University* (Providence, R. I., 1896), VI, 33.

36. HSP, Hepburn Collection, Barry Papers, China Letter Book, John Barry, Canton, to Mrs. Isaac Hazlehurst, Philadelphia, January 8, 1789.

37. LCP, Waln Papers, McNeilledge, "Notes," p. 31.

38. PMS, Ship *Minerva* Papers, Ward, Notebook, Canton, 1809.

39. Shaw, pp. 199–200. Shaw continued: "Thus far, it may be supposed, the fellow's remarks pleased me. Justice obliges me to add his conclusion—'All men come first time China very good gentlemen, all same you. I think two three time more you come Canton, you make all same Englishman too.'"

# *NOTES*

## *to Chapter IV*

1. Mrs. Jacques Noel Jacobsen, "Lowestoft China," *Antiques*, LII (July, 1947), 32.

2. William Bowyer Honey, *European Ceramic Art from the End of the Middle Ages to about 1815* (London, 1952), pp. 36, 376. See also Wolf Mankowitz and Reginald G. Haggar, *The Concise Encyclopedia of English Pottery and Porcelain* (New York, [1957]), pp. 7, 135; and George Savage, *18th-Century English Porcelain* (New York, 1952), pp. 266–71.

3. Mankowitz and Haggar, p. 135. See also Homer Eaton Keyes, "Lowestoft: What Is It? I. Concerning a Number of Misapprehensions," *Antiques*, XIII (March, 1928), 210.

4. John Goldsmith Phillips, *China-Trade Porcelain; an Account of Its Historical Background, Manufacture, and Decoration and a Study of the Helena Woolworth McCann Collection* (Cambridge, Mass., 1956).

5. John Robinson, "Blue and White 'India-China,'" *Old-Time New England*, XIV (January, 1924), 99.

6. William Milburn, *Oriental Commerce . . .* (London, 1813), II, 504–5.

7. Robinson, pp. 100, 104. Canton should be pronounced with the accent on the second syllable. Actually, most Americans in China-trade days pronounced it with the accent on the first syllable. See Chapter V for sources for the names of different wares.

8. See quotation from Hone, p. 124.

9. This subject will be discussed further in Chapter XI.

10. See Chapters VII and X for examples.

11. This development is also discussed in Chapter XI.

# NOTES

## to Chapter V

1. John Goldsmith Phillips, *China-Trade Porcelain* (Cambridge, Mass., 1956), p. 2.
2. *Ibid.*, p. 10. See also Soame Jenyns, *Later Chinese Porcelain, the Ch'ing Dynasty (1644–1912)* (London, 1951), pp. 9–11. For dating of dynasties, see L. Carrington Goodrich, *A Short History of the Chinese People* (3d ed.; New York, 1959), pp. 259–60.
3. Phillips, p. 10. See also Jenyns, pp. 17–26.
4. Jenyns, pp. 28–56.
5. *Ibid.*, pp. 62, 67, 72.
6. *Ibid.*, pp. 10–11, 13.
7. Phillips, pp. 4–6. See also Jenyns, pp. 13–14.
8. Phillips, p. 5. See also Jenyns, p. 13.
9. Phillips, p. 5. See also Jenyns, pp. 11, 13.
10. Phillips, pp. 5, 8.
11. Jenyns, p. 13.
12. Geoffrey R. Sayer, *Ching-tê-chên T'ao-lu; or the Potteries of China, Being a Translation with Notes and an Introduction* (London, 1951), pp. 28–30. See also Jenyns, p. 13; and Phillips, p. 6.
13. Sayer, pp. 4–5, 28–30. See also Jenyns, p. 6.
14. W. Winterbotham, *An Historical, Geographical and Philosophical View of the Chinese Empire* . . . (Philadelphia, 1796), II, 177. See also Sayer, p. 5; and Phillips, p. 6.
15. Phillips, p. 6.
16. Sayer, pp. 4–10, 27–38.
17. *Ibid.*, p. 3.
18. Phillips, p. 8.
19. Jenyns, p. 6.
20. Phillips, pp. 8–9.
21. Sayer, pp. 5–6.
22. Jenyns, p. 7.
23. Sayer, p. 32. In the late eighteenth century Lan P'u, a native of Ching-tê Chên, wrote most of the *T'ao Lu*, considered by the Chinese to be one of the two standard works by Oriental writers on the pottery of Ching-tê Chên (the other being the *T'ao Shuo*, by Chu T'ung-ch'uan, published in 1774). After his master's death, a pupil of Lan P'u completed the work on the *T'ao Lu* for publication in 1815. (See also Sayer, pp. xv–xvi, xxiii, 125; and Jenyns, p. 15.)
24. Sayer, pp. 31–32.
25. *Ibid.*, pp. 33–34. The rough wares, however, were often improved by special

workmen whose shops were colloquially called "the shops that smooth the rough edges" (*ibid.*, p. 37).

26. Jenyns, p. 10.

27. Phillips, pp. 7–8. See also Jenyns, p. 10.

28. J. A. Lloyd Hyde, "The Yesterday and Today of Oriental Lowestoft," *Antiques*, XIX (June, 1931), 447.

29. William Hickey, *Memoirs of William Hickey, 1749–1809*, ed. Alfred Spencer (New York, 1921), p. 210.

30. Letter, John R. Latimer, Canton, to his mother, Wilmington, Delaware, October 19, 1815, quoted by Charles F. Hummel, "John R. Latimer and the China Trade," *Winterthur Newsletter*, IV (December, 1958), 2.

31. *Ibid.*

32. Samuel Shaw, *The Journals of Major Samuel Shaw, the First American Consul at Canton*, edited with a life of the author by Josiah Quincy (Boston, 1847), pp. 198–99.

33. The Library Company of Philadelphia, Waln Papers, Robert Waln, Jr., "China; Comprehending a View of the Origin, Antiquity, History . . . written on the ship *Caledonia* at Sea, February 2, 1820."

34. Jenyns, pp. 2, 79–84. See also John Robinson, "Blue and White 'India-China,'" *Old-Time New England*, XIV (January, 1924), 108.

35. Marco Polo, *The Book of Ser Marco Polo*, translated and edited by Sir Henry Yule (London, 1871), II, 186.

36. Jenyns, pp. 80–81. See also Joseph T. Butler, "Chinese Porcelain Figures of Westerners," *Antiques*, LXXIX (February, 1961), 170–73.

37. Jenyns, p. 83.

38. *Ibid.*, pp. 79–80, 84. See also Sir Harry Garner, *Oriental Blue and White* (London, 1954), pp. 54–57.

39. Robinson, p. 110.

40. Phillips, pp. 8, 59–60. It is interesting to note that John R. Latimer, in writing to his mother from Canton in 1815, said, "The ware called Nankin is produced from a superior kind of clay only found in the Province of Nankin where the china is made and the first glazing put on; some is left white for penciling; the other is blue and white" (see Hummel, p. 2). That Latimer was misinformed both as to the origin of the porcelain and the location of Nanking (actually in the province of Kiangsu) is understandable in light of the fact that the foreign traders were closely confined to a small area in Canton and therefore knew little of the interior of China.

41. Robinson, p. 116.

42. Homer Eaton Keyes, "Lowestoft: What Is It? III. Centres of Manufacture, and a Classification," *Antiques*, XIV (November, 1928), 422.

43. Jenyns, pp. 12, 71–73.

44. G. A. R. Goyle, letter, quoted by Keyes, p. 426.

45. The New York Public Library, Constable-Pierrepont Collection, Hezekiah B. Pierrepont, "Notes of the Trade of China, taken chiefly from Observations made at Canton in the Season of 1796 & corrected in London, June 1798." 2d copy.

46. Latimer letter, October 19, 1815, quoted by Hummel, p. 2.

# NOTES

## to Chapter VI

1. Edward Dillon, *Porcelain* (New York, 1904), pp. 209–15. See also Homer Eaton Keyes, "Lowestoft: What Is It? II. Several Whys and Wherefores," *Antiques*, XIII (May, 1928), 384–88.
2. Robert Schmidt, *Porcelain as an Art and a Mirror of Fashion*, trans. W. A. Thorpe (London, 1932), p. 48.
3. Dillon, pp. 218–19.
4. *Ibid.*, pp. 220–23.
5. *Ibid.*, pp. 242–43. See also Rodris Roth, "Tea Drinking in 18th-Century America: Its Etiquette and Equipage," *United States National Museum Bulletin 225; Contributions from the Museum of History and Technology*, Paper 14 (Washington, D. C., 1961), pp. 61–64.
6. Marshall Davidson, "The China Trade," *Antiques*, XXXIX (May, 1941), 235. For an opposite view, see Dillon, p. 227.
7. Davidson, p. 235.
8. Daniel Defoe, *A Tour Through the Whole Island of Great Britain* (London, 1724), Vol. I, Letter 2, p. 122.
9. Dillon, p. 227.
10. *Ibid.*, p. 230.
11. Kamer Aga-Oglu, "Late Ming and Early Ch'ing Porcelain Fragments from Archaeological Sites in Florida," *The Florida Anthropologist*, VIII (December, 1955), 107.
12. *Ibid.*, p. 104.
13. Roth, pp. 74–75.
14. Aga-Oglu, p. 105.
15. *Ibid.*, p. 106.
16. R. T. H. Halsey and Charles O. Cornelius, *A Handbook of the American Wing*, ed. Joseph Downs (7th ed.; New York, 1942), p. 34. See also Esther Singleton, *Social New York under the Georges, 1714–1776* (New York, 1902), pp. 119–22; and Alice Winchester, "Antiques," *Antiques*, LXXIX (February, 1961), 165 (Butler quotation).
17. The New York Public Library, MS Ledger, Philip Cuyler, 1763–1794.
18. Rita S. Gottesman, *The Arts and Crafts in New York, 1777–1799; Advertisements and News Items from New York City Newspapers* (New York, 1954), p. 102.
19. John Goldsmith Phillips, *China-Trade Porcelain; an Account of Its Historical Background, Manufacture, and Decoration and a Study of the Helena*

*Woolworth McCann Collection* (Cambridge, Mass., 1956), p. 13. For description and pictures of the Lee coat of arms, see Cazenove Gardner Lee, Jr., *Lee Chronicle: Studies of the Early Generations of the Lees of Virginia*, ed. Dorothy Mills Parker (New York, 1957), pp. 11, 47; Plates V, VI; Frontispiece.

20. Lee, pp. 4–5, 19–28, 348–49.
21. Alice Morse Earle, *China Collecting in America* (New York, 1892), pp. 56, 57, 60.
22. Alfred Coxe Prime, *The Arts and Crafts in Philadelphia, Maryland, and South Carolina, 1786–1800*, Series Two (Topsfield, Mass., 1932), p. 147.
23. Maryland Hall of Records, Baltimore County (Maryland) Inventories, 1772–1801 (microfilm copy, Joseph Downs Manuscript Library, Winterthur Museum). See also Earle, p. 67.
24. Samuel W. Woodhouse, Jr., "Grandmother's China," *House Beautiful*, LXXII (July, 1932), 33.
25. Lee, pp. 235–36.
26. Mary James Leach, "From Kentucky's Collectors," *Antiques*, LII (November, 1947), 354. The bowls belong to his great-granddaughter, Mrs. Howard Evans.
27. Kenneth Scott Latourette, "The History of Early Relations Between the United States and China, 1784–1844," *Transactions of the Connecticut Academy of Arts and Sciences*, XXII (August, 1917), 140. For example, a large number of important Boston shipping records no longer exist.
28. Number of piculs listed by Samuel W. Woodhouse, Jr., "The Voyage of the *Empress of China*," *The Pennsylvania Magazine of History and Biography*, LXIII (January, 1939), 30. Number of chests from the manifest of the *Empress of China*, November, 1784 (MS in possession of Mr. Carrow Thibault).
29. Woodhouse, "Voyage of the *Empress*," p. 30.
30. Foster Rhea Dulles, *The Old China Trade* (Boston, 1930), p. 44. See also Essex Institute, MS Account Book of Elias Hasket Derby, 1785–1796, Ship *Grand Turk* Invoice No. 15, December, 1786, and March, 1787.
31. Library Company of Philadelphia, Waln Papers, Robert Waln, "Collections for the Formation of Letters from Canton from various Authors . . . ," pp. 95–96.
32. NYPL, Constable-Pierrepont Collection, William Bell, Account Books, Ship *Canton*, Notebook, 1809.
33. Peabody Museum of Salem, George Hodges MSS, Ship *Union* Accounts, Invoice of China for Capt. Ichabod Smith, November 14, 1802.
34. NYPL, Constable-Pierrepont Collection, William Bell, Account Books, Ship *Eliza*, Memo of China Ware for Peter McKinley, May 9, 1806.
35. *Ibid.*, Ship *Eliza*, Memo of China Ware for Thomas Chrystie, May 9, 1806.
36. *Ibid.*, Ship *Canton*, Invoice of Merchandise, 1809.
37. *Ibid.*, Ship *Canton*, Invoice of China Ware for Albert Christie, November 1, 1816.
38. *Ibid.*, Ship *William and John*, Invoice of China Ware for John Jacob Astor, 1816.

39. The Historical Society of Pennsylvania, Woodhouse Collection, Ships' Papers, Ship *Caledonia*, George L. Small, Report and Manifest of the Cargo on board the Ship *Caledonia*, 1817.

40. Homer Eaton Keyes, "Quality in Oriental Lowestoft," *Antiques*, XXXII (December, 1937), 292–93.

41. LCP, Waln Papers, Robert Waln, Jr., "China; Comprehending a View of the Origin, Antiquity, History . . . written on the Ship *Caledonia* at Sea, February 2, 1820."

42. *Ibid.*

43. Keyes, p. 294.

44. LCP, Waln, "Collections . . . ," taken from C. L. J. de Guignes, *Voyages à Péking, Manille et L'ille de France* (Paris, 1808), II, 241–46.

45. PMS, Benjamin Shreve MSS, Accounts for Brig *New Hazard*, Ropes, Pickman and Company to Benjamin Shreve, May 30, 1815.

46. NYPL, Constable-Pierrepont Collection, William Bell, Account Books, Ship *William and John*, Joseph Minturn, New York, to William Bell, Canton, December 24, 1815.

47. PMS, Benjamin Shreve MSS, Accounts for Brig *Canton*, John Prince, Jr., Salem, to Benjamin Shreve, Canton, October 25, 1821.

48. Geoffrey R. Sayer, *Ching-tê-chên T'ao-lu; or the Potteries of China. Being a Translation with Notes and an Introduction* (London, 1951), p. 72.

49. Sir Henry Yule (ed.), *The Book of Ser Marco Polo* (London, 1871), II, 186. The exact city cannot be identified from Marco Polo's rendering of the name, but it was apparently in Fukien, near Zayton, through which port its wares were shipped to other parts of Asia.

50. Benjamin Franklin, *The Writings of Benjamin Franklin, 1783–1788*, ed. Albert Henry Smyth (New York, 1906), IX, 207.

51. Samuel Shaw, *The Journals of Major Samuel Shaw, the First American Consul at Canton*, edited with a life of the author by Josiah Quincy (Boston, 1847), p. 229.

52. Homer Eaton Keyes, "The Chinese Lowestoft of Early American Commerce," *Antiques*, XVI (November, 1929), 382–83.

53. NYPL, Constable-Pierrepont Collection, Hezekiah B. Pierrepont, "Notes of the Trade of China, taken chiefly from Observations made at Canton in the Season of 1796 & corrected in London, June 1798." 2d copy.

54. PMS, Benjamin Shreve MSS, Accounts for Brig *New Hazard*, Benjamin Shreve, Notebook, 1815.

55. PMS, George Hodges MSS, Ship *Union* Accounts, Sales and Estimates of the Profits of the Adventure of Benjamin Pickman, Canton, July 20, 1803.

56. *Stephens's Philadelphia Directory, for 1796* . . . (Philadelphia, [1796]), p. 232.

57. LCP, Waln Papers, Robert Waln, "Collections . . ." The Tariff of 1842 placed a 30 per cent ad valorem duty on chinaware; a specific duty on cassia, mace, and ginger; and a 20 per cent duty on all unenumerated goods, which must have included teas and silks. A 10 per cent additional duty was placed on all goods imported from the East. This may have meant that the chinaware from Canton at this time was not only of poorer quality than the porcelains of Europe, but also more expensive. (Latourette, p. 79.)

58. Girard College Library, Stephen Girard MS Collection, Arthur Grelaud and Robert Wilson, Canton, to Stephen Girard, Philadelphia, March 12, 1812.

59. Connecticut Historical Society, Photostat of MS Account Book, Amos Porter, 1802.

60. C. Northcote Parkinson, *Trade in the Eastern Seas, 1793–1813* (Cambridge, England, 1937), p. 203.

61. *Ibid.*

62. Haverford College Library, The Charles Roberts Autograph Collection, James Josiah, Ship *Asia*, to John Barry, Canton, September 25, 1788.

63. Gertrude S. Kimball, "The East-India Trade of Providence from 1787–1807," *Papers from the Historical Seminary of Brown University*, VI (Providence, R. I., 1896), 15–16.

64. NYPL, Constable-Pierrepont Collection, Pierrepont, "Notes on the Trade in China. . . ."

65. PMS, Benjamin Shreve MSS, Accounts for Brig *New Hazard*, Joseph Peabody, William Ropes and Company, Salem, to Benjamin Shreve, Canton, May 8, 1816.

# *NOTES*

## *to Chapter VII*

1. The *Hope* was the second ship, taking Shaw on his second trip. See Robert E. Peabody, *The Log of the Grand Turks* (Boston, 1926), p. 75.

2. Charles H. P. Copeland, "To the Farthest Port of the Rich East," *American Heritage*, VI (February, 1955), 114–15.

3. Foster Rhea Dulles, *The Old China Trade* (Boston, 1930), p. 29.

4. Copeland, p. 115.

5. Kenneth Scott Latourette, "The History of Early Relations Between the United States and China, 1784–1844," *Transactions of the Connecticut Academy of Arts and Sciences*, XXII (August, 1917), 64.

6. James D. Phillips, "East India Voyages of Salem Vessels Before 1800," *The Essex Institute Historical Collections*, LXXIX (April, July, October, 1943), 117, 222, 331.

7. Samuel Eliot Morison, *The Maritime History of Massachusetts, 1783–1860* (Boston, 1921), p. 217.

8. *Ibid.*

9. Latourette, p. 65.

10. Ralph D. Paine, "The Tragedy of the 'Friendship,' " *The Ships and Sailors of Old Salem* (New York, 1909), pp. 508–35.

11. Homer Eaton Keyes, "American Ship Lowestoft," *Antiques*, XIX (June, 1931), 441, 443. Keyes states that the *Friendship* was built in Portland, Maine, in 1815, and was owned by the Silsbees, of Salem. There were several ships with the same name, however, and the plate might have been made for any of them. Its wide border, as ornate in style as mandarin ware, suggests a date after 1820.

12. Latourette, p. 64.

13. Copeland, p. 115.

14. Peabody, p. 91.

15. *Ibid.*, pp. 102–4.

16. Essex Institute, MS Account Book of Elias Hasket Derby, 1785–1796, Invoice No. 15 of sundry merchandize shipped on Board ship Grand Turk . . . for Account & Risque of Elias Hasket Derby, Esq., of Salem, North America marked and numbered . . . December 1786 and March 1787.

17. Peabody, p. 94.

18. William Hutchinson, *A Treatise on Practical Seamanship* . . . (London, 1777). The same source was no doubt used for three similar bowls, two made for Commodores Richard Dale and John Barry and a third for John Lamb, the collector of the port of New York. The Dale bowl has its owner's initials on the outside, while Barry's bowl bears a ribbon reading *John Barry, Esq.* *Alliance. Commander.* See also Samuel W. Woodhouse, Jr., "Punch and Punchbowls," *Antiques*, XXIX (February, 1936), 56–57.

19. EI, MS Account Book of Elias Hasket Derby, 1785–1796, Ship *Grand Turk* Invoice No. 15, December 1786 and March 1787.

20. Peabody Museum of Salem, George Hodges MSS, Ship *Union* Accounts, Invoice of the ship *Union*, November 14, 1802.

21. PMS, Ship *Minerva* Papers, Canton, 1809, Invoice of Thomas W. Ward, November 20, 1809.

22. PMS, Benjamin Shreve MSS, Accounts for Brig *New Hazard*, Ropes, Pickman and Company, Boston, to Benjamin Shreve, Canton, May 2, 1815.

23. *Ibid.*, Benjamin Shreve, Canton, to Ropes, Pickman and Company, Boston, November 13, 1815.

24. *Ibid.*, Benjamin Shreve, Directions for the Investment of One Thousand Specie Dollars for the Account of William Reed of Marblehead, Notebook, 1815.

25. *Ibid.*, Benjamin Shreve, Memo Book, 1815.

26. PMS, Benjamin Shreve MSS, Accounts for Brig *Governor Endicott*, Benjamin Shreve, Memo Book, 1819–1821.

27. Latourette, pp. 65–66.

28. *Ibid.*, p. 66.

29. *Ibid.*

30. Morison, p. 274.

31. *Ibid.*, p. 275.

32. *Ibid.*, p. 84.

33. The home of John P. Cushing, to which he retired after 1830, was supposedly screened by a Chinese porcelain wall. (Morison, p. 240.)

34. Harrison Gray Otis House, Accessions Records.

35. Boston Museum of Fine Arts, Accessions Records.

36. Massachusetts Historical Society, Thomas W. Ward Papers (1760–1816), William Ward, Canton, to Nancy Ward, Boston, January 10, 1800.

37. MHS, Thomas H. Perkins MSS, E. Bumstead, Journal A, Invoice of China Ware, August 20, 1804.

38. MHS, Thomas H. Perkins MSS, E. Bumstead, Blotter A, Invoice of China Ware, November 17 and December 30, 1804.

39. MHS, Thomas H. Perkins MSS, J. and T. H. Perkins and Sons, Invoices Inward, Invoice of China Ware, about 1805.

40. MHS, Thomas H. Perkins MSS, J. and T. H. Perkins and Sons, Invoice of China Ware, January 7, 1826.

41. Latourette, p. 67.

42. Tyler Dennett, *Americans in Eastern Asia; a Critical Study of the Policy of the United States with Reference to China, Japan, and Korea in the 19th Century* (New York, 1922), p. 10.

43. Latourette, p. 67.

44. James B. Hedges, *The Browns of Providence Plantations, Colonial Years* (Cambridge, Mass., 1952), pp. 19–20.

45. Latourette, p. 67.

46. *Ibid.*, p. 68. See also Hugh Gourley, III, "History in Houses: Carrington House, Providence, Rhode Island," *Antiques*, LXXIX (February, 1961), 182–86.

47. Gertrude S. Kimball, "The East-India Trade of Providence from 1787–1807," *Papers from the Historical Seminary of Brown University*, VI (Providence, R. I., 1896), 6.

48. *Ibid.*, p. 32.

49. *Ibid.*, p. 16.

50. The John Carter Brown Library (hereafter cited as JCBL), Brown Papers, Letter, Brown and Ives, Providence, to John Bennock, Newport, May 11, 1797.

51. Frances Little, "America's East Indiamen and the China Trade," *Antiques*, XV (January, 1929), 27–31.

52. JCBL, Brown Papers, Ship *Ann and Hope* MSS, Christopher Bentley, Division of the Cargo of the Ship *Ann and Hope*, 1799.

53. JCBL, Brown Papers, Ship *Ann and Hope* MSS, Invoice Book, 1800–1801.

54. Little, p. 30.

55. Latourette, p. 68.

56. Connecticut Historical Society, Photostat of MS Account Book, Amos Porter, 1802.

57. Latourette, p. 68.

58. Dulles, p. 62. See also Robert Greenhalgh Albion, *The Rise of New York Port (1815–1860)* (New York, 1939), p. 197.

59. Latourette, p. 69.

60. *Ibid.* See also Albion, p. 198.
61. Albion, pp. 198–200.
62. *Ibid.*, p. 201.
63. *Ibid.*, pp. 200–201.
64. *Ibid.*
65. University of Delaware, Memorial Library, Latimer Papers, John R. Latimer, Canton, to Henry Latimer, Wilmington, November 30, 1832.
66. Samuel W. Woodhouse, Jr., "The Voyage of the *Empress of China,*" *The Pennsylvania Magazine of History and Biography*, LXIII (January, 1939), 32–35.
67. MS Collection of Mr. Carrow Thibault, Manifest of the Ship *Empress of China*, November, 1784.
68. Letter from B. MacDonald Steers, Director, Mystic Seaport, Mystic, Connecticut, July 10, 1956.
69. Rita S. Gottesman, *The Arts and Crafts in New York, 1777–1799; Advertisements and News Items from New York City Newspapers* (New York, 1954), p. 101.
70. The New York Public Library, MS Letter Book of Samuel Fleming (1782–1790), Samuel Fleming, New York, to Captain Thomas Randall, Canton, February 5, 1788.
71. NYPL, Constable-Pierrepont Collection, William Bell, Account Books, Ship *Eliza*, Memo for John H. Titus, 1806.
72. *Ibid.*, Memo for William Bayard, 1806.
73. Gottesman, p. 100.
74. The New-York Historical Society (hereafter cited as N-YHS), Oliver Wolcott and Company, Account Book (1804–1810), pp. 180–83.
75. *Ibid.*, Account Book (1808–1815), pp. 120, 136.
76. "The City Punch Bowl," *Bulletin of the Metropolitan Museum of Art*, VII (September, 1912), 165.
77. Homer Eaton Keyes, "Lowestoft: Exclusively American," *Antiques*, XXI (April, 1932), 171–75.
78. The Library of Congress, Latimer Papers, Ship *Washington* MS, Invoice of China Ware for Floyd S. Bailey, November 14, 1825.
79. Winterthur Museum, Joseph Downs Manuscript Library, Inventory of the Estate of John C. Vanden Heuvel, May, 1826. The pagoda pictured in Figure 47 is one of two matching ones at Winterthur Museum. The pair are similar to, but smaller than, the pair of pagodas in Augustus Pugin's signed drawing of the music room of the Pavilion at Brighton at the time that the Pavilion was remodeled in the Oriental style by the architect John Nash between 1816 and 1823. (See Edward Wedlake Brayley, *Illustrations of Her Majesty's Palace at Brighton; Formerly the Pavilion: Executed by the Command of King George the Fourth, under the Supervision of John Nash, Esq., Architect* [London, 1838], Plate 17.)
80. Latourette, pp. 13–18.
81. Dennett, p. 10. See also Latourette, pp. 69–70.
82. Dennett, p. 6.
83. Albion, pp. 394–95. See also Dulles, pp. 113–14.

84. The Historical Society of Pennsylvania, MS Letter Book of Benjamin Fuller (1784–1787), Benjamin Fuller, Philadelphia, to Thomas Truxtun and Jonathan Frazier, Canton, December 31, 1785.

85. *Ibid.*

86. *Ibid.*, Benjamin Fuller, Philadelphia, to Colonel John Mitchell, Charleston, April 6, 1787.

87. HSP, MS Letter Book of Benjamin Fuller (1787–1791), Benjamin Fuller, Philadelphia, to Thomas Truxtun, Canton, December 8, 1787.

88. *Ibid.*

89. *Ibid.*

90. Harrold E. Gillingham, "A Lost Set of Eighteenth-Century Oriental Lowestoft," *Antiques*, XXXIV (October, 1938), 198–99.

91. HSP, MS Letter Book of Benjamin Fuller (1787–1791), Benjamin Fuller, Philadelphia, to Thomas Truxtun, Canton, December 12, 1789.

92. HSP, Hepburn Collection, Barry Papers, China Letter Book, Hugh Doyle, Philadelphia, to John Barry, Canton, December 14, 1787.

93. *Ibid.*, James Hill, Philadelphia, to John Barry, Canton, December 13, 1787.

94. *Ibid.*, Henry Gurney, Tusculam, to John Barry, Canton, December 11, 1787.

95. *Ibid.*, John Nixon, Philadelphia, to John Barry, Canton, December 11, 1787.

96. Stephen Decatur, "The Commodore Decatur Punchbowl," *Antiques*, XXXII (December, 1937), 296–97.

97. HSP, Woodhouse Collection, Ships' Papers, 1783–1811.

98. *Ibid.*, Ship *Fame*, Bill of Lading, January, 1801.

99. The Library Company of Philadelphia, Waln Papers, Robert Waln MSS, Letter Book (1802–1806), Robert Waln, Philadelphia, to Redwood Fisher, Canton, June 14, 1805.

100. *Ibid.*, Letter Book (1808–1814), Robert Waln, Philadelphia, to Charles Ross and John C. Smith, Canton, May 20, 1811.

101. *Ibid.*, Letter Book (1805–1819), Robert Waln, Philadelphia, to William Chaloner and Robert Wells, Canton, August 16, 1816. See also Waln Memo Book, Canton, September 16, 1819.

102. HSP, Woodhouse Collection, Ships' Papers, Ship *Rousseau*, Manifest, Canton, March 9, 1804.

103. Girard College Library, Stephen Girard MS Collection, Invoice Book, Stephen Girard, 1811–1823, pp. 98–99.

104. Record of history of the chinaware contained in a letter in the files of Dr. John B. Carson, Newtown Square, Pennsylvania.

105. Letter from Mrs. Alfred Coxe Prime, Paoli, Pennsylvania, November 7, 1956 (in files of the author).

106. Hamilton Owens, *Baltimore on the Chesapeake* (Garden City, N. Y., 1941), p. 142.

107. Thomas Courtenay Jenkins Whedbee, *The Port of Baltimore in the Making, 1828 to 1878* (Baltimore, 1953), p. 69. In 1807 an association of merchants formed the Baltimore East India Company, with plans for extensive commerce; however, when their ships, the *London Packet* and the *William Bingham*, returned during the Embargo, the company split the profits of their cargoes; the company was then dissolved. (J. Thomas Scharf, *The*

*Chronicles of Baltimore, Being a Complete History of "Baltimore Town" and Baltimore City* [Baltimore, 1874], p. 300.)

108. Whedbee, pp. 47, 52.
109. "Baltimore," *The North American Review*, XLVI (January, 1825), 108.
110. Maryland Historical Society (hereafter cited as MdHS), Charles Ridgely MSS, Charles Ridgely, Account with Peter Frick, January 13, 1797, to March 22, 1797; see also Account with Peter Frick, December 7, 1790, to January 24, 1792.
111. Maryland Hall of Records, Baltimore County Inventories, 1797–1801 (microfilm copy, Joseph Downs Manuscript Library, Winterthur Museum).
112. *Federal Gazette & Baltimore Daily Advertiser*, July 1, 1808, p. 3.
113. MdHS, Accessions Records.
114. Latourette, p. 70.
115. UD, Latimer Papers, John R. Latimer, Canton, to Henry Latimer, Wilmington, October 23, 1826: "When I came out last, I thought that the prospect of doing well, was so great that I was induced to take an interest in the voyage of the Splendid far exceeding what prudence would dictate, the long detention of that ship at New Orleans & her late arrival here—occasioned me to pay very high for her cargo."
116. Albion, pp. 96–100.
117. *Ibid.*, pp. 98, 100.
118. *Ibid.*, pp. 117–18.
119. *Ibid.*, p. 397, figures for 1835.
120. EI, MS Account Book of Elias Hasket Derby, 1785–1796, Invoice No. 15 of sundry merchandise shipped on Board ship Grand Turk . . . for Account & Risque of Elias Hasket Derby, Esq., of Salem, North America, marked and numbered . . . December 1786 and March 1787.
121. JCBL, Brown and Ives, Providence, to Hazard and Robinson, Charleston, June 11, 1791.
122. *Ibid.*, Hazard and Robinson, Charleston, to Brown, Benson, and Ives, Providence, October 5, 1793.
123. Alfred Coxe Prime, *The Arts and Crafts in Philadelphia, Maryland, and South Carolina, 1786–1800*, Series Two (Topsfield, Mass., 1932), p. 150.
124. Whedbee, p. 65.
125. William M. Lytle, *Merchant Steam Vessels of the United States, 1807–1868* (Mystic, Conn., 1952), p. 151. See also James W. Foster, Director of Maryland Historical Society, summary of research on Steamboat *Philadelphia*, contained in letter dated October 17, 1956 (in files of Winterthur Museum). See also Fred E. Dayton, *Steamboat Days* (New York, 1925), pp. 288–89.

# NOTES

## to Chapter VIII

1. The Library Company of Philadelphia, Waln Papers, Robert Waln, Jr., "China: Comprehending a View of the Origin, Antiquity, History, . . . (written on the Ship *Caledonia* at sea, February 2, 1820)."

2. Tyler Dennett, *Americans in Eastern Asia; a Critical Study of the Policy of the United States with Reference to China, Japan, and Korea in the 19th Century* (New York, 1922), p. 70.

3. *Ibid.*, p. 73.

4. Robert Greenhalgh Albion, *The Rise of New York Port (1815–1860)* (New York, 1939), pp. 202–3.

5. *Ibid.*, pp. 196–97.

6. The four new ports were Amoy, Foochow, Ningpo, and Shanghai. See Kenneth Scott Latourette, "The History of Early Relations Between the United States and China, 1784–1844," *Transactions of the Connecticut Academy of Arts and Sciences*, XXII (August, 1917), 140.

7. *Ibid.*, pp. 140–43.

8. D. Mackensie Brown (ed.), *China Trade Days in California* (Berkeley, Cal., 1947), p. 4.

9. University of Delaware, Memorial Library, Latimer Papers, "Statement of the American Trade with the Port of Canton during the Season of 1833–34, ending June 30th, 1834."

10. Foster Rhea Dulles, *The Old China Trade* (Boston, 1930), p. 211.

11. John Goldsmith Phillips, *China-Trade Porcelain* (Cambridge, Mass., 1956), p. 41.

12. [R.] Soame Jenyns, *Later Chinese Porcelain, the Ch'ing Dynasty (1644–1912)* (London, 1951), p. 72.

13. UD, Latimer Papers, John Latimer, Canton, to Henry Latimer, Wilmington, December 2, 1822.

14. The Library of Congress, Latimer Papers, Matthew Ralston, Philadelphia, to John Latimer, Canton, July 18, 1827.

15. Geoffrey Bemrose, *Nineteenth Century English Pottery and Porcelain* (London, 1952), p. 23.

16. W. B. Honey, *French Porcelain of the 18th Century* (London, 1950), pp. 30–40. See also, Albion, p. 74; and Phillips, p. 50.

17. Harold Donaldson Eberlein and Roger Wearne Ramsdell, *The Practical Book of Chinaware* (New York, 1925), pp. 294–95. See also Arthur W. Clement, *Notes on American Ceramics, 1607–1943* (Brooklyn, N. Y., 1944), p. 26.

18. John Spargo, *Early American Pottery and China* (New York, 1926), pp. 232–36. See also Clement, pp. 28–29.

19. Spargo, pp. 256–74. See also Lura Woodside Watkins, *Early New England Potters and Their Wares* (Cambridge, Mass., 1950), pp. 211–13.

20. Dulles, p. 118.

21. Marshall Davidson, "The China Trade," *Antiques*, XXXIX (May, 1941), 235.

# *N O T E S*

## *to Chapter IX*

1. Europe also imported more tableware than any other type of export porcelain. See John Goldsmith Phillips, *China-Trade Porcelain* (Cambridge, Mass., 1956), p. 52.

2. An evening set was probably a small dinner service.

3. William Bell brought home for John McVickar, in December, 1799, a blue-and-white breakfast set of sixty-three items, which included coffee cups and a butter boat and stand. (The New York Public Library, Constable-Pierrepont Collection, William Bell, Account Books, Ship *Mary*, Invoice of China Ware for John McVickar, December 4, 1799.) William Milburn lists a set of twenty pieces with only half the usual number of cups. See William Milburn, *Oriental Commerce* . . . (London, 1813), II, 504.

4. The John Carter Brown Library, Brown Papers, Ship *Ann and Hope* MSS, Christopher Bentley, Invoice Book, 1801, p. 68.

5. Milburn, II, 504.

6. Connecticut Historical Society, Photostat of MS Account Book, Amos Porter, 1802.

7. Homer Eaton Keyes, "Lowestoft: What Is It? II. Several Whys and Wherefores," *Antiques*, XIII (May, 1928), 386.

8. Milburn, II, 504. See also JCBL, Brown Papers, Ship *Ann and Hope* MSS, Christopher Bentley, Invoice Book, 1801, p. 68.

9. NYPL, William Law Mercantile Papers, Letters and Accounts of Ship *Lion* (1807–1817), William Law, Invoice of China Ware, 1815.

10. Often a fish dish and drainer are listed in porcelain accounts.

11. Peabody Museum of Salem, Benjamin Shreve MSS, Accounts for Brig *New Hazard*, J. W. Rogers, Boston, to Benjamin Shreve, Canton, May 1, 1815.

12. *Ibid.*, Accounts for Brig *New Hazard*, Mrs. Joseph Peabody, Salem, to Benjamin Shreve, Canton, May 1, 1815.

13. A dish of this last sort with the Nanking pattern is shown in John Robinson, "Blue and White 'India-China,'" *Old-Time New England*, XIV (January, 1924), 115.

14. NYPL, William Law Mercantile Papers, Letters and Accounts of Ship *Lion* (1807–1817), William Bell, Invoice of China Ware for Mr. Christie, 1816.

15. PMS, George Hodges MSS, Accounts for Ship *Union*, Benjamin Hodges, Invoice of China Ware, November 18, 1802.

16. A standing cup is illustrated in *Antiques*, LVI (October, 1949), 248.

17. NYPL, Constable-Pierrepont Collection, William Bell, Account Books, Ship *Eliza*, Invoice of China Ware for John H. Titus, 1806.

18. *Ibid.*

19. *Ibid.*, Invoice for Thomas C. Pearsall, 1806.

20. NYPL, William Law Mercantile Papers, Letters and Accounts of Ship *Lion* (1807–1817), William Law, Invoice of China Ware, October, 1816.

21. MS Collection of Mr. Carrow Thibault, Manifest of the *Empress of China*, November, 1784.

22. NYPL, William Law Mercantile Papers, Letters and Accounts of Ship *Lion* (1807–1817), William Law, Invoice of China Ware, October, 1816.

23. Walter Muir Whitehill, *The East India Marine Society and the Peabody Museum of Salem: A Sesquicentennial History* (Salem, Mass., 1949), facing p. 16.

24. *Ibid.*, pp. 3, 16.

# *N O T E S*

## *to Chapter X*

1. Benjamin Shreve bought a breakfast service of blue-and-white Fitzhugh pattern for himself in 1822. (Peabody Museum of Salem, Benjamin Shreve MSS, Accounts for Brig *Comet*, Invoice, October 17, 1822.)

2. Samuel Chamberlain, *Salem Interiors* (New York, 1950), p. 36.

3. John Robinson, "Blue and White 'India-China,'" *Old-Time New England*, XIV (January, 1924), p. 100. See also John Goldsmith Phillips, *China-Trade Porcelain* (Cambridge, Mass., 1956), p. 58.

4. This fabricated legend is narrated in Harry Barnard, *The Story of the Willow Pattern Plate*, published by Josiah Wedgwood & Sons (Stoke on Trent, n.d.). It is also presented in W. H. Ukers, *All about Tea* (New York, 1935), II, 476.

5. Another pronounced difference between the English "willow pattern" and the

patterns on the Canton ware is that the former was applied to the porcelain by a transfer method, while the latter were always painted on, freehand.

6. J. A. Lloyd Hyde, *Oriental Lowestoft, Chinese Export Porcelain . . .* (Newport, Monmouthshire, 1954), p. 52, and W. G. Gulland, *Chinese Porcelains* (London, 1911), pp. 449–51. It is sometimes said that "Fitzhugh" is a corruption of Foochow, the name of a famous river port in Fukien; this seems highly unlikely.

7. Robinson, p. 100, tries to interpret the Fitzhugh border by giving the explanation which Gulland, *ibid.*, gave in describing the central motif. Thus it is an inaccurate explanation of the border.

8. Hyde, pp. 71–72. See also Phillips, pp. 59–60. Fitzhugh china may not have been made at Ching-tê Chên. Canton ware may have been made at the factories of Shaouking, west of Canton.

9. Soame Jenyns, *Later Chinese Porcelain, the Ch'ing Dynasty (1644–1912)* (London, 1951), pp. 6–8.

10. This process, described by Père d'Entrecolles in the early eighteenth century (1712), is detailed in R. L. Hobson, *The Later Ceramic Wares of China* (London, 1925), pp. 5–6.

11. Geoffrey R. Sayer, *Ching-tê-chên T'ao-Lu; or the Potteries of China. Being a Translation with Notes and an Introduction* (London, 1951), p. 31.

12. That is to say, the Fitzhugh wares were often sent down from the factories without any center pattern, and these were added in Canton in overglaze painting, which was set by a second firing.

13. Jenyns, p. 32.

14. *Ibid.*, p. 33.

15. As the Chinese artists often copied Occidental prints and engravings, which they did not fully understand, in these penciled wares they did not show their best efforts or full capabilities.

16. The New York Public Library, William Law Mercantile Papers, Letters and Accounts of Ship *Lion* (1807–1817), William Law, Invoice of China Ware, July 1, 1815.

17. Sayer, pp. 21, 31.

18. Peabody Museum of Salem, Benjamin Shreve MSS, Accounts for Brig *Comet*, John Prince, Jr., Salem, to Benjamin Shreve, Canton, October 25, 1821.

19. Jenyns, pp. 71–73.

20. PMS, Benjamin Shreve MSS, Accounts for Ship *China*, Benjamin Shreve, Invoice of China Ware, 1817.

21. Montroville Wilson Dickeson, *The American Numismatical Manual of the Currency or Money of the Aborigines, the Colonial, State, and United States Coins* (Philadelphia, 1859), Plates XII and XIV.

22. Homer Eaton Keyes, "American Eagle Lowestoft," *Antiques*, XVII (June, 1930), 531.

23. This particular design with fifteen stars indicates a date after 1792, when Kentucky was admitted, and before 1796, when Tennessee was admitted as the sixteenth state. This seal might have been used on documents for many years, however, without a change in its design for accuracy; nevertheless, the number of stars does fix the earliest date that it could have appeared.

24. Keyes, p. 530.

25. NYPL, William Law Mercantile Papers, Letters and Accounts of Ship *Lion* (1807–1817), National Insurance Company Policy for the Ship *Lion*, March 30, 1816.

26. Dickeson, Plate XIII, Figure 12.

27. Keyes, pp. 531–32.

28. Homer Eaton Keyes, "American Ship Lowestoft," *Antiques*, XIX (June, 1931), 444–45.

29. Irving S. Olds, *Bits and Pieces of American History as Told by a Collection of American Naval and Other Historical Prints and Paintings, Including Portraits of American Naval Commanders and Some Early Views of New York* (New York, 1951), pp. 216, 218–19.

30. The engagement actually took place on September 5.

31. Record of original ownership held in the files of the Peabody Museum of Salem.

32. Ruth Ralston, "Early Republican Decoration on Chinese Lowestoft," *Bulletin of the Metropolitan Museum of Art*, XXII (July, 1927), 191. See also Edgar A. Werner, *Civic List and Constitutional History of the Colony and State of New York* (2d ed.; Albany, N. Y., 1886), Plate I.

33. The colors differ slightly from one service to another, but are fairly standard. Usually Liberty is dressed in dark blue, with a red sash or red-brown cap; Justice is in green, varying from emerald to pale canary, or in yellow or yellow-brown, probably to suggest gold. (Ralston, p. 190.)

34. Homer Eaton Keyes, "State Arms on Chinese Lowestoft," *Antiques*, XVIII (October, 1930), 321.

35. *Ibid.*, p. 323.

36. Hyde, p. 156.

37. Although the author has not found export porcelain with other states' arms reproduced as closely as the New York, Pennsylvania, and New Jersey examples cited, there are extant pieces decorated with elements from other state seals; two known examples are from the seals of New Hampshire and Maryland.

38. Homer Eaton Keyes, "The Cincinnati and Their Porcelain," *Antiques*, XVII (February, 1930), 132–33.

39. *Ibid.*, p. 133.

40. *Ibid.* See also William Sturgis Thomas, *Members of the Society of the Cincinnati, Original, Hereditary and Honorary, with a Brief Account of the Society's History and Aims* (New York, 1929), pp. 7–8, 12.

41. Keyes, "The Cincinnati and Their Porcelain," p. 133.

42. Samuel Shaw, *The Journals of Major Samuel Shaw, the First American Consul at Canton*, edited with a life of the author by Josiah Quincy (Boston, 1847), pp. 198–99. Quincy explained in a footnote (*ibid.*, p. 198) that the "military man" referred to by Shaw was the Count d'Estaing, at the taking of Grenada.

43. Keyes, "The Cincinnati and Their Porcelain," p. 135.

44. "George Washington's Cincinnati Porcelain," *Antiques*, XXXI (May, 1937), 233–34.

45. Hazel E. Cummin, *Handbook, Concord Antiquarian Society* (3d ed.; 1948), p. 53.
46. Claude M. Fuess, "William Eustis," *Dictionary of American Biography*, VI, ed. Allen Johnson and Dumas Malone (New York, 1931), 193–95.
47. Charles H. Hart, *Catalogue of the Engraved Portraits of Washington* (New York, 1904), p. 354.
48. Dickeson, p. 127 and Plate XI, Figure 7.
49. The print was done by the Englishman David Edwin.
50. "Made in China," *Antiques*, XXIX (February, 1936), 52–53.
51. Robert L. Harley, "George Washington Lived Here. Some Early Prints of Mount Vernon, Part I," *Antiques*, XLVII (February, 1945), 105.
52. Samuel W. Woodhouse, Jr., "Martha Washington's China and 'Mr. Van Braam,'" *Antiques*, XXVII (May, 1935), 186–88.
53. *Ibid.*, p. 186.
54. George R. Loehr, "A. E. Van Braam Houckgeest, the First American at the Court of China," *Princeton University Library Chronicle*, XV (Summer, 1954), 183.
55. William A. Crozier, *A Registry of American Families Entitled to Coat Armor from the Earliest to the Present Time* (New York, 1904), p. 47.
56. Ada Walker Camehl, *The Blue-China Book* (New York, 1948), p. 252.
57. "Chinese Export Porcelain . . . ," *Antiques*, LVIII (September, 1950), 2.
58. Stephen Decatur, "The Commodore Decatur Punchbowl," *Antiques*, XXXII (December, 1937), 296–97.
59. "Historic Tea Service to Be Displayed . . . ," *Antiques*, LII (October, 1947), 278.
60. Waldo Hopkins, "General John Stark's Tea Service," *American Collector*, IX (November, 1940), 7.
61. Hyde, p. 83.
62. Homer Eaton Keyes, "The Chinese Lowestoft of Early American Commerce," *Antiques*, XVI (November, 1929), 383.
63. Albert Post, *Popular Freethought in America, 1825–1850* (New York, 1943), Chapter I.
64. Thomas G. Morton, *The History of the Pennsylvania Hospital, 1751–1895* (Philadelphia, 1895), pp. 322–23.
65. *Ibid.*, pp. 324–26.
66. Francis R. Packard, *Some Account of the Pennsylvania Hospital from Its First Rise to the Beginning of the Year 1938* (Philadelphia, 1938), pp. 93–95.
67. Hyde, p. 96. Also, "The Frontispiece," *Antiques*, XXXIV (November, 1938), 237. A punch bowl in the possession of the Germantown Fire Insurance Company is painted with Masonic emblems and the initials *JAP*, probably for Julia Ann Price, who married Thomas Adriance in 1823. See also Wilmington Society of Fine Arts, *Chinese Export Porcelain and Enamels* (Wilmington, Del., 1957), No. 180; and Alan Gowans, "Freemasonry and the Neoclassic Style in America," *Antiques*, LXXVII (February, 1960), 172–75.
68. "A Bonaparte Relic," *The Antiquarian*, II (April, 1924), 17.

*Appendixes*

# APPENDIX I

*Calculations for the Sloop* Experiment, *1786*
*Captain Stewart Dean* *

| | | |
|---|---:|---:|
| Sloop *Experiment* first Cost & outfit | | £ 2200 |
| 20 Shares 1000 Dollars | | 8000 |
| 3000 bbs Ginsang 5/ | | 7500 |
| Madeira Wine & other Goods | | 2300 |
| | | £20000 |
| | | |
| Premium on Dollars 6 pr Ct | £ 480 | |
| ditto of Insurance on £22000 a 10 p Ct | 2200 | |
| Interest for 2 Years on £22680 | | |
| 7 pr Ct per Annum | 3175.4 | 5855.4 |
| | | £25855.4 |
| Sales etc in Canton | | |
| 30000 bls Ginsang a 4/ | | £12000 |
| 20000 Dollars a 4/ | | 8000 |
| Madeira Wine & other Goods | | 3400 |
| | | £23400.4 |
| Off Expenses in Canton | | 2400 |
| to be laid out in Canton | | 21000.4 |
| | | |
| Purchase of Cargo in Canton | | |
| 600 Chests of best Hyson Tea a £ 16 | | 9600 |
| 30000 ps Nankeens     4/6 | | 6750 |
| Taffaties & other Fine Goods | | 4000 |
| China | | 650 |
| | | £21000 |
| Sales in N York | | |
| 600 Chest Hyson Tea at 30 | | £18000 |
| 30000 ps Nankeens     9/ | | 13000 |
| Taffaties & other Fine Goods | | 6000 |
| China | | 1300 |
| | | £38300 |
| Deduct first Cost Vessel & Cargo | £24855.5 | |
| do Agents Coms 5 pr Ct | 1915. | |
| Vessel to pay Portage Bill | | 27770.4 |
| Profits & to pay Interest for 2 Years near 40 pr Ct. | | 10529.16 |

* MS, New-York Historical Society.

[ 227 ]

# APPENDIX II

*Price Current at Canton for Chinaware in 1797 from the Notebook of an Anonymous American Trader of Providence, Rhode Island*

| Exports          Articles | Doll$^s$ | Tale | M | C | Qty |
|---|---|---|---|---|---|
| Tea & Coffee setts of old fashioned 81 p$^s$ | 6 to 9 | | | | Sett |
| Large Urns or flower Jars, richly gilt 2 to 3 feet high | 6 to 17 | | | | each |
| Jars & Tumblers for ornaments to a Chimney, 6 to 18 inch high, 5 in a sett | ¾ to 5 | | | | sett |
| Blue & White dishes, with covers, 3 to a sett | 3 | | | | " |
| Blue round butter tureens, covers & stands | 2 | | | | pair |
| Blue pint sneakers, with covers, handles & plates | 1½ | | | | " |
| Jars, 12, 14 & 18 inches High elegantly ornamented with the Federal Eagle in front—3 to a sett | 14 to 18 | | | | sett |
| Red and White breakfast cups & saucers, gilt | 8 to 9 | | | | 100 ps |
| do tea cups & saucers | 5 to | 4 | 5 | | 100 ps |
| pencil & gilt-do | 4¾ to | 4 | 5 | | " |
| Blue & White do | 5 to | 4 | 5 | | " |
| do large, breakfast tea cups & saucers | 9 to 9½ | | | | " |
| do large, Coffee cups & saucers | 8 to 9 | | | | " |
| Red & White pint bowls, gilt | 7 to 9 | | | | " |
| Blue & White do          do | 8 to 9 | | | | " |
| do 3 pint bowls | 22 | | | | " |
| do 1½ pint do | 9 to 10 | | | | " |
| do quart bowls gilt | | 12 to 13 | | | " |
| do 4 quart do | | 35 to 65 | | | " |
| do 6 do    do    best kind | | 95 to 100 | | | " |
| do 8 do    do        " | 2 to 3 | | | | each |

| Exports          Articles | Doll^s | Tale | M | C | Qty |
|---|---|---|---|---|---|
| Blue & White & red & white Patty pans 3 to a sett | | | 2 | 2 | sett |
| Blue & White desert plates 8 Inches flat | | 5 | | | 100 ps |
| Blue & White desert plates 8 Inches deep | | 5 | 6 | | " |
| Blue & White desert plates 6 Inches flat | | 4 | | | " |
| Blue & White desert plates 6 Inches deep | | 4 | 5 | | " |
| Blue & White dinner plates     flat | | 5 | 8 | | " |
| "        "        "        "        deep | | 6 | 8 | | " |
| Blue & White dinner plates common flat | | 4 | 5 | | 100 ps |
| Blue & White dinner plates common deep | | 5 | | | " |
| Blue & White desert plates common flat | | 4 | | | " |
| Blue & White desert plates common ¼ inch deep | | 4 | 5 | | " |
| Blue & White desert plates common 6 inch flat | | 4 to 3 | 9 | | " |
| Blue & White desert plates common deep | | 4 | | | " |
| 2 quart punch bowls 5 inches deep | | | | 5 | each |
| 4 quart " " common | | 27 | | | 100 |
| Enamelled blue & gilt stem porter cups ½ pint | | 20 | | | " |
| Enamelled blue & gilt stem porter with Fed. Eagle | 40 to 50 | | | | " |
| Nankin blue & white dishes, 6 to a sett viz 1 of 18, 1 of 16, 1 of 14, 1 of 12, & 1 of 10 inches | | 1 | 4 | 4 | sett |
| Nankin blue & White do 10 to a sett viz $\frac{2}{14}$ $\frac{2}{12}$ $\frac{2}{10}$ & $\frac{2}{8}$ Inches | | 2 | 4 | | " |
| Do 12 to a sett $\frac{2}{12}$ $\frac{4}{10}$ & $\frac{6}{8}$ Inch | | 2 | 3 | | " |
| Do 3 Do 1 of 16 1 of 14 & 1 of 10 | | 4 small to 5.5 | | | " |
| Blue & white large high sallad bowls | | | 7 | 5 | each |
| do square beef steak dishes & covers | | | 9 | | " |
| do oval beef steak dishes & covers | | | 7 | 1 | " |

| Exports          Articles | Doll⁸ | Tale | M | C | Qty |
|---|---|---|---|---|---|
| do oval beef steak dishes & covers | | 1 | | | each |
| do Octagon pudding dishes, 3 to a sett | | | 5 | 5 | sett |
| do oval pudding dishes, 3 to a sett | | | 5 | 5 | " |
| do round scalloped & fluted | | | 4 | 0 | " |
| Common blue & white custard cups with tops | 3 to 7 | | | | 100 ps |
| Nankin blue & White, gilt breakfast sett, best kind, viz—12 large cups & saucers 24 | | | | | |
| 1 teapot & top 2 | | | | | |
| 1 sugar dish | | | | | |
| top & stand 3  } 32 ps | 5 | | | | sett |
| 1 bowl & plate 2 | | | | | |
| 1 milk pot 1 | | | | | |
| a set of 36 ps has cake plates & coffee pot over | 4 | | | | " |
| A Tea set of Nankin blue & white gilt | | | | | |
| 12 tea cups & saucers 24 | | | | | |
| 12 coffee do 24 | | | | | |
| 2 cake plates 2 | | | | | |
| 1 slop bowl & saucer 2 | | | | | |
| 1 large tea pot, top & stand 3 | | | | | |
| 1 smaller do do 3  } 65 ps | 6½ | | | | Sett |
| 1 Coffee pot, top & stand 3 | | | | | |
| 1 sugar dish, do do 3 | | | | | |
| 1 milk pot 1 | | | | | |
| A dinner sett, Nankin blue & white China, viz, | | | | | |
| 6 doz. large flat plates 72 | | | | | |
| 2 doz " soup " 24 | | | | | |
| 2 doz small desert do 24 | | | | | |
| 8 pudding dishes 8 | | | | | |
| 2 large Tureens, dishes & tops 6  } 172 ps | 22 | | | | " |
| 2 smaller do do 6 | | | | | |
| 16 dishes various sizes 16 | | | | | |
| 6 sauce boats & stands 12 | | | | | |
| 4 Salts 4 | | | | | |
| Large Nankin Blue & White tureens, dish & top 3 ps | | 1 | 4 | | each sett |

| Exports       Articles | Doll[s] | Tale | M | C | Qty |
|---|---|---|---|---|---|
| do . . . . second size do do | | 1 | | | "   " |
| do Hot water plates, large size | | | 4 to 3 | | each |
| Blue & White fruit baskets, handles & stands, open work, 2 to a set | 2 to 4.00 | | | | sett |
| Tea setts of China, agreeable to Pattern, figure & painting | various prices | | | | |
| Breakfast setts of Canton, blue & gilt | 2¼ to 3 | | | | " |
| Common blue & white Breakfast setts, viz— | | | | | |
| 6 large coffee cups & saucers  12 | | | | | |
| 1 Teapot  2 | | | | | |
| 1 Bowl & plate  2  } 20 ps | 2 | | | | " |
| 1 milk pot  1 | | | | | |
| 1 sugar dish top & stand  3 | | | | | |
| Tea setts of china Common, viz— | | | | | |
| 12 tea cups & saucers  24 | | | | | |
| 6 coffee cups  6 | | | | | |
| 1 sugar dish top & stand  3 | | | | | |
| 1 tea pot top & stand  3 | | | | | |
| 1 tea Cannister, top & stand  3  } 43 ps | 1¾ to 2½ | | | | Sett |
| 1 bowl & saucer  2 | | | | | |
| 1 cake plate—1 milk pot  2 | | | | | |
| A Tea sett of china of 45 ps contains 1 tea cup more than a sett of 43 ps | 1¾ to 3 | | | | " |
| A do of 49 ps contains 6 coffee cups more than 1 of 43 ps | | | | | |
| Tea setts of China of 53 pieces, viz. | | | | | |
| 12 tea cups & saucers  24 | | | | | |
| 12 coffee cups & 6 do  18 | | | | | |
| 2 cake plates  2 | | | | | |
| 1 bowl & saucer  2  } 53 ps | 4 to 6 | | | | " |
| 1 teapot, top & stand  3 | | | | | |
| 1 sugar dish, top & stand  3 | | | | | |
| 1 Milk pot  1 | | | | | |
| Tea setts of China 45 ps same as mentioned | 4¾ to 7 | | | | " |
| Nankin blue & white gilt custard cups, tops & handles | | 10 | | | 100 |

| Exports            Articles | Doll$^s$ | Tale | M | C | Qty |
|---|---|---|---|---|---|
| Wash hand basons | 1 | | | | each |
| Large China spitting Jars | 3 | | | | pair |
| Chimney pieces | 3 | | | | " |
| ½ pint mugs elegantly flowered & gilt, with Fed. eagle | 3 | | | | " |
| Nankin blue & white common Table setts China 168 ps | | 15 | | | sett |
| Nankin blue & white common Table half setts viz. | | | | | |
| 8 dishes                8 ⎫ | | | | | |
| 1 large Tureen         3 ⎪ | | | | | |
| 3 doz flat plates      36 ⎪ | | | | | |
| 1 doz. soup–do       12 ⎬ 67 ps | | 7 | | | " |
| 2 pudding dishes     2 ⎪ | | | | | |
| 2 Salts                  2 ⎪ | | | | | |
| 4 Butter boats        4 ⎭ | | | | | |
| Best enamelled mugs, 3 to a sett, 1 qt, 1 pt, 1 of ½ pint | ¾ to 1 | | | | " |
| Pencil tea cups & saucers, small | | | 4 | | 100 ps |
| Small Butter Turreens with tops & stands | 8 | | | | " |
| Blue & White tea pots, large size | | 1 | 7 | | each |
| Sauce Boats | | 1 | | | each |
| Large pint Bowles with Saucers | 14 | | | | 100 ps |
| Sallad or deep pudding dishes, 2 to a sett | | | 3 | 3 | sett |
| Common China Mugs, 3 to a sett, 2 1 pt & ½ pt | | | 4 | 3 | " |
| Blue & White teapots, 3 to a sett 3 sizes | | | 6 | 3 | " |
| Best Nankin, blue & white, gilt, tea setts of 45 ps | 5 | | | | Sett |
| Small Oyster Turreens, tops & stands | | 10 | | | 100 ps |
| Large   do   do next to soup  do | | 30 | | | " |
| Egg Cups | | 6 to 8 | | | " |
| Masonic Bowls from 1 to 1½ gallons | 2 to 3 | | | | each |
| do    Mugs  3 in a sett | 1¾ | | | | sett |
| do    Pint Mugs | 20 | | | | 100 ps |
| Lacquered knife Cases & for Spoons | 14 | | | | pair |

# Bibliography

# MANUSCRIPTS

The manuscript material consulted and used in this study is located in various libraries, historical societies, and museums, as well as in private collections; hence the arrangement of this bibliography is according to location.

## I. IN PRIVATE COLLECTIONS

Porter, Amos. Account Book, 1802. In possession of Mrs. Harold H. Winship, Wethersfield, Connecticut. (Photostat at The Connecticut Historical Society, Hartford, Connecticut.)

Ralston, R., Jr. Invoice of China Ware, Canton, January 15, 1817, on ship *Pacific*. In possession of Mrs. Benjamin Rush, Philadelphia, Pennsylvania.

Ship *Empress of China*. Manifest, Canton, November, 1784. In the possession of Mr. Carrow Thibault, Ardmore, Pennsylvania.

## II. THE JOHN CARTER BROWN LIBRARY, BROWN UNIVERSITY, PROVIDENCE, RHODE ISLAND

Brown Papers:
    Ship *Ann and Hope* MSS.
        Division of China Ware, 1796–1799. V-A65 (1800).
        Invoice Book, 1800.
        Invoice Book, 1801.

    Ship *Arthur* MSS.
        Account Book, 1803–1804.
        Transactions, September, 1807, to June, 1809.

Brown and Ives, Providence, to John Bennock, Newport: November 18, 1796; May 11, 1797.

Brown and Ives, Providence, to Charles C. Hoskins and Company, Newport: September 3, 1807; October 6, 1807; May 4, 1809; July 12, 1809; July 17, 1809; July 27, 1809.

Brown and Ives, Providence, to Hazard and Robinson, Charleston: June 11, 1791; November 14, 1793.

Hazard and Robinson, Charleston, to Brown, Benson and Ives, Providence, October 5, 1793.

Hoskins, Charles C., and Company, Newport, to Brown and Ives, Providence, September 29, 1807.

III. ESSEX INSTITUTE,

SALEM, MASSACHUSETTS

Derby, Elias Hasket. Account Book, 1785–1796.
Pickman, Benjamin, Jr. Invoice Book, 1789–1791.
Waldo, Charles F. "Remarks on a voyage from Boston to Canton." Ship *Indus.*
    1802.

IV. GIRARD COLLEGE LIBRARY,

PHILADELPHIA, PENNSYLVANIA

Girard, Stephen. Invoice Book, 1811–1823.
———. Bills and Receipts, China and Glassware, 1788–1827.

V. HAVERFORD COLLEGE LIBRARY,

HAVERFORD, PENNSYLVANIA

The Charles Roberts Autograph Collection:
    James Josiah, ship *Asia*, to John Barry, Canton, September 25, 1788. (Courtesy
    of William Bell Clark.)

VI. THE HISTORICAL SOCIETY OF PENNSYLVANIA,

PHILADELPHIA, PENNSYLVANIA

Fuller, Benjamin. Letter Books: June 5, 1784, to August 9, 1787; August 18, 1787,
    to September 24, 1791.
Graff, Charles. "Diary of Chas. Graff of Phila. 1804–1805." Ship *China Packet,*
    1804–1805.
Hepburn Collection, Barry Papers:
    Barry, John. Memorandum relating to the trade at Canton. January 7 to June 4,
        1789.
    China Letter Book:
        John Barry, Canton, to Mrs. Isaac Hazlehurst, Philadelphia, January 6,
            1789.
        Hugh Doyle, Philadelphia, to Barry, Canton, December 14, 1787.
        James Hill, Philadelphia, to Barry, Canton, December 13, 1787.
        Henry Gurney, Tusculam, to Barry, Canton, December 11, 1787.
        John Nixon, Philadelphia, to Barry, Canton, December 11, 1787.
Society Collection:
    Bill of Lading on Six Cases of China Ware shipped to Messrs. Fletcher and
        Gardiner, Philadelphia, October 25, 1825, New York.
Woodhouse Collection, Ships' Papers:
    Ship *America*. Inward Entry, 1800.
    Ship *Argonaut*. Invoice, 1793.

# Bibliography

Ship *Caledonia*. Report and Manifest of Cargo, 1817.
Ship *Fame*. Bill of Lading, 1801.
Ship *Hebe*. Manifest, 1806.
Ship *Ohio*. Manifest, 1804.
Ship *Rousseau*. Manifest, 1804.
Ship *Wooddrop Sims*. List of Goods Imported, 1797.

## VII. THE LIBRARY OF CONGRESS, MANUSCRIPT DIVISION, WASHINGTON, D. C.

Latimer, John R. Correspondence and Business Papers, 1820–1833.
Russell, Samuel, and Company. Letters, 1818–1840.

## VIII. THE LIBRARY COMPANY OF PHILADELPHIA, PHILADELPHIA, PENNSYLVANIA

Waln Papers:
  McNeilledge, Alexander. "Notes on the China Trade, May 1, 1818."
  Waln, Robert, Jr. "China: Comprehending a View of the Origin, Antiquity, History, Religion, Morals, Government, Laws, Population, Literature, Drama, Festivals, Women, Infanticide, Beggars, Manners, Customs, etc. of that Empire with Remarks on the European Embassies to China, and the Policy of sending a Mission from the United States to the Court of Pekin, to which is added, a Commercial Appendix containing a Synopsis of the Trade of Portugal, Holland, England, France, Denmark, Ostend, Sweden, Prussia, Trieste, & Spain in China & India and an Account of the Commerce of the United States in the East; with a full description of the American Trade to Canton, its Rise, Progress, & present State; with mercantile information useful to the Chinese Trader & General Merchant. Written on the ship *Caledonia* at Sea, February 2, 1820."
  Waln, Robert, MSS: "Collections for the Formation of Letters from Canton from various Authors, not to be made use of without reference to the original, December 20, 1819."
  Letter Books: September 24, 1784, to February 23, 1808; January 1, 1798, to June 8, 1802; June 10, 1802, to December 12, 1806; February 27, 1808, to December 30, 1814; January 4, 1805, to May 12, 1819.
  Memo Book, September, 1819, to January, 1820.

## IX. MARYLAND HALL OF RECORDS, ANNAPOLIS, MARYLAND

Baltimore County, Maryland, Inventories, 1772–1801. (Microfilm copy, Joseph Downs Manuscript Library, Winterthur Museum.)

### X. MARYLAND HISTORICAL SOCIETY, BALTIMORE, MARYLAND

Baltimore Exchange Reading Room Records of Arrivals and Clearances, July 23 to November 11, 1835.

Baltimore East India Company. Draft of Articles of Association, January 27, 1807.

Baltimore Entry Records, 1833–1835.

Buckler, William. Account Books, 1788–1832; Journal, 1790–1796.

Davidson, John and Samuel. Ledger, 1787–1795, Annapolis.

Ship *Pallas*. Manifest, 1785.

Ridgely, Charles, MSS:
    Bill with Frederick Thornhill, January 29, 1796.
    Account with Peter Frick, January 13, 1797, to March 22, 1797.
    Account with Peter Frick, December 7, 1790, to January 24, 1792.

### XI. MASSACHUSETTS HISTORICAL SOCIETY, BOSTON, MASSACHUSETTS

Perkins, Thomas H., MSS, 1789–1853:
    Bumstead, E. Blotter A.
    ———. Journal A.
    Perkins, C. J. and T. H., and Sons. Invoice Inward.
    Perkins, J. and T. H., and Sons. Invoice Inward.
    ———. Extracts from Letter Book, 1786–1838.
Ward, Thomas W. Papers, 1760–1816.

### XII. THE NEW-YORK HISTORICAL SOCIETY, NEW YORK, N. Y.

Sloop *Experiment*. Calculations of Captain Stewart Dean, 1786.

Wolcott, Oliver, and Company. Account Books: 1804–1810; 1808–1815.

### XIII. THE NEW YORK PUBLIC LIBRARY, MANUSCRIPT DIVISION, NEW YORK, N. Y.

Constable-Pierrepont Collection:
    Bell, William. Account Books.
        Ship *Washington*, 1790.
        Ship *Mary*, 1799.
        Ship *Devotion*, 1803.
        Ship *Eliza*, 1805; 1806.
        Ship *Canton*, 1809.
        Ship *William and John*, 1816.

Pierrepont, Hezekiah B. "Notes on the Trade of China, taken chiefly from Observations made at Canton in the Season of 1796 & corrected in London, June 1798." 2d copy.

Cuyler, Philip. Ledger, 1763–1794.

Fleming, Samuel. Letter Book, 1782–1790.

Fogg Brothers (Merchants of Boston) Mercantile Papers:
Ayres, Howard. Memorandum on Trade between the United States and China, 1840–1910, for the New York Public Library, 1932. Typed copy.

Hill, Samuel. "Journal and Log of the *Ophelia* and *Packet*, 1815–1822."

Law, William, Mercantile Papers. Letters and Accounts, ship *Lion*, 1807–1817.

Low, A. A. and Seth, Mercantile Papers. Bills of Lading, 1834–1875.

Wolcott, Oliver. Letter Book, March 16, 1803, to December 5, 1808.

XIV. PEABODY MUSEUM OF SALEM,
SALEM, MASSACHUSETTS

Hodges, Benjamin, MSS:
Ships *Betsey*, *Astrea*, and others. Accounts, 1781–1803 and 1784–1801.
Ship *Astrea*. Accounts, 1787.
Brig *William and Henry*. Accounts, 1788–1789.
Ship *Three Sisters*. Accounts, 1788.
Ship *Grand Turk*. Accounts, 1792.

Hodges, George, MSS:
Ship *Union*. Accounts, n.d. [c. 1802–1804] and 1802–1803.

Shreve, Benjamin, MSS:
Brig *New Hazard*. Accounts, 1815.
Brig *Canton*. Accounts, 1817.
Brig *Governor Endicott*. Accounts, 1819–1821.
Brig *Comet*. Accounts, 1822.
Ship *Minerva*. Accounts, 1813.
Ship *China*. Accounts, 1817.
Ship *Packet*. Accounts, n.d.
Waldo, Edward W., Salem, to Shreve, Canton, March 16, 1815.

Ward, Thomas W. Ship *Minerva* Papers, Canton, 1809.

XV. RHODE ISLAND HISTORICAL SOCIETY,
PROVIDENCE, RHODE ISLAND

Notebook of an Anonymous American Trader, of Providence, Rhode Island, 1797. (Microfilm M–6, Joseph Downs Manuscript Library, Winterthur Museum.)

XVI. UNIVERSITY OF DELAWARE,
MEMORIAL LIBRARY, NEWARK, DELAWARE

Latimer Papers. Correspondence and Business Papers of John R. Latimer, 1821–1834.

XVII. WINTERTHUR MUSEUM,
JOSEPH DOWNS MANUSCRIPT LIBRARY,
WINTERTHUR, DELAWARE

Microfilm copy of Baltimore County, Maryland, Inventories, 1772–1801. (Originals, Maryland Hall of Records, Annapolis, Maryland.)
Microfilm copy of the notebook of an anonymous trader, of Providence, Rhode Island, 1797. (Original, Rhode Island Historical Society.)
Vanden Heuvel, John. Inventory of Estate, New York, May, 1826.

# NEWSPAPERS

*Federal Gazette & Baltimore Daily Advertiser*, July 1, 1808.
*The Maryland Journal, and the Baltimore Advertiser*, September 15, 1785.
*The Pennsylvania Gazette*, June 24, 1789.
*The Pennsylvania Packet, and Daily Advertiser*, May 16, 1785, and August 8, 1787.

# BOOKS

Albion, Robert Greenhalgh. *The Rise of New York Port (1815–1860)*. New York, 1939.
Barnard, Harry. *The Story of the Willow Pattern Plate*. Stoke on Trent, England, n.d.
Bayer, Herbert (ed.). *World Geographic Atlas, a Composite of Man's Environment*. Chicago, 1953.
Bemrose, Geoffrey. *Nineteenth Century English Pottery and Porcelain*. London, 1952.
Blunt, Joseph. *The Shipmaster's Assistant and Commercial Digest* . . . 12th ed. New York, 1864.
Bolton, Charles Knowles. *Bolton's American Armory; a Record of Coats of Arms Which Have Been in Use Within the Present Bounds of the United States*. Boston, 1927.
Brayley, Edward Wedlake. *Illustrations of Her Majesty's Palace at Brighton; Formerly the Pavilion: Executed by the Command of King George the Fourth under the Supervision of John Nash, Esq., Architect; to Which Is Prefixed, a History of the Palace*. London, 1938.
Brown, D. Mackensie (ed.). *China Trade Days in California; Selected Letters from the Thompson Papers, 1832–1863*. Berkeley, Cal., 1947.
Burke, Edmund. *Speeches and Letters on American Affairs*. "Everyman's Library." London, 1908.
Burling, Judith, and Hart, Arthur. *Chinese Art*. New York, 1953.
Camehl, Ada Walker. *The Blue-China Book*. New York, 1948.

# Bibliography

Cammann, Schuyler. *China's Dragon Robes.* New York, 1952.

Chamberlain, Samuel. *Salem Interiors; Two Centuries of New England Taste and Decoration.* New York, 1950.

Clark, William Bell. *Gallant John Barry, 1745–1803; the Story of a Naval Hero of Two Wars.* New York, 1938.

Clement, Arthur W. *Notes on American Ceramics, 1607–1943.* Brooklyn, N. Y., 1944.

Crozier, William A. *A Registry of American Families Entitled to Coat Armor from the Earliest to the Present Time.* New York, 1904.

Cummin, Hazel E. *Handbook, Concord Antiquarian Society.* 3d ed. Concord, Mass., 1948.

Danton, George H. *The Culture Contacts of the United States and China; the Earliest Sino-American Culture Contacts, 1784–1844.* New York, 1931.

Dayton, Fred E. *Steamboat Days.* New York, 1925.

Defoe, Daniel. *A Tour Through the Whole Island of Great Britain.* London, 1724.

Dennett, Tyler. *Americans in Eastern Asia; a Critical Study of the Policy of the United States with Reference to China, Japan, and Korea in the 19th Century.* New York, 1922.

Dickeson, Montroville Wilson. *The American Numismatical Manual of the Currency or Money of the Aborigines, and Colonial, State, and United States Coins.* Philadelphia, 1859.

Dillon, Edward. *Porcelain.* New York, 1904.

Downs, Joseph, and Scherer, Margaret R. *The China Trade and Its Influences.* New York, 1941.

Dulles, Foster Rhea. *The Old China Trade.* Boston, 1930.

Earle, Alice Morse. *China Collecting in America.* New York, 1892.

Eberlein, Harold Donaldson, and Ramsdell, Roger Wearne. *The Practical Book of Chinaware.* New York, 1925.

Fanning, Edmund. *Voyages Round the World, with Selected Sketches of Voyages to the South Seas, North and South Pacific Oceans, China. . . .* New York, 1833.

Felt, Joseph B. *An Historical Account of Massachusetts Currency.* Boston, 1839.

Franklin, Benjamin. *The Writings of Benjamin Franklin, 1783–1788.* Edited with a life and introduction by Albert Henry Smyth. Vol. IX. New York, 1906.

Garner, Sir Harry. *Oriental Blue and White.* London, 1954.

Goodrich, L. Carrington. *A Short History of the Chinese People.* 3d ed. New York, 1959.

Gottesman, Rita S. *The Arts and Crafts in New York, 1777–1799; Advertisements and News Items from New York City Newspapers.* New York, 1954.

Greenbie, Sydney, and Greenbie, Marjorie Barstow. *Gold of Ophir; the China Trade in the Making of America.* 2d ed. New York, 1937.

Gulland, W. G. *Chinese Porcelains.* London, 1911.

Gützlaff, Charles. *A Sketch of Chinese History, Ancient & Modern; Comprising a Retrospect of the Foreign Intercourse and Trade with China.* 2 vols. London, 1834.

Halsey, R. T. H., and Cornelius, Charles O. *A Handbook of the American Wing.* Edited by Joseph Downs. 7th ed. New York, 1942.

Hart, Charles H. *Catalogue of the Engraved Portraits of Washington*. New York, 1904.

Hayes, Carlton J. H., Baldwin, Marshall Whitehead, and Cole, Charles Woolsey. *History of Europe*. New York, 1949.

Hedges, James B. *The Browns of Providence Plantations, Colonial Years*. Cambridge, Mass., 1952.

Henderson, Daniel. *Yankee Ships in China Seas; Adventures of Pioneer Americans in the Troubled Far East*. New York, 1946.

Hickey, William. *Memoirs of William Hickey, 1749–1809*. Edited by Alfred Spencer. New York, 1921.

Hirth, Friedrich, and Rockhill, W. W. *Chau Ju-Kua: His Work on the Chinese and Arab Trade in the Twelfth and Thirteenth Centuries*. St. Petersburg, Russia, 1911.

Hobson, R. L. *The Later Ceramic Wares of China*. London, 1925.

Honey, W. B. *The Ceramic Art of China and Other Countries of the Far East*. London, 1949.

———. *European Ceramic Art from the End of the Middle Ages to about 1815*. London, 1952.

———. *French Porcelain of the 18th Century*. London, 1950.

Hunt, Freeman. *Lives of American Merchants*. New York, 1858.

Hunter, William C. *The Fan Kwae at Canton Before Treaty Days, 1825–1844*. Hong Kong, 1911.

Hutchinson, William. *A Treatise on Practical Seamanship*. . . . London, 1777.

Hyde, J. A. Lloyd. *Oriental Lowestoft, Chinese Export Porcelain, Porcelaine de la C^ie des Indes; with Special Reference to the Trade with China and the Porcelain Decorated for the American Market*. Newport, Monmouthshire, England, 1954.

Jenyns, [R.] Soame. *Later Chinese Porcelain, the Ch'ing Dynasty (1644–1912)*. London, 1951.

Jourdain, Margaret, and Jenyns, R. Soame. *Chinese Export Art in the Eighteenth Century*. London, 1950.

Kirkland, Edward C. *A History of American Economic Life*. New York, 1932.

Krout, John Allen, and Fox, Dixon Ryan. *The Completion of Independence, 1790–1830*. Vol. V of *A History of American Life*. New York, 1944.

Latourette, Kenneth Scott. *The Chinese, Their History and Culture*. 3d ed. New York, 1957.

———. *A Short History of the Far East*. New York, 1946.

Lee, Cazenove Gardner, Jr. *Lee Chronicle: Studies of the Early Generations of the Lees of Virginia*. Edited by Dorothy Mills Parker. New York, 1957.

Lindsey, Benjamin J. *Old Marblehead Sea Captains and the Ships in Which They Sailed*. Marblehead, Mass., 1915.

Loines, Elma (ed.). *The China Trade Post-Bag of the Seth Low Family of Salem and New York, 1829–1873*. Manchester, Maine, 1953.

Lytle, William M. *Merchant Steam Vessels of the United States, 1807–1868*. Mystic, Conn., 1952.

McMaster, John Bach. *The Life and Times of Stephen Girard, Mariner and Merchant*. 2 vols. Philadelphia, 1918.

# Bibliography

Mankowitz, Wolf, and Haggar, Reginald G. *The Concise Encyclopedia of English Pottery and Porcelain.* New York, [1957].

Milburn, William. *Oriental Commerce; Containing a Geographical Description of the Principal Places in the East Indies, China, and Japan; with Their Products, Manufactures, and Trade. . . .* Vol. II. London, 1813.

Monkhouse, Cosmo. *A History and Description of Chinese Porcelain.* London, 1901.

Morison, Samuel Eliot. *The Maritime History of Massachusetts, 1783–1860.* Boston, 1921.

Morse, Hosea Ballou. *The Chronicles of the East India Company Trading to China, 1635–1834.* Vols. II–V. Cambridge, Mass., 1926–1929.

———. *The Gilds of China, with an Account of the Gild Merchant or Co-hong of Canton.* London, 1909.

———. *The Trade and Administration of the Chinese Empire.* London, 1908.

Morse, Hosea Ballou, and MacNair, Harley Farnsworth. *Far Eastern International Relations.* Boston, 1931.

Morton, Thomas G. *The History of the Pennsylvania Hospital, 1751–1895.* Philadelphia, 1895.

Olds, Irving S. *Bits and Pieces of American History as Told by a Collection of American Naval and Other Historical Prints and Paintings, Including Portraits of American Naval Commanders and Some Early Views of New York.* New York, 1951.

Olschki, Leonardo. *Marco Polo's Precursors.* Baltimore, 1943.

Orange, James. *The Chater Collection: Pictures Relating to China, Hongkong, Macao, 1655–1860.* London, 1924.

Owens, Hamilton. *Baltimore on the Chesapeake.* Garden City, N. Y., 1941.

Packard, Francis R. *Some Account of the Pennsylvania Hospital from Its First Rise to the Beginning of the Year 1938.* Philadelphia, 1938.

Paine, Ralph D. *Ships and Sailors of Old Salem; the Record of a Brilliant Era of American Achievement.* New York, 1909.

Parkinson, C. Northcote. *Trade in the Eastern Seas, 1793–1813.* Cambridge, England, 1937.

Peabody, Robert E. *The Log of the Grand Turks.* Boston, 1926.

Phillips, John Goldsmith. *China-Trade Porcelain; an Account of Its Historical Background, Manufacture, and Decoration and a Study of the Helena Woolworth McCann Collection.* Cambridge, Mass., 1956.

Pitkin, Timothy. *A Statistical View of the Commerce of the United States of America. . . .* 2d ed. New York, 1817.

Polo, Marco. *The Book of Ser Marco Polo.* Translated and edited with notes by Sir Henry Yule. 2 vols. London, 1871.

———. *The Description of the World.* Translated and annotated by A. C. Moule and Paul Pelliot. London, 1938.

Post, Albert. *Popular Freethought in America, 1825–1850.* New York, 1943.

Prime, Alfred Coxe. *The Arts and Crafts in Philadelphia, Maryland, and South Carolina, 1786–1800.* Series Two. Topsfield, Mass., 1932.

Ritter, Abraham. *Philadelphia and Her Merchants. . . .* Philadelphia, 1860.

Rydell, Raymond A. *Cape Horn to the Pacific; the Rise and Decline of an Ocean Highway.* Berkeley, Cal., 1952.

Savage, George. *18th-Century English Porcelain.* New York, 1952.

——. *Porcelain Through the Ages.* New York, 1952.

Sayer, Geoffrey R. *Ching-tê-chên T'ao-lu; or the Potteries of China. Being a Translation with Notes and an Introduction.* London, 1951.

Scharf, J. Thomas. *The Chronicles of Baltimore, Being a Complete History of "Baltimore Town" and Baltimore City.* Baltimore, 1874.

Schmidt, Robert. *Porcelain as an Art and a Mirror of Fashion.* Translated by W. A. Thorpe. London, 1932.

Seybert, Adam. *Statistical Annals of the United States. . . .* Philadelphia, 1818.

Shaw, Samuel. *The Journals of Major Samuel Shaw, the First American Consul at Canton.* Edited with a life of the author by Josiah Quincy. Boston, 1847.

Simpson, Henry. *The Lives of Eminent Philadelphians, Now Deceased, Collected from Original and Authentic Sources.* Philadelphia, 1859.

Singleton, Esther. *Social New York under the Georges, 1714-1776.* New York, 1902.

Spargo, John. *Early American Pottery and China.* New York, 1926.

——. *The Potters and Potteries of Bennington.* Boston, 1926.

*Stephens's Philadelphia Directory, for 1796. . . .* Philadelphia, [1796].

Thomas, William Sturgis. *Members of the Society of the Cincinnati, Original, Hereditary and Honorary, with a Brief Account of the Society's History and Aims.* New York, 1929.

Tudor-Craig, Sir Algernon. *Armorial Porcelain of the Eighteenth Century.* London, 1925.

Ukers, W. H. *All about Tea.* Vol. II. New York, 1935.

Watkins, Lura Woodside. *Early New England Potters and Their Wares.* Cambridge, Mass., 1950.

Werner, Edgar A. *Civic List and Constitutional History of the Colony and State of New York.* 2d ed. Albany, N. Y., 1886.

Wescott, Thompson. *The Historic Mansions and Buildings of Philadelphia with Some Notice of Their Owners and Occupants.* Philadelphia, 1895.

Whedbee, Thomas Courtenay Jenkins. *The Port of Baltimore in the Making, 1828 to 1878.* Baltimore, 1953.

Wheeler, Sir Robert Eric Mortimer. *Rome Beyond the Imperial Frontiers.* New York, 1954.

Whitehill, Walter Muir. *The East India Marine Society and the Peabody Museum of Salem: A Sesquicentennial History.* Salem, Mass., 1949.

The Wilmington Society of the Fine Arts. *Chinese Export Porcelain and Enamels.* Wilmington, Del., 1957.

Winterbotham, W. *An Historical, Geographical and Philosophical View of the Chinese Empire. . . .* Vol. II. Philadelphia, 1796.

Zeis, Paul Maxwell. *American Shipping Policy.* Princeton, N. J., 1938.

Zieber, Eugene. *Heraldry in America.* Philadelphia, 1895.

# Bibliography

## ARTICLES

Aga-Oglu, Kamer. "Late Ming and Early Ch'ing Porcelain Fragments from Archaeological Sites in Florida," *The Florida Anthropologist*, VIII (December, 1955).

Berkley, Henry J. "A Register of the Cabinet Makers and Allied Trades in Maryland, as Shown by the Newspapers and Directories, 1746 to 1820," *Maryland Historical Magazine*, XXV (March, 1930), 1–27.

"A Bonaparte Relic," *Antiquarian*, II (April, 1924), 17.

Brunhouse, R. L. "Lascars in Pennsylvania: A Side-Light on the China Trade," *Pennsylvania History*, VII (January, 1940), 20–30.

Buhler, Kathryn C. "A Recent Gift of Chinese Export Porcelain," *Bulletin of the Boston Museum of Fine Arts*, LIII (February, 1955), 10–11.

Butler, Joseph T. "Chinese Porcelain Figures of Westerners," *Antiques*, LXXIX (February, 1961), 170–73.

Cammann, Schuyler. "The Interchange of East and West," *Asia in Perspective* (Philadelphia, 1959).

"The China Trade of Baltimore, an Exhibition Illustrating 165 Years of Commerce with the Orient at the Maryland Historical Society, June 15 to October 15, 1950," *Maryland History Notes*, VIII (August, 1950), 1–4.

"A Chinese Lowestoft Punch Bowl," *Bulletin of the Metropolitan Museum of Art*, XXVII (March, 1932), 82–83.

"The City Punch Bowl," *Bulletin of the Metropolitan Museum of Art*, VII (September, 1912), 165.

Copeland, Charles H. P. "To the Farthest Port of the Rich East," *American Heritage*, VI (February, 1955), 10–18, 114, 115.

Cornelius, Charles O. "Sino-Lowestoft," *Bulletin of the Metropolitan Museum of Art*, XXI (November, 1926), 264–66.

Cutler, Carl C. "A Brief Survey of the Early Shipping Industry in the Northern States," *Marine Historical Association Publication*, I (March, 1932), 63–83.

Davidson, Marshall. "The China Trade," *Antiques*, XXXIX (May, 1941), 234–37.

Decatur, Stephen. "The Commodore Decatur Punchbowl," *Antiques*, XXXII (December, 1937), 296–97.

Downs, Joseph. "The China Trade," *Bulletin of the Metropolitan Museum of Art*, XXXVI (July, 1941), 156–58.

———. "Designs on a Punch Bowl," *Bulletin of the Metropolitan Museum of Art*, XXVIII (August, 1933), 146.

———. "Reinstallation of a Chinese Lowestoft Service," *Bulletin of the Metropolitan Museum of Art*, XXXV (October, 1940), 205.

"The Editor's Attic: Chinese Export Porcelain," *Antiques*, XL (August, 1941), 108.

"The Editor's Attic: The Frontispiece [Cincinnati Porcelain]," *Antiques*, XXX (October, 1936), 148–50.

"The Editor's Attic: The Frontispiece [Masonic Porcelain]," *Antiques*, XXXIV (November, 1938), 236–38.

"The Editor's Attic: George Washington's Cincinnati China," *Antiques*, XXXI (May, 1937), 233–34.

"The Editor's Attic: Made in China," *Antiques*, XXIX (February, 1936), 52–53.

Fairbank, J. K., and Teng, S. Y. "On the Ch'ing Tributary System," *Harvard Journal of Asiatic Studies*, VI (June, 1941), 135 ff.

"Five American Rooms," *Antiques*, L (October, 1946), 244.

Fuess, Claude M. "William Eustis," *Dictionary of American Biography*, VI (New York, 1931), 193–95.

Gillingham, Harrold E. "A Lost Set of Eighteenth-Century Oriental Lowestoft," *Antiques*, XXXIV (October, 1938), 198–99.

Gourley, Hugh, III. "History in Houses: Carrington House, Providence, Rhode Island," *Antiques*, LXXIX (February, 1961), 182–86.

Gowans, Alan. "Freemasonry and the Neoclassic Style in America," *Antiques*, LXXVII (February, 1960), 172–75.

Harley, Robert L. "George Washington Lived Here. Some Early Prints of Mount Vernon, Part I." *Antiques*, XLVII (February, 1945), 103–5.

"Historic Tea Service to Be Displayed," *Antiques*, LII (October, 1947), 278.

Hopkins, Waldo. "General John Stark's Tea Service," *American Collector*, IX (November, 1940), 7.

Hummel, Arthur W. "The Journal of Harriet Low," *The Library of Congress Quarterly Journal*, II (June, 1945), 45–60.

Hummel, Charles F. "John R. Latimer and the China Trade," *Winterthur Newsletter*, IV (December 10, 1958), 2.

Hyde, J. A. Lloyd. "The Yesterday and Today of Oriental Lowestoft," *Antiques*, XIX (June, 1931), 447–48.

Jacobsen, Mrs. Jacques Noel. "Lowestoft China," *Antiques*, LII (July, 1947), 31–33.

Jones, Edward S. "The Willow Pattern: New Legends for Old," *Antiques*, LXVII (January, 1955), 50–52.

Keyes, Homer Eaton. "American Eagle Lowestoft," *Antiques*, XVII (June, 1930), 530–33.

———. "American Ship Lowestoft," *Antiques*, XIX (June, 1931), 441–46.

———. "The Chinese Lowestoft of Early American Commerce," *Antiques*, XVI (November, 1929), 381–85.

———. "The Cincinnati and Their Porcelain," *Antiques*, XVII (February, 1930), 132–36.

———. "Lowestoft: Exclusively American," *Antiques*, XXI (April, 1932), 171–75.

———. "Lowestoft: What Is It? I. Concerning a Number of Misapprehensions," *Antiques*, XIII (March, 1928), 206–10.

———. "Lowestoft: What Is It? II. Several Whys and Wherefores," *Antiques*, XIII (May, 1928), 384–88.

———. "Lowestoft: What Is It? III. Centres of Manufacture, and a Classification," *Antiques*, XIV (November, 1928), 422–26.

———. "Lowestoft: What Is It? V. Genre Designs." *Antiques*, XV (June, 1929), 487–92.

———. "Lowestoft: What Is It? VI. Ship Designs," *Antiques*, XVI (August, 1929), 109–11.

——. "Quality in Oriental Lowestoft," *Antiques*, XXXII (December, 1937), 290–94.

——. "State Arms on Chinese Lowestoft," *Antiques*, XVIII (October, 1930), 321–23.

Kimball, Gertrude S. "The East-India Trade of Providence from 1787–1807," *Papers from the Historical Seminary of Brown University*, VI (Providence, R. I., 1896).

Kimball, Marie G. "The Original Furnishings of the White House," *Antiques*, XV (June, 1929), 481–86.

Latourette, Kenneth Scott. "The History of Early Relations Between the United States and China, 1784–1844," *Transactions of the Connecticut Academy of Arts and Sciences*, XXII (August, 1917), 1–209.

——. "Voyages of American Ships to China, 1784–1844," *Transactions of the Connecticut Academy of Arts and Sciences*, XXVIII (April, 1927), 237–71.

Leach, Mary James. "From Kentucky Collectors," *Antiques*, LII (November, 1947), 350–55.

Lee, George L. "Thank God for Tea," *Bulletin of the Brooklyn Museum*, XVI (Winter, 1955).

Little, Frances. "America's East Indiamen and the China Trade," *Antiques*, XV (January, 1929), 27–31.

Loehr, George R. "A. E. Van Braam Houckgeest, the First American at the Court of China," *Princeton University Library Chronicle*, XV (Summer, 1954), 179–93.

Lunny, Robert M. "The Great Sea War," *American Heritage*, VII (April, 1956), 12–21.

Norman-Wilcox, Gregor. "American Ships in the China Trade," *Bulletin of the Los Angeles County Museum*, VII (Winter, 1955).

——. "Antiques," Los Angeles *Times*, May 13, 1956, Magazine Section, pp. 11, 56.

Phillips, James D. "East India Voyages of Salem Vessels Before 1800," *The Essex Institute Historical Collections*, LXXIX (April, 1943), 117–32; (July, 1943), 222–45; (October, 1943), 331–65.

"Porcelain for the Collector," *Antiques*, XLVIII (November, 1945), 258, 260.

Priest, Alan. "A Note on Houqua," *Bulletin of the Metropolitan Museum of Art*, XXXVI (September, 1941), 191.

"Principal Accessions, Bequest of James T. Woodward," *Bulletin of the Metropolitan Museum of Art*, V (November, 1910), 257.

Ralston, Ruth. "Early Republican Decoration on Chinese Lowestoft," *Bulletin of the Metropolitan Museum of Art*, XXII (July, 1927), 190–91.

Ranshaw, Carol J. "Calendar of the University of Delaware Collection of the John R. Latimer China Trade Papers, 1821–1834." Unpublished Master's thesis, School of Library Science, Drexel Institute of Technology, Philadelphia, 1953.

Robinson, John. "Blue and White 'India-China,'" *Old-Time New England*, XIV (January, 1924), 99–121.

Roth, Rodris. "Tea Drinking in 18th-Century America: Its Etiquette and Equipage," *United States National Museum Bulletin 225: Contributions from the*

*Museum of History and Technology*, Paper 14 (Washington, D. C., 1961), pp. 61–91.

Rutter, Frank R. "South American Trade of Baltimore," *Johns Hopkins Studies in Historical and Political Science*, IX (September, 1897), 1–49.

"Shop Talk: Chinese Export Porcelain," *Antiques*, LVIII (September, 1950), 162.

"Show Business," *Antiques*, LVI (October, 1949), 248.

"Silver Jubilee Exhibitors," *Antiques*, LX (October, 1951), 248.

Snyder, James W., Jr. "A Bibliography for the Early American China Trade, 1784–1815," *Americana*, XXXIV (April, 1940), 297–345.

——. "Marine Insurance on Early American Voyages," *Fair Winds*, II (January, 1940), 20–22, 30.

Spendlove, F. G. "Eastern and Western Ceramics," *Bulletin of the Royal Ontario Museum of Archaeology*, XIX (September, 1952), 6–18.

Thomas, Gertrude Z. "Cane, a Tropical Transplant," *Antiques*, LXXIX (January, 1961), 92–95.

"A Trip to the Fair," *Antiques*, LVIII (October, 1950), 244.

Tudor-Craig, Sir Algernon. "Chinese Armorial Porcelain; Some Eighteenth-Century Borders," *Antiques*, XIV (August, 1928), 124–28.

Winchester, Alice. "Antiques," *Antiques*, LXXIX (February, 1961), 165.

Woodhouse, Samuel W., Jr. "Grandmother's China," *House Beautiful*, LXXII (July, 1932), 33, 34, 54.

——. "Lowestoft Bowl Can Be Dated," New York *Sun*, May 13, 1933, p. 12.

——. "Martha Washington's China and 'Mr. Van Braam,'" *Antiques*, XXVII (May, 1935), 186–88.

——. "Punch and Punchbowls," *Antiques*, XXIX (February, 1936), 56–59.

——. "The Voyage of the *Empress of China*," *The Pennsylvania Magazine of History and Biography*, LXIII (January, 1939), 24–36.

# UNPUBLISHED MATERIAL

Background material has been found in unpublished notes and papers in various institutions. Histories of particular pieces of porcelain, in some cases, came from letters and notes in the files of private owners of the porcelain and from museum accessions records.

Bissell, Mr. and Mrs. Alfred E., Wilmington, Delaware. Record of history of chinaware originally owned by Henry Chanopin Belin.

Carson, Dr. John B., Newtown Square, Pennsylvania. Record of history of chinaware originally made for Isaac and Mary (Hollingsworth) Morris.

Creer, Doris. "Americans at Canton: The Development of American Trade with China." Unpublished paper at the University of Delaware, 1956.

Foster, James W., Director, Maryland Historical Society. Summary of research on history of Union Line and Packet *Philadelphia* contained in a letter dated October 17, 1956, in the files of the Winterthur Museum.

Harrison Gray Otis House, Boston. Accessions Records.

# Bibliography

Holland, Eugenia Calvert. "Notes on the China Trade and the Port of Baltimore—1785–1850." Unpublished file of research notes compiled and used in the preparation of the exhibition: *The China Trade of Baltimore / 165 Years of Commerce with the Orient / The Maryland Historical Society / June 15 to October 15, 1950.*

Maryland Historical Society. Accessions Records.

Museum of Fine Arts, Boston. Accessions Records.

Mystic Seaport, Mystic, Connecticut. Accessions Records.

Peabody Museum of Salem, Salem, Massachusetts. Accessions Records.

Peterson, Charles E. "Notes on the Voyage to Canton and Return, 1787–1788, of Ship *Alliance*." In the files of the Historical Society of Pennsylvania.

Prime, Mrs. Alfred Coxe, Paoli, Pennsylvania. Summary of history of chinaware made for three nineteenth-century Philadelphia families (in letters dated November 7, 1956, and October 3, 1959, in the files of the author).

Winterthur Museum. Accessions Records.

# Index

A

Acapulco, Mexico, seaport, 6, 65
Adams, John Quincy, 154
Adriance, Thomas, 222
Advertisements (notices), *see* Newspaper advertisements
Albany, New York, 66–67
*Alexander* (ship), 107
Allen, Robert, 41
*Alliance* (ship), 15, 98, 101, 212
*America* (banner), 146
*America* (ship), 101
American bald eagle, eagle design, 143–145, 181
  (on) box, covered, 4-legged, (*see in* Fig. 136)
  chinaware prices at Canton (*1797*), 228–232
  Cincinnati, Society of the, 149–152; Figs. 42, 46, 105, 106, 107
  (on) coins and seals, 143, 144–145
  (on) cup, double-handled, 144; Fig. 82
  (on) cup and saucer, 143; Fig. 81
  (on) cup and tray, 148; Fig. 104
  (in) Declaration of Independence painting on screen, (*see in* Fig. 138)
  (on) dinner service (Ridgway family), 145; Fig. 87
  (on) dish, with 2 flags and elaborate border, 185
  (on) Fitzhugh ware, 129, 141, 142, 145; *frontispiece* and Figs. 63, 90
  (on) flagon, 144; Fig. 84
  flying with pinions extended, 145; Fig. 92
  (on) fruit compote, 130, Fig. 65
  (on) garniture, 144; Fig. 86
  (on) goblets, 131; Fig. 68
  (on) goglet (guglet), 185; Fig. 134
  L'Enfant, Pierre-Charles, suggestion of, 149
  (on) Massachusetts coinage, 143

American bald eagle (*cont.*)
  (on) mourning set, Washington's tomb, Fig. 110
  (on) mug, 144; Fig. 84
  (on) National Insurance Company policies, 145; Fig. 88
  (on) plate (Franklin Pierce), 144; Fig. 85
  (on) punch bowl, grasping trophy of war, 147; Fig. 101
  (on) punch bowl (Henry Smith), (*see in* Fig. 40)
  (on) quarter-eagle minted in 1792, 145; (*see in* Fig. 91)
  (on) saucer, 144–145; Fig. 89
  (on) tea service, with banner *In God We Hope*, 145; Fig. 92
  (on) tea service (Isaac Hull), (*see in* Fig. 116)
  variations on, 144
American emblems and symbols, 44, 70, 139, 185
  Battle of Bennington, 155; Fig. 117
  chain of states, 152, 153; Figs. 107, 112
  Cincinnati, Society of the, *see* Cincinnati
  coat of arms, *see* Coats of arms
  Declaration of Independence, *see* Declaration
  *E Pluribus Unum*, 145
  eagle, *see* American bald eagle
  Erie, Lake, Battle of, 147
  flag, *see* American flag
  naval engagements, 147; Fig. 100
  seal (great) of the United States, *see* Seal
  stars, *see* Stars
  states' coats of arms, *see* Coats of arms
  War of 1812, 147, 154; Fig. 100
  (on) Washington, Martha, tea set, 153; Fig. 112

# Index

# Index

China (*cont.*)

Peking, *see* Peking

porcelain manufacture, *see* Porcelain manufacture

ports, opening of, 10, 24, 124

position in East Asia, 9

routes to, 18, 19–20, 21–22

shapes and motifs typical of, 44, 185

superiority attitude, 9, 44

*China* (ship), 219

China-trade porcelain (term), x, 41–42

Chinaware (term), x, 42; *references to*, 22, 34–36

Chinese court, Imperial use, 4, 5, 8–9, 10, 44, 45–46, 50, 74

Chinese export porcelain, ix–x, 41–44

dating of, 46, 139, 180–187

European interest in, 63–64

export to America, 69–73, 123–127

inferior materials used in, 44, 49–50

ingredients, 47–48

manufacture of, *see* Porcelain manufacture in China

merchants, *see* Hong merchants

money involved in, 18

ownership of, 42–43

patterns of, *see* Patterns

prices of, *see* Prices

procurement of, 32–36

production of, *see* Porcelain manufacture in China

purchasing, 36–38

quality of, 73–76, 125–127

quantities of, 68–73

shapes and sizes (forms), 48, 100, 128–133, 180, 228–232

shipping costs of, 79

significance of, 42–44

sources of, 54–56

trade decline, 123–127, 180

Chinese flag, 186; Fig. 134

Chinese merchants, *see* Hong merchants

Chinese people:

aesthetic qualities, 43

American attitude toward, 9–10, 28, 37

English treatment of, 7, 8, 10

Chinese people (*cont.*)

imitation, 53, 125, 150, 183

(in) Manila, 6

original genius, 53, 150

Portugese treatment of, 6, 8

restraint, 44

self-sufficiency, 18

Spanish treatment of, 6, 8

Ch'ing dynasty, 45–46, 64–65

Ching-tê Chên, 45–56, 141–142, 220

Canton, distance from and routes to, 50–52; *map* (Fig. 8)

Chinkiang, 50

Chinoiserie style, 64

Chioqua (linguist), 29

Chocolate pot, 101

pear-shape, 131; Fig. 69

"Chop," 29

*Chow chow*, 95

Christian, Fletcher, 89

cup supposedly belonging to, Fig. 37

Christie, Mr., 130

Chrystie, Albert, 72–73

Chrystie, Thomas, 72, 97

Chu T'ung-ch'uan, 206

Ch'üan Chou (Zayton), 4, 5, 198, 210

Chusan, 7

Cider jugs, *see* Flagons

Cincinnati, Society of the, emblem, 149–152; Figs. 42, 46, 105–107, *frontispiece*

(on) basket on stand (Samuel Shaw), 150; Fig. 42

(on) cup and saucer (Samuel Shaw dinner service), 53, 149–150; Fig. 105

(on) dinner service (George Washington), 150–151; *frontispiece*

(on) punch bowl (Richard Varick), 97; Fig. 46

(on) punch bowl with bust of George Washington, 152; Fig. 107

Ciphers, monograms, or initials, 42–43, 153–155

*B* (William Bayard), 96

*BCW* (Benjamin Chew Wilcocks), 152

# Index

# Index

# Index

# Index

# Index

# Index

# Index